Helion & Company Limited
26 Willow Road
Solihull
West Midlands
B91 1UE
England
Tel. 0121 705 3393
Fax 0121 711 4075
email: info@helion.co.uk
website: www.helion.co.uk
Twitter: @helionbooks
Visit our blog http://blog.helion.co.uk

Published by Helion & Company 2017
Designed and typeset by Farr out
    Publications, Wokingham, Berkshire
Cover designed by Paul Hewitt, Battlefield
    Design (www.battlefield-design.co.uk)
Printed by Henry Ling Limited, Dorchester,
    Dorset

Text © Alexander Mladenov 2016
Photographs © as individually credited
Colour profiles drawn by Peter Penev ©
    Helion & Company 2017

ISBN 978-1-911096-45-0

British Library Cataloguing-in-Publication
    Data
A catalogue record for this book is available
    from the British Library

For details of other military history titles
published by Helion & Company Limited
contact the above address, or visit our
website: http://www.helion.co.uk
We always welcome receiving book
proposals from prospective authors.

CONTENTS

LIST OF ABBREVIATIONS

AAA	anti-aircraft artillery		kt	knots
AAH	Army Attack Helicopter programme		LLLTV	Low-light-level television
AB	Air Base		LoS	Line of Sight
AEW	airborne early warning		MAP	Ministry of Aircraft Industry
ATGM	anti-tank guided missile		MAWS	missile approach warning sensors
AVMF	Russian Naval Aviation Service		MB	Brazilian Navy
BAA	Army Aviation Brigade		MBT	main battle tank
BT	armour-piercing/tracer		MoD	Ministry of Defence
C2	command and control		MTBF	mean time between failures
CAS	close air support		MTOW	maximum take-off weight
CO	Commanding Officer		Nm	nautical miles
CoG	centre of gravity		NoE	nap-of-the-earth
CSG	Combat Strike Group		NVG	Night vision goggles
DoD	US Dept of Defense		OEI	one engine inoperative
ECG	Experimental Combat Group		OFZ	fragmentation/high explosive/incendiary
FLIR	forward-looking infrared		OGE	Out of Ground Effect
f/m	feet per metre		OT	fragmentation/tracer
FoV	Fields of View		OVP	Independent Helicopter Regiment
f/s	feet per second		RAA	Russian Army Aviation
FSB	Federal Security Service		RFP	Request for Proposals
FTS	Flight Test Station		RPKB	Ramenskoye Instrument-Making Design Bureau
GLITs	VVS flight test centre		RSRA	Rotor Systems Research Aircraft
GOES	Gyro-stabilised electro-optical systems		RuAF	Russian Air Force
GSE	ground servicing equipment		RuASF	Russian Air and Space Force
HMCDS	Helmet-mounted cueing and display system		SAM	Surface-to-air missile
HMCS	Helmet-mounted cueing system		SOF	Special operations forces
HMOSP	Helicopter Multi-mission Optronic Stabilised Payload system		SSM	Undersecretary of Defence Industry (Turkey)
			TAI	Turkish Aerospace Industry
HOCAS	Hands on Collective and Stick		TBO	times between overhaul
HUD	Head-up display		TOW	Tube-launched, Optically tracked, Wire-guided
IAI	Israel Aircraft Industries		TsBPiPLS	344th Combat Training and Aircrew Conversion Centre
IFV	infantry fighting vehicles			
IIVP	Research Instructor Helcopter Regiment		UAV	unmanned air vehicles
IHS	Integrated Helmet System		UOMZ	Urals Optical-Mechanical Plant
IR	infrared		UV	Ultraviolet
IRHS	Instructor Research Helicopter Squadron		VAP	Helicopter Aviation Regiment
ISA	International Standard Atmosphere		VVS	Soviet Air Force
JGF	Joint Group of Forces		WSO	Weapons system operator
KBP	Instrument Design Bureau			

INTRODUCTION

The Ka-50 and Ka-52 coaxial armoured attack helicopters are widely regarded as the crowning achievement of Dr Sergey Viktorovich Mikheev, the long-time designer-general of the Lyubertsi-based (a Moscow suburb) Kamov Experimental Design Bureau (colloquially known as the Kamov OKB). A well-deserved patriarch of the company, he put all his efforts and all his prestige into demonstrating that a coaxial attack helicopter could be definitely superior to a conventional layout (using main and tail rotors) in terms of flight performance and overall combat-effectiveness.

This superiority was clearly demonstrated back in 1987 when the Ka-50 won the head-to-head competitive evaluation with the Mi-28 and claimed victory in the hotly contested tender for a Mi-24 replacement. The military team conducting the flight testing and evaluation effort found that the Kamov's single-seat, coaxial design is faster and more agile, its unguided weapons are more accurate and it comes armed with a longer-range anti-tank guided missile system than its rival Mi-28. Furthermore, the Ka-50 boasted a considerably better overall combat damage resistance thanks to its extensive armour protection, flight-critical system redundancy and lack of a tail rotor and associated transmission components.

Today, Mikheev is a charismatic industry veteran and recipient of the extremely prestigious Hero of Russia Golden Star – the highest state award in today's Russia. Aged 79 and still fit, the patriarch remains firmly at the helm of the Kamov company and is widely known as the

longest-lasting designer general in the modern-day Russian aerospace and defence industries.

Mikheev was the principal driving force behind the development of the new-generation high-performance, heavily armoured attack helicopter, originally destined to be the successor of the omnipresent Mi-24 *Hind* in an effort to become the Soviet response to the US Army's AH-64A Apache. The overtly ambitious programme was launched in the late 1970s and the single-seat Ka-50 Black Shark (NATO codename *Hokum*), an unorthodox, heavily armoured gunship, made its maiden flight in hover in June 1982.

Prominent British aviation journalist Jon Lake characterised the new Russian attack helicopter back in 1994 with the following words in an article published in *World Air Power Journal* (Volume 19, Winter 1994): "The Ka-50 'Hokum' represents the most radical approach to the design of a modern combat aircraft, with only a single crewman to fly the aircraft, acquire and attack targets in a high-threat environment."

The day-operations-only *Hokum* pioneered the coaxial rotor scheme, combined with a highly-automated flight/navigation/attack suite and long-range anti-tank guided missiles (ATGMs). The Kamov-trademark coaxial aerodynamic layout made it a supremely agile and survivable attack platform with benign handling performance, capable of nap-of-the-earth (NoE) flying, even lower than tree-top level, popping out only to acquire the target after receiving initial information on its position and launch its guided missiles when facing

Kamov OKB's patriarch Sergey Mikheev is widely known as the chief driving force behind the design concept and real-world implementation of the unorthodox Black Shark and Alligator development programmes. (Author)

Both the single-seat Ka-50 and its two-seat derivative Ka-52, which made its first hovering flight in June 1997, were selected by the Russian MoD as new-generation attack helicopters to replace the Mi-24 *Hind* fleet serving with the Russian Army Aviation service. The second Alligator prototype, serialled '062', and the third pre-series example, '53', are seen here in formation flight during a Victory Day flypast rehearsal over Moscow in May 2010. (Dmitry Pichugin)

powerful battlefield air defences. To further increase its battlefield survivability, the rugged airframe was designed to absorb heavy punishment of enemy anti-aircraft weapons.

In the late 1980s, the effective and survivable Ka-50 was judged by the Soviet military leadership and the Soviet Air Force's flight testing authority as being definitely superior to its competitor, the Mil Mi-28 (NATO codename *Havoc*), and was subsequently ordered for large-scale serial production. The first production-standard machine made its maiden flight in May 1991 and the new attack rotorcraft type was formally commissioned into Russian Army Aviation (RAA) service in August 1995.

The unorthodox and highly-automated Ka-50, however, appeared at just the wrong time, during the inglorious demise of the Soviet Union and the onset of abrupt cuts in the defence budget of its successor, Russia. This caused a good many troubles to the Ka-50 programme, which was postponed for more than a decade, and the last three aircraft of the initial 12-strong production batch were eventually completed and handed over to the Russian Air Force as late as 2008–2009.

The Ka-50 received its baptism of fire during the second Chechen War in January–February 2001, where the heavily armoured and agile type performed its combat tasks over rugged terrain with finesse, often in inclement weather conditions.

The first prototype of its two-seat derivative, designated Ka-52 and named Alligator, was rolled out in November 1996, made its maiden flight in the hover on 25 June 1997 and saw a very protracted

development. The patience and persistence of Mikheev and his team at the Kamov OKB eventually paid off, and in August 2006 the Russian MoD allocated the long-awaited budget for systems development testing and evaluation — within the framework of stage two of the Ka-52's state testing effort. It also funded setting up a series production line for the type at the AAC Progress plant in Arsenyev in Russia's Far East. In the event, after almost three decades of never-ending, head-to-head competition with the Mil Moscow Helicopter Plant (MVZ Mil) developer of the Mi-28/A/N Mikheev's brainchild in its definitive two-seat attack/reconnaissance configuration was at last launched in full-scale production in 2009. By 2015, the Ka-52 had enjoyed the prestigious status of the premier and most capable new-generation attack helicopter type fielded in service with the RAA branch of the Russian Air and Space Force (RuASF).

Nowadays, Mikheev is not resting on his past achievements in the attack helicopter domain; instead, he is pushing forward with follow-on developments of the Alligator. He claims that its baseline design has ample reserves for further performance enhancements, and new development of derivatives is in the pipeline, especially in the naval aviation domain.

Regarding the land-based derivative, Mikheev admitted that he has adopted a pragmatic approach for boosting the Ka-52's mission avionics and armament operational capabilities; he says this can be best described by the motto: "Let's eat the elephant piece by piece." This could be especially true while considering its all-weather/night mission capability and radar performance, which would require further improvements in the future, together with the integration of a helmet-mounted cueing and display system and possibly longer-range all-weather anti-armour missiles.

The Alligator's two contra-rotating, three-blade coaxial rotors contribute to the compact appearance, stability of flight and high agility. Thanks to the coaxial rotors and up-rated VK-2500-01 engines, the flight performance, as Mikheev noted, will be superior to that of its US counterpart, the AH-64E Apache Guardian, especially in demanding 'hot-and-high' environments. It is no secret, however, that the Alligator still has a long way to go to compete with the overall mission avionics capability of today's Apache Guardian, especially in terms of day/night sensor suite performance and all-weather targeting and weapons capability.

1

HOW IT ALL BEGAN

New attack helicopters for the Red Army

A talented engineer and well-recognised leader, when he took over the management of the Kamov OKB on 19 April 1974, 36-year-old Sergey Mikheev was the youngest design bureau head in the history of the then mighty Soviet aerospace and defence industry initially as chief-designer and since 1987 being promoted to designer-general. He was appointed at the helm of the helicopter design company soon after the death of its founder, Nikolay Kamov. In the first days in his new position, he set the task to expand the activities of the experimental design bureau and its experimental plant used to design, build and test prototype rotorcraft.

During an interview just before being appointed as chief-designer, Mikheev claimed in front of Ivan Serbin, the all-powerful chief of the defence department of the Central Committee of the Communist Party of the Soviet Union, that he was committed to develop a new-generation combat rotorcraft with better performance than the attack machines developed at that time in the USA under the Army Attack Helicopter (AAH) programme. Mikheev promised to submit the technical concept of this state-of-the-art attack rotorcraft within four months. He saw this new machine as a second-generation dedicated attack helicopter for the Soviet military.

The original concept of introducing into the then Soviet Armed Forces a new class of armour-protected battlefield helicopters to be used as flying infantry fighting vehicles (IFV) referred to as the first generation of attack rotorcraft was born in the early 1960s. Its main purpose was to deliver troops on the battlefield quickly and precisely, and also to provide on-demand close air support (CAS) to the advancing ground troops, knocking out armoured targets at the forward edge of the battle area, both stationary and moving ones.

Back in 1967, a programme was initiated by the Soviet Ministry

Kamov OKB's Sergey Mikheev and his counterpart, MVZ Mil's Marat Tishtchenko (on the left), sitting side-by-side at an official event in the mid-1970s. (Sergey Mikheev archive)

The Ka-25F was a coaxial attack helicopter to be derived from the Ka-25 shipborne submarine hunter, but remained only as a deck-size mock-up as it lost the Soviet attack helicopter competition to the Mi-24 *Hind*. (Kamov OKB)

A Soviet Air Force production-standard Mi-24A *Hind-A* attack helicopter armed with 16 and 32-round packs for firing S-5 57mm rockets. (Author)

of Defence to develop a new-generation combat rotorcraft with combined attack and assault transport capabilities. Initially, only the MVZ Mil (then known as the OKB-329) was ordered to work on this, on 29 March 1967. Soon afterwards, Nikolay Kamov asked the Central Committee of the Communist Party if his design bureau (then known as the OKB-2, renamed in 1967 as the Ukhotomsky Helicopter Plant, abbreviated in Russian as *UVZ*) could also join the effort, and not after long he got corresponding approval from the Soviet Minister of Defence, Marshall Dmitry Ustinov.

This way, both the MVZ Mil and Kamov OKB, the two principal helicopter design bureaux in the Soviet Union, began competing head-to-head in the late 1960s in offering their designs for heavily armoured battlefield helicopters to fit into the Soviet understanding of the flying IFV concept.

Kamov OKB's design team, however, chose to follow a rather conservative path by offering a derivative of its then-new Ka-25 (NATO codename *Hormone*) coaxial multifunctional naval helicopter, heavily modified for CAS and assault transport roles and designated Ka-25F. It had a maximum take-off weight of 7,500kg (16,530lb), was equipped with skid landing gear and armed with one 23mm GSh-23 rapid-fire cannon with 400 rounds, six 16-round packs for firing 57mm rockets and six 3M11 Falanga anti-tank guided missiles, in addition to free-fall iron bombs or cluster bombs weighting up to 250kg (551lb) each. Without armaments, the Ka-25F was offered for assault transport, with a cabin capable of accommodating eight troops.

In the event, MVZ Mil's twin-engine clean sheet project dubbed V-24 was considered by the Soviet military in May 1968 to be better and much more promising than that offered by Kamov OKB. The V-24 design was finalised in February 1969 and final assembly of the first prototype commenced shortly afterwards at MVZ Mil's experimental plant in Panki near Moscow. The new helicopter made its maiden hovering flight in the capable hands of MVZ Mil test pilot German Alferov on 19 September 1969.

The V-24, still in a partially complete weapon system configuration, eventually entered its state testing and evaluation phase with the Soviet Air Force's State Research-Test Red Banner Institute (abbreviated in Russian as *GNIKI*) in June 1970, and was completed within a year and a half. However, production of the new attack helicopter type, which received the in-service designation Mi-24 (NATO codename *Hind*), followed the usual Soviet procurement practice as it was launched in 1970, well before completion of the type's state testing and evaluation effort.

Between late 1970 and late 2015, some 3,500 examples of all *Hind* variants had been produced at two plants situated in Arsenyev and Rostov on Don. At present, the type's production line at the latter location is still active due to continuing demand for the latest Mi-24 derivatives from both domestic and export customers.

AAH programme features

The Soviet requirement for a new attack helicopter for the Army Aviation service, as a replacement for the mass-produced *Hind*, was heavily influenced by the US AAH programme. This effort originally foresaw development of a well-armoured anti-tank helicopter with a maximum take-off weight (MTOW) of 7.26 tonnes, armed with a 30mm cannon and long-range ATGMs.

The official Request for Proposals (RFP) of the US Department of Defense (DoD) AAH programme was issued in August 1972. It called for a clean-sheet design attack helicopter with a maximum cruse speed of 269km/h (145kt) when carrying eight BGM-71 TOW anti-tank guided missiles (or a minimum expendable warload of 453kg [1,000lb]) for a mission duration of 1.9 hours. The performance requirements (set at 1,220m/4,000ft altitude and an ambient air temperature of 35°C/95°F) called for a maximum speed of 323km/h (175kt) and a maximum rate of climb (vertical speed) of 2.53m/s (500f/m). The operational *g*-limits were set at +3.5 and -1.5. The helicopter structure was required to be resistant to hits from 12.7mm

The Hughes YAH-64 prototype took to the air in its maiden flight in September 1975. By that time, the Soviet military leadership had already considered launching a wide-ranging effort to counter the US AAH programme. (Boeing)

armour-piercing incendiary projectiles, while the rotor head was to be able to survive a hit from a 23mm high-explosive incendiary round. In addition, the new attack helicopter for the US Army had to be protected from heat-seeking surface-to-air missiles (SAMs), featuring a drastically reduced infrared (IR) signature and equipped with chaff/flare dispensers. The radically enhanced crew survivability was among the chief requirements, with the crewmen able to survive crash landings at a speed of up to 48km/h (26kt), with vertical rate of descent of up to 12.8m/s (48f/s) at a forward speed of up to 28km/h (15kt).

The first Hughes YAH-64 prototype took to the air in its maiden flight on 30 September 1975, followed by the Bell YAH-63 the next day. On 10 December 1976, the Secretary of the Army announced that the Hughes AH-64 had been selected as the winner of the AAH tender, preferred to the Bell YAH-63 due to its better combat damage resistance and better stability when on the ground. During the comparative tests, the YAH-64 demonstrated a maximum speed of 362km/h (196kt), while the rate of climb was 4.06m/s (800f/m).

The first production-standard AH-64 made its maiden flight on 31 October 1979. The US Army's requirements changed several times, and in 1982 the order was set at 515 aircraft, with the first of these rolled out on 30 September 1983. The US Army took on strength its first AH-64A on 26 January 1984.

The production-standard Apaches were armed with the all-new Rockwell Hellfire (HELIopter-Launched, FIRE-and-forget) supersonic ATGM, using semi-active laser guidance and an effective engagement range of 6km (3.7 nautical miles [nm]). The Martin-Marietta TADS/PNVS advanced day/night targeting system installed on the helicopter comprised two parts independent from each other.

The TADS unit integrated a dual forward-looking infrared (FLIR) sensor for pilot and gunner, with additional optical sensors and a laser rangefinder/designator. The PNVS is a steerable system used by the pilot, providing him with FLIR imagery. He was equipped with the IHADSS helmet with a sight for the right eye where PNVS imagery can be displayed, together with essential flight information.

The first US Army unit to take on strength the new Apache was the 7th Battalion, 17th Calvary Brigade stationed at Fort Hood, Texas, which commenced its conversion training on the new attack helicopter type in April 1986. By September 1989, as many as 500 AH-64As were handed over to the US Army, increasing to no fewer than 700 in December 1992 and 800 in July 1993. The last of 821 AH-64As ordered by the US Army (excluding prototypes) was taken on strength in April 1996. In addition, by 1996, over 200 AH-64s had been ordered by export customers, and by early 1997, confirmed production for both domestic and foreign customers accounted for 1,040 examples, with the last of these slated for delivery in 2000.

Designing an Apache counterpart

Because of the traditional Soviet-era approach of separating aircraft design and production activities, the Kamov OKB was engaged in helicopter design and development activities as well as prototype-building and flight testing, while mass production of its already Soviet military tested and approved military designs was handled by a chain of purpose-built serial production plants.

One of the first new themes at the Kamov OKB under the direction of then young chief-designer Sergey Mikheev was the development of a concept for an all-new combat helicopter for the Soviet military. It was to be optimised to destroy ground targets in addition to other

Designed in the late 1970s, the AH-64 Apache has undergone two major capability improvement programmes, Longbow and Guardian, and is still the main attack helicopter of the US Army, set to remain in active service in large numbers even beyond 2030. (US DoD)

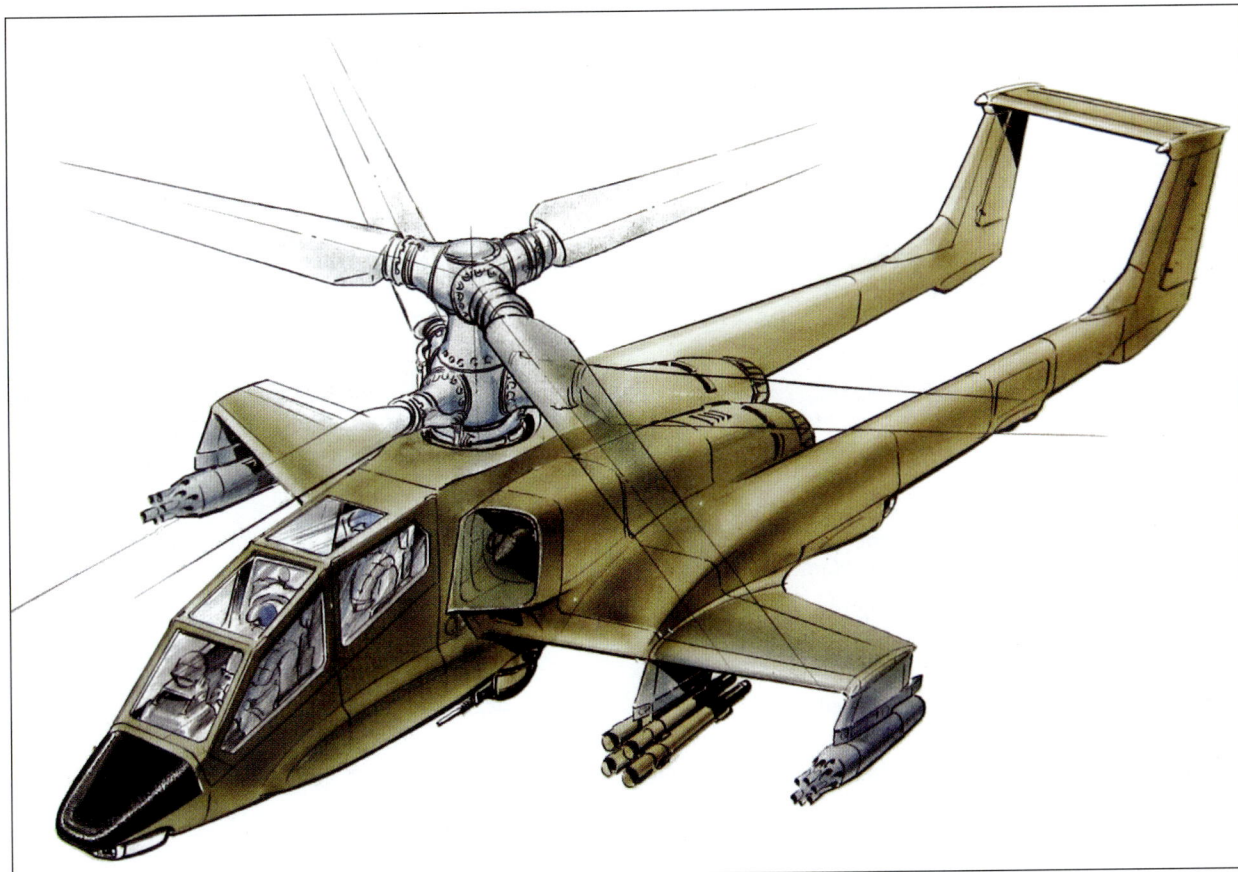

An early twin-tail concept for a coaxial attack helicopter proposed by the Kamov OKB, featuring a two-man crew, rigid rotors, wingtip-mounted rocket packs, underbelly gun turret and four-round ATGM launchers. (Sergei Fomin)

helicopters and low-flying, slow-speed, fixed-wing aircraft over the battlefield. Young and ambitious, Mikheev realised back in the mid-1970s that if the task was solved, the work on the new helicopter would grant his design bureau a promising and sustainable development base for many years to come. History showed that he had been absolutely right in this early judgment.

The new attack helicopter programme was formally launched by decree No. 1043-361 of the Council of Ministers and the Central Committee of the Communist Party of the Soviet Union, dated 16 December 1976. Instead of awarding a direct order to the MVZ Mil to develop the rotorcraft, it called for a competitive selection among the designs offered by the MVZ Mil and Kamov OKB. This was, in fact, the opening shot of an epic head-to-head competition between the two design bureaux, which has proceeded, in one form or another, until the early and mid-2010s. Furthermore, the Ka-52 and Mi-28N continued to be more or less rivals after both types were launched in wide-scale production in the second half of the 2000s for re-equipping the RAA attack helicopter squadrons previously operating the Mi-24V/P.

The specification issued by the Soviet Ministry of Defence originally called for a day/night-capable all-weather helicopter, much better than the Mi-24 in terms of range, flight performance, firepower and armour protection; it was also required to be supremely agile for safe manoeuvring in NoE flight. At the same time, the new attack rotorcraft was not required to feature a transport cabin, like that of the Mi-24, but instead had to be provided with much more extensive armour protection for the cockpit area, fuel tanks and the most vulnerable airframe and powerplant areas. The armour protection was required to provide resistance to hits from 7.62mm and partially from 12.7mm rounds. Finally, the military requirements also insisted than the new attack rotorcraft design should outperform the modern-day

Western helicopters, especially the Hughes AH-64A Apache.

Initial design works at the Kamov OKB commenced in March 1977, with the collection and in-depth analysis of all available information about the YAH-64 and AH-64A gathered from a wide variety of sources. From the very beginning, Kamov OKB's design team was tasked to compete with the Hughes instead of with their colleagues from the MVZ Mil. On this occasion, Sergey Mikheev noted that in case of war, the AH-64 Apache would be the real enemy and therefore the new helicopter being developed at the Kamov OKB should outperform its American rival in the first place. This way, the Apache had been designated to be the designer's benchmark, as Mikheev was ready and willing, from the very beginning, to dispute the claim of the AH-64 Apache to be the best attack helicopter in the world.

The main design drivers, as outlined in the military technical and tactical requirements issued by the Soviet military, called for a high cost/effectiveness ratio, while crew survivability was placed at a premium and had to be granted literally in any critical situation. The helicopter was to be capable of autonomous operation for prolonged periods while utilising a bare minimum of ground support equipment; it was also required to be easy and affordable for servicing in the field. The new machine had to be equipped with a highly automated targeting system and armed with powerful precision-guided weapons. At the same time, the number of crewmen on board was not specified in the list of requirements. Perhaps nobody in the Soviet MoD had realised at the time that a single crewman onboard could fly and fight with the helicopter, since the US Army's new-generation attack helicopter sported a two-man crew.

The design team at Kamov had to solve a highly complex task while facing a skilled and experienced domestic competitor enjoying the solid support of the VVS (*Voenno Vozdushnie Sily* Soviet Air Force) and MoD, and boasting a lot of expertise and experience in designing,

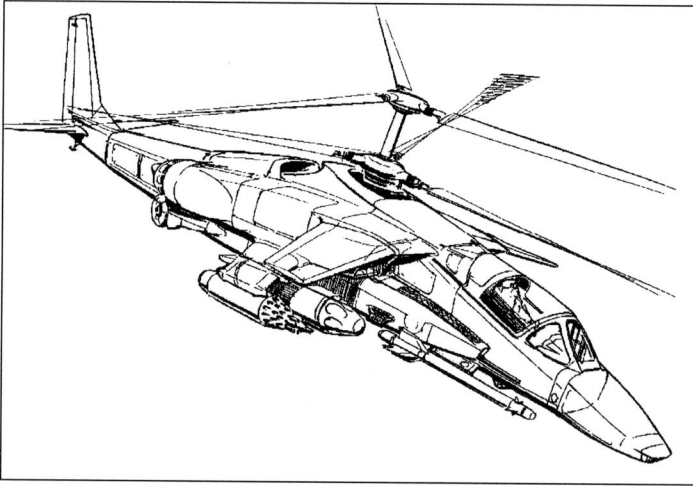

An early layout of the single-seat attack helicopter concept as proposed by Kamov OKB's concept designer Sergey Fomin, featuring a notably streamlined fuselage. (Kamov OKB)

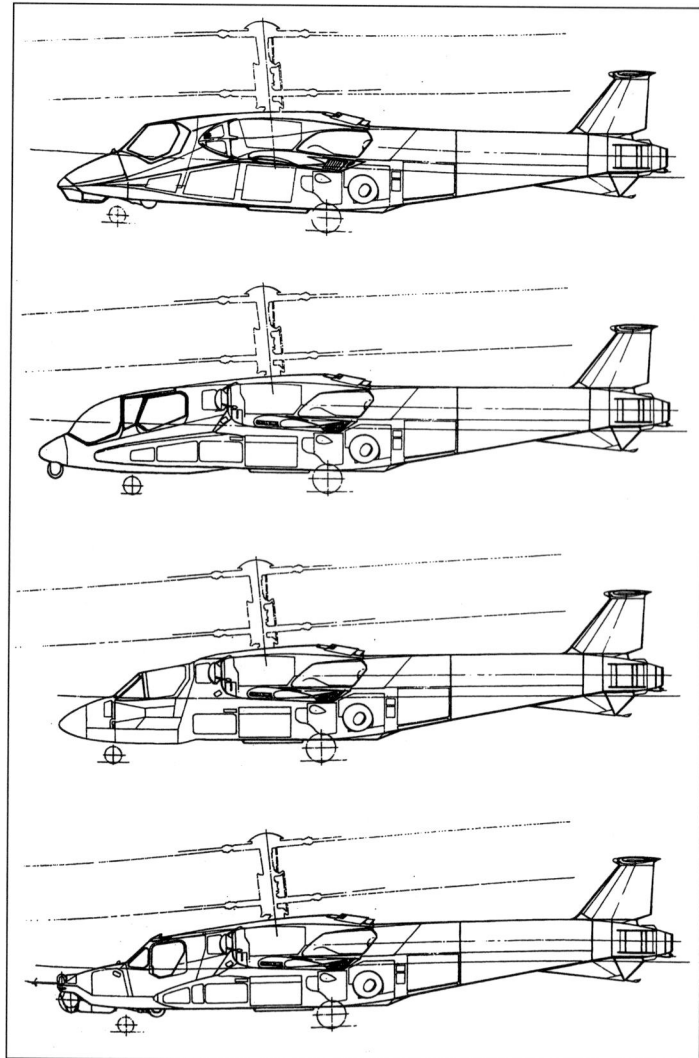

These four different early layouts for the Kamov OKB's new attack helicopters were proposed for review but had never been approved for further development. Three of them (Nos 1, 3 and 4) are single-seaters, while No. 2 is a two-seater. (Kamov OKB)

testing, launching into production and refining the legendary *Hind*, including operations in real-world war conditions. But it should be noted here that the first of the many *Hind* versions to be launched in serial production, the Mi-24A, had reportedly failed to fully meet the technical and tactical requirements at the time. Then, in a desperate attempt to solve this acute issue, the MVZ Mil had adopted specific tactics, also pursued in follow-on programmes. It called initially for pushing the fielding into military service of its new models (despite the serious shortcomings that had been revealed during the state testing and evaluation programme) and then continuing to improve the flawed designs as long as necessary in order to make them fully compliant with the original technical specification.

At the beginning of this new competition, the MVZ Mil leadership saw itself as the undisputed front-runner and promoted its concept for a new-generation attack rotorcraft featuring the conventional scheme with main and tail rotors, while also offering an alternative concept with a two-rotor lateral layout design; it was a combination of the Mi-24's fuselage and the rotor scheme borrowed from the V-12 design,

An early full-scale mock-up of the Mi-28 built in the late 1970s, which is very different to the definitive prototype which flew for the first time in 1982 and copied many design features from the AH-64 Apache. (MVZ Mil)

but this had been discarded at an early stage.

In the event, the configuration of the eventual design concept at the MVZ Mil followed somewhat slavishly the US attack helicopter configuration. The new angular and awkward-looking helicopter, later designated Mi-28, used most if not all of the design features that can be found in the AH-64 Apache. As sources from the Kamov OKB tended to comment, all these features had been directly copied from the Apache, without being analysed in any depth. That way, the eventual Mi-28 had resembled pretty closely the US attack helicopter's general layout, with a sleek fuselage, stepped tandem cockpit, widely spaced podded engines, tailwheel undercarriage arrangement, four-bladed main rotor and a gun turret installed under the forward fuselage. The resultant design, however, proved to be considerably heavier and bulkier than its US counterpart and original; as could be expected, the Mi-28 suffered from inferior flight performance, while the mission avionics were also seriously underperforming.

Nowadays, the Mi-28N, in the form of the production-standard day/ night attack helicopter dubbed *Night Hunter*, officially commissioned by the RAA service not before 2014, is known as the only Russian-made rotorcraft without a nose steering wheel. It has to be moved on the ground with its tail forward, connected to the towing bar, because of the specifics of its tailwheel undercarriage arrangement, and received the popular nickname *Rat*. Generally speaking, the MVZ Mil attempt, dating back from the late 1970s, to design a superior helicopter by directly and uncritically copying most if not all of the design features of the original (i.e. the AH-64 Apache) had definitely failed to bring any impressive results.

Single-seat attack helicopter concept 2

Strongly motivated to win the tender, the design team at the Kamov OKB had evaluated a good many design layouts, and in the event decided to utilise the company's trademark coaxial scheme, combined with a fixed-wing aircraft-lookalike fuselage.

The next issue to be solved was to cope with the weight penalty imposed by the Soviet-made defence electronics, capable of facilitating day-only combat operations. It had reportedly failed to produce state-of-the-art electro-optical systems that would allow the V-80 to locate, identify and engage the enemy at night. In stark contrast, its arch-rival AH-64 Apache benefited from very modern lightweight and small-size day/night targeting and observation systems, while their Soviet day-only equivalents, as well as the navigation/flight avionics and engines, proved noticeably heavier and bulkier. This issue, in turn, had threatened to result in a considerably heavier and larger attack helicopter with inferior performance, rendering it impossible for the new Kamov attack machine to outperform the Apache, as had expressly been requested by the Soviet military in the technical specification. Facing this big and virtually unsolvable challenge, Mikheev took an uneasy and bold decision to offer a single-seat helicopter. Such a design solution would promise savings of around 1.5 tonnes of dry weight compared to the two-seat alternative. "So, the single-seater proved to be the only readily available option at the time, making us sure that we [could] achieve better performance than that of the Apache," Mikheev said 35 years later.

The implementation of the single-seat concept had become possible thanks to the benign handling characteristics of the coaxial rotor scheme combined with a highly automated mission suite. This novel design solution proposed by Mikheev was keenly supported by the Kamov OKB's test-pilot, Evgeny Laryushin, who claimed at the time: "Yes, I can demonstrate you even tomorrow a terrain-following flight at an altitude of [only] 5m (16ft)."

His confidence that he could do this with ease it was based upon the fact that the coaxial helicopter was not prone to losing altitude while manoeuvring in the horizontal plane, unlike the conventional single-rotor scheme, because it retains automatically the set lift of the rotor system. This design feature enables the coaxial rotorcraft to be agile enough for safe manoeuvring in NoE flight around forests, hills and avoiding any kind of natural or man-made vertical obstacles in front of it.

"I may strike an obstacle with the tail and tear it. But what would follow next? Anyway, I will be able to return to base and make a safe landing with such damage," Laryushin said. His words proved prophetic – two decades later, one of the Ka-50s operated by the RAA's Torzhok training centre lost its rudder while flying a cross-country mission. The pilot failed to notice that the rudder had separated due to hinge failure. The helicopter continued its flight without any stability and control disturbances related to the rudder loss. The Ka-50 pilot only eventually realised the rudder had been lost when a warning was issued from the regiment commanding officer (CO), flying behind him.

Mikheev recalled that a couple of weeks after this statement of Laryushin's, he received permission to conduct a demo flight with the coaxial Ka-27. Mikheev said:

Evgeny Ivanovich [Laryushin] flew at an altitude of about 5m (16ft), well below the tree canopy and right over a field featuring a system of trenches. He was escorted by another helicopter, used as a camera ship, with video- and photo-operators onboard. The test flight was conducted in a bright sunny day and the helicopter's shadow was clearly visible running below it on the ground. After all, this experimental flight had played a pivotal role as the pilot managed to convince us that in complicated NoE flight conditions the coaxial [attack] helicopter would be noticeably better than the conventional one.

The revolutionary single-seat concept embraced by Mikheev then had to be sold to the military and MAP leadership as a doable and effective solution for boosting the flight performance of the future attack helicopter. The analyses of the all available information gathered at the OKB Kamov, including the published US research in this area, together with research works undertaken by the Moscow Aviation Institute and the *30 TsNII* scientific-research institute of the Soviet MoD, motivated Mikheev to claim that the high level of system automation would boost the pilot's situation awareness. This, in turn, would make it possible to design an operationally effective single-seat attack helicopter. The pilot of such a machine would need reliable targeting information, as well as a good situational awareness of terrain features, threats, navigation environment and operability of the helicopter's systems. In addition, he had to be supplied with information about the position of other helicopters in the group conducting coordinated attack operations. These tasks, according to Mikheev, could be solved by using the technologies available in the late 1970s, in terms of high-performance sensors and advanced system automation. He was confident that the technology level attained in the Soviet Union at the time would allow the design of a single-seat helicopter. His confidence had been reinforced by the excellent controllability and stability performance of the coaxial rotor design, which would allow implementation of a high level of automation in the air vehicle's control system. This feature had already been implemented on the Ka-27PL *Helix-A* anti-submarine helicopter, boasting highly automatic modes of flight that were useful when the machine was engaged in group anti-submarine search operations and when returning to the ship.

Kamov's head, Sergey Mikheev, presents the V-80's full-scale mock-up to the VVS CinC, Aviation Marshal Pavel Kutakhov. (Kamov OKB)

Later on, the coaxial, single-seat concept proposed by the Kamov OKB was warmly embraced by the VVS Commander-in-Chief (CinC), Aviation Marshal Pavel Kutakhov. A fighter pilot, he was awarded the highest Soviet decoration, the Hero of the Soviet Union, for his extraordinary Second World War air combat exploits, which included shooting down 28 enemy aircraft solo, plus 14 more when fighting in a group. When he saw for the first time the mock-up of the Kamov's new attack machine, Aviation Marshal Kutakhov tended to comment in a straightforward manner: "It's the right layout for me! I'm the king in the air and why [do] I have to take a passenger with me? [It would only make me] responsible for his life."

The first images of the new coaxial attack helicopter wearing the preliminary designation V-80 were made by Sergey Fomin, a talented designer from the general layouts department of the Kamov OKB. The lighter single-pilot scheme allowed for an increase of the static ceiling by some 1,500m (4,920ft) and doubled the rate of climb compared a heavier two-seat helicopter, powered by the same engines. These are the key performance parameters, then and now, setting out the helicopter's offensive tactics and enabling it to mount attacks from ambush position while remaining as briefly as possible inside the lethal envelope of the enemy anti-aircraft systems.

The aircrew rescue system was another important novelty conceived for the V-80. Here, Mikheev had again relied on the published US experience, based on the information released on the test of the Sikorsky S-72, developed under the wide-ranging Rotor Systems Research Aircraft (RSRA) programme. A unique vehicle created to test advanced helicopter rotors in flight, the S-72 was also used to evaluate the suitability of introducing an aircrew escape system similar to those used on fixed-wing aircraft. It had been discovered that the downward ejection of crew members would not be acceptable due to the acceleration forcing the blood into their head; furthermore, helicopters as a rule operate close to the ground, precluding the downward direction of escape. So the crew escape system tested on the S-72 relied on small rockets fired upwards to pull the crew out of the helicopter, rather than the more conventional seat-installed rocket booster as used in fixed-wing aircraft ejection systems. Before ejection, the rotor blades had to be jettisoned i.e. blown away from the aircraft to allow a safe exit of the aircrew dragged by a rocket.

The RSPA programme had demonstrated the first crew escape system in the world specifically for use on rotorcraft, with a full-scale test at speed conducted by using a rocket sled at Holloman Air Force Base in New Mexico. US research had shown that the crew ejection system integrated on attack helicopters could increase the crew's overall combat effectiveness, as the crew members would have increased chances of survival in case of serious combat damage such as detached blades, main gearbox failure, control system failure or a fire on board that was impossible to extinguish. In addition, the crew ejection system allowed a reduction in the strength and dimensions of the undercarriage and the bottom fuselage structure.

The requirement for a crew escape system was also included in the Soviet specification for the new-generation attack helicopter. The MVZ Mil, however, was unwilling to adopt the aircrew ejection seat concept, once again citing data originating from other US research, which had shown that terrain-following low-level flight would render the crew ejection technically impossible, because pilots would lack the time to use the escape system. Hughes designers had also managed to prove that the use of a crew escape system on the AH-64 Apache would be impossible; instead, they had introduced a strengthened main landing gear with shock struts to absorb impact during hard landing, together with energy-absorbing (stroking) crew seats and deformable structural members which changed shape on impact and absordedb energy to enable crew survival in case of a crash landing. The Mi-28 used all these design features, together with inflatable slides to allow crew members the chance to escape the helicopter with parachutes at higher altitude.

Coaxial scheme advantages

The coaxial system is a trademark of almost all helicopter models developed by the Moscow-based experimental design bureau founded in 1947 by the talented Russian engineer, Nikolay Ilych Kamov. The development of such complex systems was a notably protracted process involving enormous design and testing efforts and immense funding. The coaxial rotor system was initially used in light piston-powered helicopters such as the Ka-8, Ka-10, Ka-15 and Ka-18. Coaxial rotors were later utilised successfully on the turbine-powered Ka-25 and Ka-27 series of naval helicopters.

A significant advantage of the coaxial rotor configuration mastered by the Kamov OKB is the compact overall dimensions it allows for a helicopter. The excellent stability and manoeuvrability performance conferred by the aerodynamic symmetry of the configuration were appreciated by the then Soviet Naval Aviation service, which put Kamov OKB's designs to good use in many shipborne roles. The coaxial advantages proved highly valuable for safe operations on rolling and pitching ship decks in rough seas. Finally, in the early 1980s, the coaxial rotor design had found its way onto the new V-80 armoured attack helicopter.

The coaxial rotor configuration creates lift, and at the same time eliminates the torque reaction and the resultant requirement for a tail rotor. Two identical three-blade main rotors, installed on a common rotor mast (often referred to by the Russians as a rotor column) turn in opposite directions (contra-rotating design), mutually cancelling the torque thanks to their common axis of rotation. In this way, torque is countered without any loss of power. In conventional helicopters i.e. those using the so-called classic main and tail rotor system the tail rotor is used to counter torque reaction (the so-called reactive momentum), which is created by the main rotor tending to turn the fuselage in the opposite direction.

In conventional-layout helicopters, any change in power (and associated change in the amount of lift created by the rotor system) would result in an imbalance of yaw, which must be countered by application of pedal to control the pitch (and thus thrust) of the tail rotor. Pilots of conventional helicopters are required to constantly adjust the thrust created by the tail rotor in order to keep the helicopter balanced all the time, and this design feature incurs a number of negative consequences.

According to Dr Eduard A. Petrosyan, Kamov OKB's deputy designer-general, from an energy point of view, the optimal rotorcraft design would transform all available power to lift and propulsive force in any given flight regime. Comparing coaxial and conventional designs (assuming the same amount of power is consumed for auxiliary needs such as generators and hydraulic pumps, etc.), the coaxial system has no losses, since all of the available power is used for generating lift. However, a conventional design requires power to drive the tail rotor typically between 10 and 12 percent of the total power supplied to the main rotor shaft. From a lift point of view, this power is considered a complete loss.

With a coaxial rotor configuration, there is no imbalance of yaw with changes in power. The pedals are used to create a difference in torque between the two rotors to produce yaw.

Flight test experiments and other research has shown that coaxial rotors boast between six and 10 percent better aerodynamic efficiency than conventional rotor configurations. When this is combined with the power consumed for driving the tail rotor, the overall efficiency advantage of the coaxial over conventional configurations is between 16 and 22 percent. In practical terms, this advantage would translate into a static ceiling of 500–1,000m (1,600–3,280ft) higher, and a rate of climb between 4 and 5m/s (780 and 980f/m) faster than conventionally configured machines.

As might be expected, the notably taller rotor mast of coaxial helicopters creates more drag. Kamov designers spent a good many efforts to reduce drag created by the V-80, which proved to be 30 percent less than that created by the Ka-27, enabling the V-80 to hit a maximum speed of 310km/h (167kt) in level flight, while in shallow dive the helicopter demonstrated 395km/h (213kt).

In the event, flight tests of both attack helicopter competitors, the Mi-28 (conventional rotor design) and V-80 (coaxial rotor design), had demonstrated in the early 1980s that there was no difference between these two types in the power settings required to maintain the same forward speeds. This can be explained by the phenomenon of positive mutual interference of both rotors in horizontal flight using the so-called 'biplane box' effect created by the coaxial system, which results in a fraction less power being required to create lift (so-called inductive power). In addition, the coaxial scheme has none of the power losses associated with driving a tail rotor, none of the additional drag created by the tail rotor (especially in relation to the negative interference between the tail rotor and the fin), or the additional drag created by the forced sideslip inherent to the flight behaviour of all conventional-layout helicopters (in order to eliminate this sideslip, a pilot has the option of banking the helicopter). It is also possible to reduce the drag of the coaxial helicopter even further by incorporating a retractable undercarriage a notable feature of the V-80, which has the same top speed as that of its conventional counterpart, the Mi-28.

Furthermore, the coaxial rotor scheme allows for smaller dimensions and weights than those of conventional designs. In the case of coaxial and conventional helicopters of identical weights, with identical engine power, the overall dimensions of the coaxial machine can be made around 35–40 percent smaller.

Among the factors contributing to the reduction in overall dimensions is the ability to reduce rotor diameter in the more efficient coaxial system. With no tail rotor, a coaxial machine also needs no tail boom and associated complex transmission components extending beyond the main rotor's diameter.

If a coaxial and conventional helicopter were to use main rotors of the same diameter, as a rule, the latter would have a lower take-off weight because of the lower aerodynamic efficiency and the inevitable

The Ka-27 *Helix* is a typical representative of Kamov OKB's trademark coaxial rotor scheme, suitable for demanding shipborne operations due to its superior controllability and stability characteristics, even in strong crosswind and tailwind conditions. (Sergey Mikheev)

The drag of the rotor column of the V-80 was significantly reduced compared to that of the Ka-27; in combination with the streamlined fuselage, it provides reasonably high cruise and maximum speeds that are comparable with those of both the Mi-28 and AH-64 Apache. (Author)

The aerodynamically symmetrical coaxial rotors are free of cross-channel control influences, which greatly simplifies handling. (Sergey Nosov archive)

power losses associated with the tail rotor assembly. With the need to mount and drive its tail rotor, the conventional helicopter's dimensions would be approximately 20 percent larger than those of the coaxial design with the same rotor diameter.

The coaxial helicopter also boasts less longitudinal and directional inertial momentums, which would in turn entail better stability and controllability performance.

Kamov OKB's Petrosyan also notes that the most important consideration in assessing the stability and controllability performance of the coaxial helicopter relates to its aerodynamic symmetry. This can be explained by the fact that the aircraft's aerodynamic symmetry provides a set of important handling qualities and, most importantly, simplicity of control.

Symmetry is clearly evident in fixed-wing aircraft, which all have symmetrical properties in terms of dimensions, weight and thrust. It would be difficult to imagine, as Petrosyan pointed out, the existence of fixed-wing aircraft with different wings or powered by engines developing different thrust. Should this be the case, such a non-symmetrical aircraft would have to fly all the time either with bank or sideslip, and the relationships (couplings) arising from the alterations in thrust, directional and lateral balancing would make its handling unusual and difficult compared to symmetrical machines.

Nevertheless, most of the helicopter-makers worldwide have embraced the non-symmetrical (i.e. conventional) design because of a perceived simplicity, which is in fact illusory, as it is always a complex and costly undertaking to design an effective tail rotor and transmission with acceptable service life and performance.

The aerodynamic symmetry of the coaxial design is possible thanks to the lack of torque reaction on the helicopter's fuselage, with the relative proximity of the top and bottom rotors, and their positive mutual interference resulting in small differences in the lift they create in a balanced position. The counter-rotating rotors compensate for each other and the lateral momentum created by the difference in the height of the rotors is negligible.

With no tail rotor, there is no permanent lateral disruptive influence acting on the stabiliser, which in a conventional helicopter influences its stability and controllability. These characteristics of the latter category make their handling much more complex at low level, such as when landing in confined spaces, and when flying in hot and elevated environments or emergency situations. By comparison, coaxial helicopters are relatively simple to control; in terms of stability, controllability and manoeuvrability, they boast significant advantages over their conventional counterparts.

Well-known Kamov OKB test pilot Nikolay Bezdetnov (who flew the V-80 during its maiden hovering and forward flights) describes flying a coaxial helicopter as being "as easy as walking on the street, thus freeing all human resources for solving tactical tasks".

The combat effectiveness of an attack helicopter is defined by many factors, but manoeuvrability performance is undoubtedly among the most important. The manoeuvrability, in turn, is closely related to stability and controllability characteristics. Controllability performance is defined as the relationship between the movements of the controls and the resultant changes in helicopter movement parameters, while stability describes the acceptability and simplicity of controlling the helicopter. In the combat aircraft world, manoeuvrability describes the ability to place an aircraft (whether for attack or defence) into the most advantageous spatial position relative to the target. This requires changes in both the flight-path and the angular position of the aircraft relative to that flight-path.

The V-80 is reported to have introduced and mastered a brand-new 'flat' (pedal) turn manoeuvre featuring sideslip angles of up to 180° left and right at speeds of up to 90–100km/h (48–54kt), while in

The coaxial scheme allows the designing of fully symmetrical rotorcraft with fair control responses. The fixed-wing aircraft-lookalike fuselage of the V-80, combined with the retractable undercarriage, has very low drag. (Kamov OKB)

a high-speed flight, the maximum permitted sideslip is 90°, in which case the bank angle would be close to zero.

The 'flat' turn is a combat manoeuvre that allows the helicopter to point its fixed, forward-firing weapons towards a target in the shortest possible time. As a consequence, it no longer requires the helicopter to have a heavy and complex turret for pointing the gun in different directions. In addition, the 'flat' turn expands the envelope for employing the rocket armament. Overall, this manoeuvre offers significant agility advantages when attacking either air or ground targets.

Altitude does not have the effect on the directional controllability of coaxial helicopters that it does on conventional helicopters, which are severely affected with increases in altitude. At their out of ground effect ceiling, conventional helicopters cannot turn without losing altitude.

The coaxial helicopter can also use the 'flat' turn during take-off and landing irrespective of wind speed or direction, which means it can land safely even in a strong tailwind. This can be an important consideration for landing in confined spaces or when having to avoid obstacles during the final part of an approach, providing additional operational and tactical advantages.

2

BIRTH OF THE V-80

Tasked to kill tanks

In the mid-1970s, the ATGM-armed helicopter became a pretty effective and very flexible anti-tank weapon. The experimental exercises held in 1972 near Ansbach, Germany, involving US Army AH-1G Cobra helicopters armed with the Hughes BGM-71 TOW (Tube-launched, Optically-tracked, Wire-guided) anti-tank missiles, operating against German Army Leopard 1 main battle tanks (MBTs), resulted in somewhat shocking results for its organisers. The anti-tank helicopters proved extremely successful in repulsing an armoured push, demonstrating an astonishing kill ratio of 28 MBTs per single aircraft loss. In 1973 and 1974, the US Army conducted more controlled exercises of this nature, pitting attack helicopters against MBTs simulating massed attacks of Soviet tank formations. The results from these wide-scale simulations had shown that the kill ratio in the encounters varied from 3:1 to 14:1, depending on the numbers of the attack helicopters involved in the massed anti-armour operation.

The Soviet military was also aware of the results achieved during the US Army-controlled anti-armour tests in Germany, employing

ATGM-armed helicopters, and requested its prospective attack helicopters have vastly increased tank-killing abilities, turning them into potential game-changers on the battlefield.

At the same time, the battlefield air defence assets in the West were considerably strengthened thanks to the fielding of modern self-propelled low-level weapons such as the MIM-79 Chaparral, Roland and Rapier SAM and the Gepard 30mm anti-aircraft artillery (AAA) systems, augmented by the mass fielding of the FIM-43 Red Eye shoulder-launched SAM with the US Army. These lethal and highly mobile anti-aircraft systems, defending armour formations in offensive or defensive combat orders, left little or no space at all for unobstructed helicopter anti-tank battlefield operations. This fact was well understood by Mikheev, who told the VVS CinC, Aviation Marshal Pavel Kutakhov, that in duel situations (when pitted against modern mobile SAM and AAA systems), an ordinary attack helicopter could survive the heat of battle for no longer than 16 seconds. The anti-aircraft system crews, as a rule, work and fight in much more comfortable conditions than the helicopter crews in the air, and this is set to decide the outcome of encounters. That is why the key to survivability on the battlefield of the 1980s and 1990s in Central Europe would be to allow the new Kamov OKB attack machine to kill tanks and other well-protected small-size targets, by staying well outside the air defence umbrella set up over the advancing or dug-in defensive position enemy armour units. A new-generation of ATGMs was clearly needed, able to outreach the enemy battlefield air defence systems; it was also to be made fast enough to avoid exposing the launch rotorcraft for too long when conducting the target engagement cycle.

Vyacheslav Dorin, a senior designer at the Kamov OKB at the time of designing the new-generation attack helicopter in the 1970s and 1980s, recalls:

The V-80's combat employment concept, as originally conceived, has been based upon two main pillars. The first of these called for a further development of the experience in the deployment of stand-off helicopter-launched guided missiles with a range of up to 5km [2.7nm]. It was also required to feature high accuracy and concentration of the hits [when unleashing unguided ordinance]. This is a must when performing escort of columns on the move while simultaneously engaging enemy positions in close proximity by using the canon and rockets.

In such situations, as Dorin claimed, the most important consideration is to avoid fratricide and civilian casualties. Getting as accurate as possible target positional data is a prerequisite for the accurate weapon deployment at short ranges. This, in turn, requires the helicopter to be equipped with highly accurate detection and targeting systems boasting resolution performance no less than two times better than the Raduga-F/Sh direct-optics system used on the Mi-24D/V. The long-range targeting options would be greatly expanded by the means of external targeting thanks to the use of sophisticated datalinks for exchanging tactical information between helicopters, fixed-wing aircraft, command-and-control (C2) centres and forward air controllers embedded into the ground troops' combat order.

The second pillar, according to Dorin, called for mounting the attack unseen, which necessitates the helicopter to be made capable of detecting, identifying the possible targets and launching its ATGMs at the chosen targets before being detected by the enemy.

Another baseline principle for designing the weapons system for the new helicopter was set out by the military requirement it be able to undertake target search at distances up to 10km (5.4nm), with missile engagements conducted at between 6–8km (3.2–4.3nm). Such extended detection and engagement ranges would allow the attacker

Aviation Marshal Pavel Kutakhov wrote on the full-scale mock-up of the V-80 at the Kamov OKB's premises in Lyubertsi on 14 March 1981. An English translation of the text is: "Fire and forget in all weather, day and night. This shall be accelerated!" (Kamov OKB)

to remain well outside the lethal range of the vast majority of enemy's air defence systems. This particular requirement had originated from a detailed analysis of the future developments of the anti-air systems in the Western world. During this analysis, it had turned out that the reaction time of all modern SAM and AAA systems would always be shorter than that needed by the pilots of fixed-wing attack aircraft or helicopters to select those targets on the battlefield representing the biggest threats, acquire, put the sight mark on them, designate, fire the missiles and then continue tracking the target for missile guidance until impact. In case of simultaneous detection of the air defence systems (that are used to protect the enemy armour) and the attacking aircraft, the crew of the latter would retain rather small chances for a successful engagement. That is why it was deemed instrumental to extend the missile engagement zone as long as possible in a bid that the attacker be able to launch its ATGMs beyond the SAM and AAA lethal range.

In order to gain better understanding about the tank battlefield tactics and operations, Mikheev contacted Soviet MBT designers. During this effort he had several times visited Nikolay Popov, chief-designer of the Kirov Plant in Leningrad. Upon request from the Kamov OKB, Popov had made a short study and wrote a detailed letter to Mikheev explaining how he saw the role of the attack helicopter in future land battles.

Based on Popov's information, Mikheev set up a diagram on his desk, illustrating several types of combat action of the enemy armour formations at day and night, including deployment of the units and their relocation into chosen staging areas with concealing measures in a bid to avoid detection and attacks from the air. The available Soviet and Western expertise and experience in anti-tank warfare, called for specialised rotary- or fixed-wing aircraft to conduct battlefield reconnaissance and provide the initial targeting cues to the shooters, represented by aircraft armed with ATGMs fired from long distances. According to Soviet anti-tank warfare experts, the search for and detection of well-concealed tanks in their pre-attack staging areas could be possible only with the use of fixed-wing attack aircraft, because attack helicopters would suffer from considerable losses.

Detection of tanks on the move or deployed in attack formations on the battlefield could be much easier thanks to the large clouds of smoke and dust created by the moving armoured tracked monsters, easy detectable by optical and thermal imaging sensors. In this case, the search for and automatic target tracking to enable ATGM attacks would be possible to be automated to a maximum possible extent.

The long-term shaping of attack helicopter design, intended to be used mainly in the anti-tank role, was not only undertaken by Russian rotorcraft designers. Their counterparts in USA, Germany and France had done exactly the same job by designing specialised anti-tank rotary- and fixed-wing aircraft in the mid/late 1970s. But nobody had been able to predict at the time how radically things would change only 15 years later.

A complex targeting system needed

The combat employment experience gained in the 1970s demonstrated that attack helicopter survivability, when facing dense air defences, could be granted only at ultra-low level, flying NoE at heights between 5–50m (16–160ft). In such situations, the weapons system operator (WSO) becomes a mere passenger in the helicopter, as ATGM employment could be possible at altitudes of between 35–70m (115–230ft) over flat terrain and between 100–245m (328–804ft) when operating over rugged terrain. At the same time, the ATGM guidance process would be possible to be automated, with all operator tasks handed over to the pilot, who would be relieved of the pressure to

A sub-scale model of the V-80 in its initial form, with a more streamlined fuselage, large fin with rudder, ventral fin and mid-set tailplane without endplate auxiliary fins. (Viktor Bakursky archive)

handle the helicopter otherwise experienced in ultra-low-level flight. According to Dorin, by that time the design team had a clear view on the future combat employment specifics: "The pilot and helicopter have to be integrated as a single body, reacting immediately and adequately to any combat situation changes. There is no spare time and the pilot has to evaluate the situation by himself, take decisions in a prompt manner, handle the helicopter and fire the weapons."

This way, the V-80 designers had realised that they had to walk away from the then-prevailing federated systems concept (i.e. using stand-alone navigation and flight instruments, sights, etc.); instead, they had decided to implement a fully integrated flight/navigation/ attack suite, automating as much as possible the flight control processes and displaying in front of the pilot only easy-to-understand information with prompts for a faster decision-taking cycle. Increased system automation of the V-80 would also save structural weight and allow effective single-crewman combat operations in NoE flight at ultra-low level.

Mikheev tasked his team to propose a novel avionics system that would enable a single crewman to deal with the same tasks that are handled by the Apache's pilot and WSO. He and his deputy responsible for avionics, Nikolay Emelyanov, knew well that pilots of single-seat fixed-wing attack aircraft would cope well with the task of dealing with small-size targets while flying at ultra-low level, so they assumed that the same task could also be successfully handled by the pilot of a single-seat attack helicopter. Furthermore, fixed-wing attack aircraft typically fly at higher speeds and therefore their pilots have to accommodate within a shorter reaction time when searching for and firing at ground targets.

The solution to enable single-crewman operation was found in a fairly natural manner. When engaged in a head-to-head competitive tender, nobody would be willing to take the risk of developing a clean-sheet targeting system. That is why Kamov OKB's design team used as a base the Su-25T's avionics system that allows a single pilot to fly and fight at ultra-low level. Such an approach was justified by the shortage of time needed for developing an all-new system. The Soviet Communist Party and the Soviet Government were not expected to tolerate any lag in the competition with the rapidly developing anti-tank helicopter technologies in the USA. The new Soviet attack helicopter, intended to kill both the M1 Abrams and Leopard 2 MBTs, was to be fielded into service with the Soviet Red Army as soon as possible. So, in a bid to speed-up the development works, the V-80

The V-80's cockpit was designed in cooperation with the Elektroavtomatika science-research enterprise of Leningrad (now St Petersburg), based on that conceived for the Su-25T. (Alexander Papay archive)

near the tile edges, the ceramic armour protection resistance would be reduced by far. At the same time, the steel plating, albeit heavier, could sustain hits by projectiles up to 12.7mm calibre without serious damage (as armour-piercing projectiles tend to make only small holes, comparable to their calibre), while the rest of the plate would retain its full protective properties without the need for replacement.

The protection scheme proposed for the V-80 included a two-layer spaced armour design. The outer layer, without load-bearing function within the helicopter airframe structure, was made of steel plating using enhanced-resistance steel alloy. The inner layer was made of softer aluminium alloy plating. This rather thick aluminium-alloy structure also served as a load-bearing member of the airframe structure, used to form the cockpit walls.

During the tender, the Ministry of Aircraft Industry (abbreviated MAP in Russian) proposed that both bidders use a common avionics system as this would result, at least in theory, in sensible savings of development money. The Ramenskoye Instrument-Making Design Bureau (RPKB) was nominated as the developer of the future attack helicopter avionics system, but in the event this proved to be a rather risky undertaking, impossible to be achieved with the defence electronics technologies available at that time in the Soviet Union. At the same time, the single-seat V-80 necessitated a much more sophisticated avionics suite than its two-seat rival developed by the MVZ Mil, in order to achieve the conceived very high level of automation of onboard systems. To get access to a new-generation and sufficiently capable avionics system, Mikheev contacted the Leningrad-based Electroavtomatika science-production enterprise, the developer of the Su-25's and Su-25T's mission suites, asking for assistance with the V-80 project.

inherited the Su-25T's sight/head-up display and TV auto-tracking system almost unchanged it became the heart of the highly-integrated and automated flight/navigation/attack suite named PrPNK-80 Rubikon.

In the beginning, the Kamov OKB's design team also considered borrowing the Su-25's titanium bathtub protecting the pilot from projectiles and high-speed missile warhead fragments. Combat employment studies, however, showed that attack helicopters operate at relatively low speeds and predominantly at ultra-low level, so the angle of arrival of projectiles would be close to 90°. In such battle damage conditions, however, the titanium armour would fare noticeably worse than steel protection, and this revelation had motivated the design team to use extensive steel armour plating to protect the pilot and the most vulnerable fuselage zones.

There were also in-depth research and development works carried out, including full-scale testing of various types of steel and ceramic armour protection. The ceramic protection was judged as lighter but had a serious shortcoming, rendering it ill-suited for use on an attack helicopter designed to soak up heavy punishment from anti-aircraft weapons and small-arms fire. The ceramic armour had to be applied in the form of separate tiles (each measuring 100x100mm), attached to a base surface by bonding. This structure of the ceramic armour protection, using hundreds of tiles, would, however, render it practically irreparable in field conditions, as all damaged tiles should be replaced by new ones, using a very complex and temperature-sensitive bonding method. In addition, in case of hits sustained

Cannon and ATGM selection

The next task to be solved personally by Mikheev called for selecting a long-legged ATGM system for the V-80, capable to knock-out heavy-armoured new-generation MBTs from safe distances, well outside the reach of enemy battlefield air defence systems. The competitor, MVZ Mil, had already decided to team with its long-time partner, the Kolomna-based KBM design bureau, the developer of the 9M114 Shturm-V supersonic ATGM integrated on the Mi-24V/P versions. Cooperation between the KBM and MVZ Mil was well-honed during the development of the Mi-24, both design houses committed to proceed forward together during the development of the *Hind's* successor. In addition to the guided missiles, the MVZ Mil intended to arm its new-generation attack machine with a turret-mounted 23mm GSh-23 cannon.

In stark contrast, the Kamov OKB had to start from a scratch as it lacked any experience in the field of ATGM technologies and integration. To get an initial knowledge in this, for him, brand-new world, Mikheev called his counterpart at the MVZ Mil, Marat Tishtchenko, asking him to share the available information and experience on integrating ATGMs developed by KBM. In response, Mikheev heard words that he remembered for life: "Frankly speaking, I do not understand why a tender would be needed for that."

If we have to look at the root cause of the statement at that specific moment, perhaps Tishtchenko had been ahead of himself. Many years later, Mikheev openly admitted that these words from Tishtchenko had played a clearly positive role, strongly motivating him to look at solving the ATGM problem from a completely different angle.

The search for a new solution of the ATGM issue was made even more difficult due to the rather rigid position of the KBM leadership, who had hinted in a mild form in front of Mikheev that the company may engage itself with the ATGM integration on the V-80, but this could be undertaken only when it was relieved from the main workload.

The way out of this dead-end situation was prompted by the VVS CinC, Aviation Marshall Pavel Kutakhov, who advised Mikheev to contact the Tula-based KBP company. He immediately phoned the KBP leadership and soon received a warm welcome from both big guns at the company – Arkady Shipunov and Vasily Gryazev. The first meeting turned Mikheev into a keen fan of the famous Tula-based ordinance design house. He presented to Gryazev and Shipunov his novel single-seat attack-helicopter concept featuring a pretty high level of automation in search and attack operations, unseen in the Soviet Union at the time. In return Mikheev, as he recalled, was more than glad to find keen supporters in Gryazev and Shipunov, who had shared his passion and striving to search for novel solutions. They also proved to be pretty good speakers, able to convince his interlocutors in that statement whenever needed. This set of skills had already worked well during this first meeting, as Gryazev succeeded in convincing Mikheev that the only cannon that should be installed on the V-80 was the KBP's then brand-new 30mm 2A42 model, purposely developed for the BMP-2 IFV. Thirty-five years later, Mikheev recalled:

I simply fell in love with the gun. It fully coincided with my internal conviction that the cannon is a key helicopter weapon. The 30mm 2A42 is able to score accurate hits at targets at 4,000m [13,120ft] distance. But it also had a major shortcoming related to its very powerful recoil force, reaching 6.5 tonnes. This was a great engineering challenge for me as the chief-designer of the helicopter. When I saw the 2A42 for the first time I had immediately realised

that this is a huge piece of kit and should be installed right into the helicopter's centre of gravity.

It is noteworthy that this visit of Mikheev to Tula had set in motion a brand-new direction for the Soviet combat helicopter-building industry. The 2A42 was a revolutionary new cannon, offering sizeable advantages compared to traditional aviation guns despite its greater weight and much more powerful recoil forces compared to the specialised aircraft cannons (also designed by the Tula-based KBP). In the event, the 2A42 was installed on the Ka-50 and later found its place on the Mi-28, Mi-28N and Ka-52.

But these events were to take place far in the future. In the very beginning of the V-80's design process, the cannon choice proved a big surprise for the VVS and representatives of the scientific-research institutes involved in the research and development programme. As Mikheev recalls, when informed about the cannon choice for the V-80, one of the VVS senior officers involved in the process had exclaimed: "It's going to be accepted only after passing through my dead body!" Fortunately, this never happened.

Among the important advantages of the 2A42 were the dual-feed capability and reliable operation in harsh environmental conditions. According to its developers at the KBP, the operating specifics of attack helicopters are, in fact, much closer to that of MBTs rather than fixed-wing aircraft. Mikheev justified his choice of the 2A42 with the following argument:

Usually the belt that feeds traditional aviation guns contains both fragmentation/high-explosive and armour-piercing types of rounds. But this could lead to an unjustifiably high round consumption

Three legendary heads of the world-famous Soviet-era defence industry design bureaux from the left: Mikhail Kalashnikov, Arkady Shipunov and Sergey Mikheev. (Sergey Mikheev archive)

The KBP 2A42 cannon as installed in the V-80's NPPU-80 hydraulically-driven mount. (Kamov OKB)

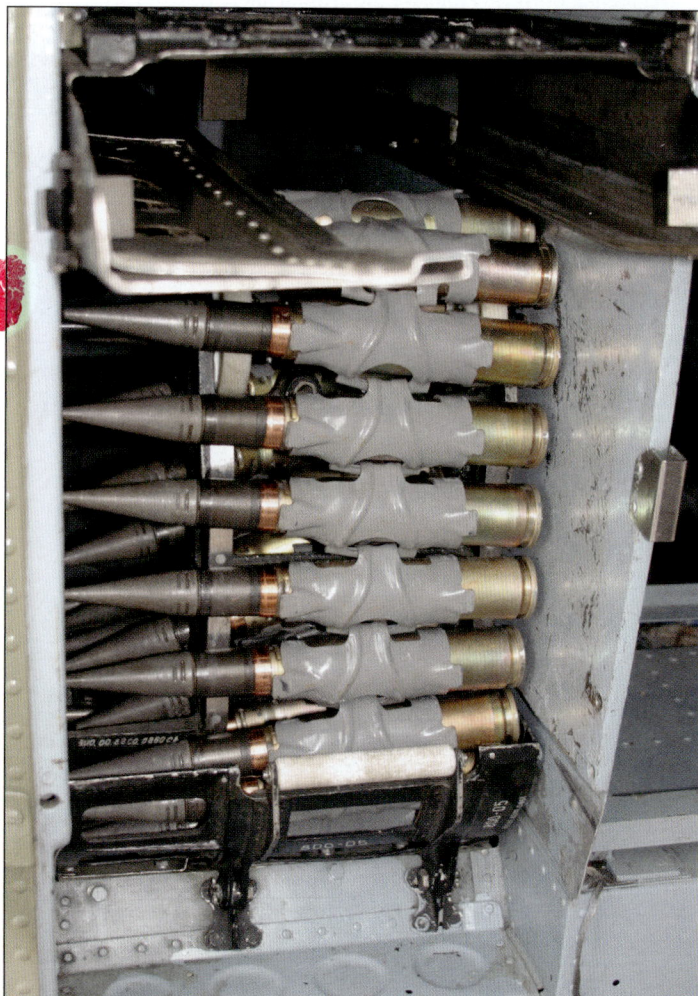

One of the two belts with 30mm rounds feeding the 2A42 dual-feed cannon. (Kamov OKB)

rate. When engaging a tank with the cannon, the fragmentation/ high explosive rounds are not effective at all. That is why we had installed two ammunition boxes on the V-80, one containing armour-piercing rounds and another with fragmentation/high-explosive ones. After selecting the target, the pilot can switch to the most appropriate ammunition for getting the best lethal effect. If an armoured target has to be engaged, he would fire armour-piercing rounds only. There was also an important consideration related to solving the cannon cooling problem. The standard aviation guns are cooled by the air stream and usually fire in short bursts. In contrast, attack helicopters are tasked to operate at low altitude, in [a] dusty atmosphere, where aviation guns cannot be used effectively [due to reliability considerations] whereas the 2A42 had been designed from the onset for prolonged usage in such difficult conditions, unleashing shells in long bursts.

The V-80's long-legged sting

Capable and resourceful, KBP's Gryazev and Shipunov also offered Mikheev an attractive solution to the main problem, a long-range ATGM system capable of engaging targets on the battlefield, well outside the lethal reach of enemy anti-aircraft weapons, represented by the new-generation self-propelled SAM and AAA systems fielded in the Western world. Shipunov already had an idea in his head for a long-range missile but lacked a suitable platform. Mikeeev, in turn, had a new helicopter under development but lacked a suitable missile. So, the two ideas met and the synergy between them resulted in the creation of the V-80's powerful and lethal anti-tank missile system.

Shipunov's new ATGM system, named Vikhr (Gale), boasted two features unique for that time – it had supersonic speed and promised effective ranges of up to 10km (5.4nm); in addition, it was intended to feature previously unseen armour penetration capability thanks to the powerful tandem warhead. The helicopter or fixed-wing aircraft launching it would achieve a decisive advantage in duel situations;

The Vikhr ATGM was a revolutionary new anti-tank guided weapon in the early 1980s, with previously unseen range, accurate guidance and lethality. (Author)

in line with Mikheev's novel idea on the V-80's combat employment method when engaging MBTs protected by modern air defences.

KBP's design team working on the Vikhr ATGM system decided to walk away from the then-modern semi-active laser guidance method because it had been considered ill-suited for mounting surprise attacks from extended ranges. All the modern MBTs would be equipped with laser warning receivers, providing the tank crew with an early warning of the incoming missile and allowing immediate use of appropriate countermeasures such as smoke grenades that would break the ATGM guidance. To avoid this, Shipunov proposed to use the well-known command guidance method, but without deploying a wire or radio beam to transmit steering commands from the helicopter to the missile. He instead offered to utilise the then-revolutionary new laser beam-riding guidance method, with a laser beam sending steering commands to the missile from launch to impact. Dorin explains: "The laser beam used for this purpose has a selectable power; it is gradually amplified after launch and therefore its effective length would accurately follow the launched missiles, without lagging behind or overtaking it. The missile looks like it is literally riding onto the laser-beam tip."

Another competitive advantage of the Vikhr missile was its high speed of 600m/s (1,968f/s), enabling it to travel 8km (4.3nm) in only 21 seconds.

The V-80 was slated to receive a highly automated TV targeting system capable of tracking the selected target and guiding a missile towards it; at the same time also displaying the aiming mark for firing with the gun. This very sophisticated electro-optical targeting system was developed by the Krasnogorsk Optical-Mechanical Plant. Named Shkval-V (Squall), in its initial form the system featured wide and narrow fields of view (FoV) TV channels together with an IR targeting channel for detecting targets featuring thermal contrast against the background (in fact, this had never been included in the production-standard system), an auto-tracking device, a laser rangefinder and an

The lethal effect of a Vikhr ATGM hit on a tank turret is clearly visible. (Kamov OKB)

This illustration made during an early test shows how deep the Vikhr's extremely powerful shaped-charge warhead could penetrate into thick armour plating. (Kamov OKB)

ATGM laser-beam guidance device. The system's optical elements were installed onto a platform provided with a two-axis gyro-stabilisation accommodated inside the helicopter nose.

The Shkval-V nav/attack system integrated a TV system, a Prichal laser rangefinder and an ATGM laser-beam missile homing system. The system's high-resolution TV sensor had a wide FoV mode, covering 36°x27° picture, which was usable for target search. The narrow FoV (1°x0.7°) was used for target tracking, providing 25x

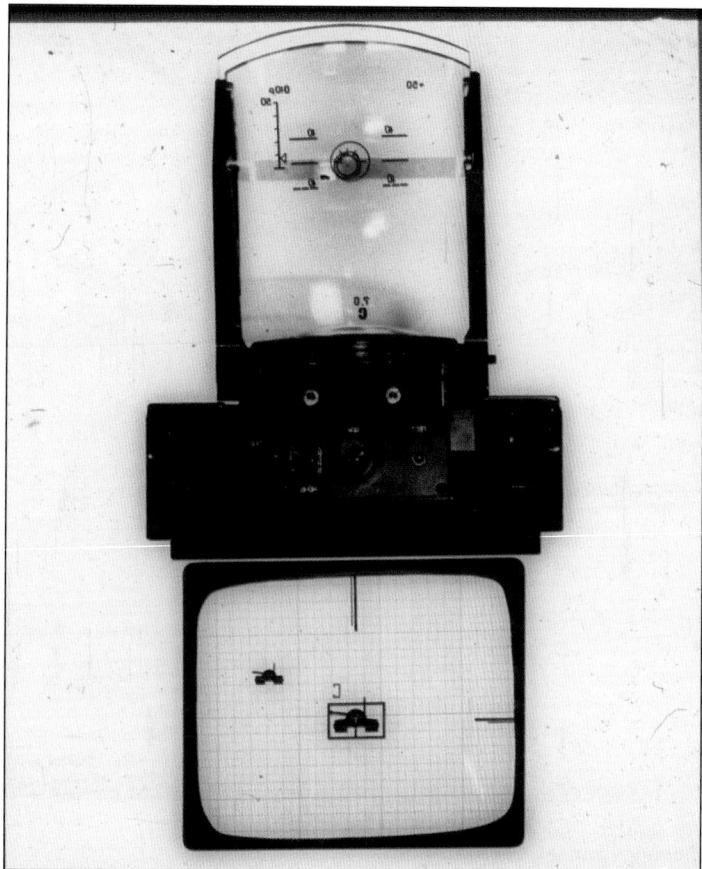

A view of the two principal displays of the Shkval-V TV/laser targeting system, with a HUD above and a TV display below, showing target acquisition and auto-tracking symbols. (Kamov OKB)]

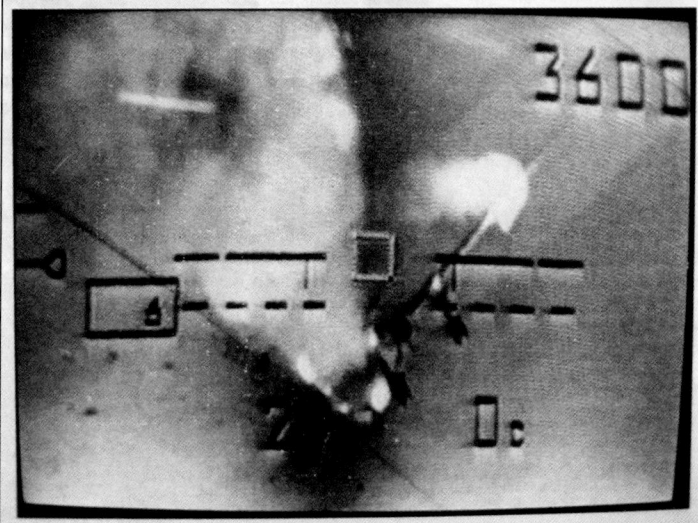

The sophisticated Shkval TV/laser targeting system in operation. The upper image displays the system tracking a MBT, while the bottom one shows a Vikhr ATGM (in this case launched by a Su-25T attack aircraft) scoring a direct hit on a Tu-16 bomber, used as an unmanned target drone. (Sukhoi OKB)

scene zoom. The system's Line of Sight (LoS) was capable of steering through 70° in azimuth (i.e. in the horizontal plane, 35° left and right) and from 15° above the centreline and 80° below (i.e. in the vertical plane). The late 1970s-vintage system was made capable of tracking moving tank-size targets and designating them for missile launch at ranges extending to 8km (4.3nm). The system was also advertised as being capable of detecting a bridge from 20–24km (11–13nm), and single buildings were detected from 15km (8.1nm). When used against air targets, the Shkval-V was capable of detecting fixed-wing jet aircraft from 10km (5.4 nm) and helicopters from 6km (3.2nm).

The engagement sequence using the Shkval-V called first for utilising the wide FoV of the TV system for target detection, starting at about 12km (6.5nm) distance from the target position. Then the pilot had to switch to the narrow FoV for target identification, followed by decision-making on whether to attack it or not. When conducting an attack, he had to put the aiming mark onto the target (shown on the IT-23M CRT display in the cockpit) by using a mini-joystick, located on the grip of the control stick, and then engaging the system's auto-tracking mode. After getting stable auto-tracking of the selected target, the pilot could launch one or two ATGMs on the target. Auto-tracking could be maintained even in the case of a brief exit of the target from the Shkval-V's narrow FoV. The system also allowed ATGM firings against air targets because it featured pretty stable and rapid-response auto-tracking capability.

3

NEVER-ENDING TENDER

Clashes from the very beginning

The tender for the new-generation attack helicopter for the Soviet Red Army created many internal clashes from the very beginning. The MVZ Mil refused to agree with the fact that the much smaller and less powerful Kamov OKB could be a true rival to the expected competition. The apparent superiority of the MVZ Mil as the Soviet Union's principal rotorcraft design house had been overwhelming at the time. This advantageous position was clearly evident in the official status of the heads of the two design bureaux. MVZ Mil's Marat Tishtchenko was titled 'designer-general', while Mikheev remained 'chief-designer' only, which entailed a lower status in the strict hierarchy of the Soviet aviation industry in the 1970s.

Following this 'logic', the first demonstration of the helicopter sub-scale models proposed by the two contenders had been organised in the headquarters of the MVZ Mil at Sokolnichesky Val in the centre of Moscow. Kamov OKB designer Evgeny Sudarev was tasked to show the mock-up, but security personnel refused to permit him to enter the building with the huge box containing the V-80 sub-scale mock-up. Sudarev was allowed in only after he told the security guards at the gate that he had been ordered to deliver this secret load for review by the VVS CinC, Aviation Marshal Pavel Kutakhov. During the display in front of the VVS commission, Marat Tishtchenko was impressed by the Kamov's novel concept, while deputy chief-designer A. Ivanov, appointed as the head of the Mi-28's design team, even noted: "Marat Nikolaevich, this would be a serious thing."

The joint VVS-Land Forces tactical-technical specification for the new-generation attack helicopter was approved, after long disputes and coordination effort, not before 2 December 1980. Four months earlier, in August that year, the Military-Industrial Commission of the Soviet Council of Ministers issued a decree obliging the bidders in the tender to build two Mi-28 and two V-80 experimental helicopters for participation in comparative trails. This was, in fact, the real launch of the Soviet Union's 'helicopter competition of the century' which continued under one form or another until the present day.

During his visit to the Kamov OKB premises in Lyubertsi on 14 March 1981, and after accepting Mikheev's report on the progress of work on the V-80, VVS CinC Kutakhov wrote spontaneously on the full-scale wooden mock-up the following instruction: "Fire-and-forget in all weathers, day and night. This shall be accelerated!"

The Kamov OKB entry was widely perceived as a revolutionary new one, with a significant use of non-metallic composite materials in the airframe design and extensive armour protection of the vulnerable areas. Colonel (Retired) Georgy Kuznetsov, an officer serving then with the GNIKI (VVS flight-test institute) recalls that he had been pretty much inspired by the V-80 when he saw it for the first time:

It was something unexpected and not looking like a helicopter at all. In fact, it was a real fighter – one pilot, accommodated in ejection seat, integrated flight/navigation/targeting suite, retractable landing gear, airplane-type empennage, perfect aerodynamic shapes and even rotor blades that would jettison in the event of ejection.

In fact, later on, Colonel Kuznetsov admitted that he had serious doubts about the Kamov OKB's chances of successfully implementing such an advanced project.

Other members of the State Mock-up Review Commission also asked many questions. Accustomed to evolutionary developments, the officers, including test pilots, lacked confidence in the revolutionary new solutions offered by the forward-thinking Kamov OKB. That is why the report of the State Mock-up Review Commission contained a text highlighting the need to provide additional information in a bid to justify some of the novel design solutions to be implemented in the V-80. This was the so-called 'constructive' critic. The commission eventually approved the V-80's definitive mock-up in early 1981 and recommended proceeding forward with the construction of a pair of experimental helicopters intended to be used in the flight test phase.

One month after, the competitor, MVZ Mil, presented the full-scale mock-up of its advanced attack helicopter. No doubt, it was a progressive design when compared to the Mi-24. But when put side by side with the V-80, it looked odd and the members of the State Mock-Up Review Commission and MVZ Mil representatives were forced to produce some notes. When asked to justify their design solutions, MVZ Mil designers explained that they had traded the aerodynamic performance of their new attack helicopter in favour of its main use, trying to boost its weapons employment effectiveness. The VVS

The first V-80 prototype, '010' (c/n 800-01), photographed at the company flight-test station in Zhulebino on the outskirts of Moscow. (Viktor Bakursky archive)

specialists, however, noticed that the Mi-28 lacked an integrated flight/navigation/attack suite; it was substituted by a bunch of individual instruments and systems. The Mil's new design also lacked a single integrator of its flight/navigation suite. It also became evident at this phase that the Mi-28's main gearbox was rated at 3,900shp, while the total power rating of the two engines amounted to 4,400shp. Colonel Kuznetsov noted at the meeting that the Mi-28, with its proposed flight performance, would lose the competition against the V-80. Marat Tishtchenko, however, replied that his design would satisfy the requirements outlined in the military specification. He added that nobody could teach him how to win competitions. It should be noted that in the event, the commission members were proved right as the MVZ Mil was eventually forced to re-work the entire main gearbox of the Mi-28.

Construction of the first V-80 at the Kamov OKB's experimental plant began in mid-1981, using some advanced manufacturing technologies. For the first time in the Soviet Union, the V-80 introduced rigid attachment of the rotor blades to the hub, with torsions (metal plates) providing the flapping during blade rotation. The rotor hub had a simplified design compared to that of the Ka-27. The production technology called for stamping it from titanium alloy in a bid to shorten the processing time at milling machines, and also to reduce the removed proportion of the rather expensive metal. The rotor column assembly, to which the two rotors are attached, also featured an all-new design, with movable swashplates in the axial direction to enhance reliability and simplify the design.

The V-80 had very compact dimensions, using a fixed-wing aircraft-lookalike fuselage and damage-tolerant structure. In an effort to reduce the fuselage weight due to the need to install heavyweight mission systems, armour protection and armament, Mikheev decided to radically increase the share of polymeric structural materials (colloquially known as composites). This way, the V-80's fuselage of mixed metallic/non-metallic construction, according to an estimate made by Kamov OKB chief-designer Alexander Vagin, has a composites share of some 36 percent. All elements used in the streamlined areas of the fuselage feature a three-layer sandwich structure with composite skin, fabricated from materials called organit, organit-glass or organit-carbon, with a honeycomb core of the PSP-1 type. The load-bearing members of the airframe were fabricated from aluminium alloys. The design team used flat panels wherever possible, or alternatively panels with constant curvature, in an effort to simplify as much of the manufacturing process as possible.

Kamov OKB test pilot Evgeny Laryushin discusses the features of the V-80 mock-up with a member of the VVS' Mock-up Review Commission. (OKB Kamov)

Flight tests

The assembly of the first prototype, designated V-80-1, serialled '010' and wearing the internal Kamov OKB c/n 800-01, was completed in early 1982. It was intended for flight performance assessment and testing the operability of various onboard systems. In addition, V-80-1 had to be tested with various types of empennages. It initially had its stub-wings with anhedral of 12°, later reduced to 6°, which necessitated reworking of the centre-wing section. V-80-1 lacked some of the systems originally intended for the attack helicopters, such as the cannon mount and the pilot ejection seat, while power was supplied by a pair of TV3-117V engines, rated at 2,200shp each, instead of the more modern TV3-117VMA.

V-80-1 was transported from the Ukhotomosk Experimental Plant in Lyubertsi to the company flight test station at Zhulebino on the edge of Moscow under tight secrecy. The short trip was made at night, and the helicopter was fully covered by tarpaulins. While at the test station, it was kept in a hangar and towed outside by a tractor for engine runs and system checks in accordance with the schedule of overflights of the US reconnaissance satellites.

The maiden flight in hover of V-80-1 was conducted on 17 June 1982, in the skilled hands of Kamov OKB test pilot Nikolay Bezdetnov. As he recalled, the flight proved to be a bit flawed as the helicopter lifted off in zero-wind weather conditions but then unintentionally rotated to the right at 10° and remained in this position until landing. The pilot had moved only the collective for vertical movement to lift off and then land, without commands for any horizontal turns. After the sortie completion, Bezdetnov reported on the strange behaviour and the post-flight check revealed that during the pre-flight inspection,

mechanics had disconnected and then simply forgot to reconnect the control linkage to the rudder. As a result, the unconnected rudder moved freely in the downwash just like a windsock or a flag in a strong wind.

V-80-1 made its maiden forward flight on 27 July 1982, on the circuit around Zhulebino, again with Nikolay Bezdetnov in the cockpit. In order to maintain secrecy and hide the true purpose of the new machine, it was painted to resemble a transport helicopter, receiving false windows and doors outlined in yellow on the fuselage sides.

The attempt to hide the true purpose of the machine from prying eyes of various Western intelligence services operating in and around Moscow had proved next to impossible. The first artworks of the V-80 were published in Western aerospace and defence magazines during 1982. The false cockpit, however, did its job as intended. There were hints in the West that the new Soviet combat helicopter had a two-seat cockpit for accommodating a pilot and a weapons system operator; the latter was said to be provided with a minimum exterior field of view in order to concentrate on the synthetic terrain and target images derived from the radar and electro-optical sensors.

Jane's All the World's Aircraft 1985–1986 then noted the existence of the new Soviet combat helicopter, as it became known that in 1984 the Kamov bureau had begun flight testing of a machine bearing the NATO-reported name *Hokum*. A side view drawing was also provided, based on a US DoD drawing, showing the basic design features such as coaxial rotor arrangement, stub-wings and podded engines; it was also portrayed as armed with a nose-mounted cannon. The text noted that no details were available except that it had coaxial

The second V-80 prototype (c/n 800-02) undergoing final assembly at the Kamov OKB's experimental plant in Lyubertsi. (Kamov OKB)

contra-rotating main rotors, while take-off weight was in the 5,450kg (12,000lb) class and the probable two-man crew was accommodated side-by-side. Duties, according to the publication, included attack and air-to-air anti-helicopter combat, with survivability enhanced by the use of IR suppressors, IR decoy dispensers and armour. The crude side elevation drawing of what purported to be the *Hokum* had been borrowed from the 1985 edition of the US DoD 'Soviet Military Power' document. It showed an aircraft with a conventional fuselage, three tail fins and a retractable tricycle landing gear. Wide vertical separation of the contra-rotating rotors hinted at a conventional drive system, as opposed to anything as advanced as Sikorsky's ABC system. However, the DoD tended to comment that the new *Hokum* would give the Soviets a significant rotary-wing air superiority capability as the system had no current Western counterpart. Estimated performance included a maximum level speed of 350km/h (189kt) and a combat radius of 250km (135nm).

The second prototype, V-80-2 (also wearing the Kamov OKB internal c/n 800-02), serialled '011', took to the air in its first flight on 16 August 1983, piloted by Evgeny Laryushin. Powered by the definitive Klimov TV3-117VMA engines, rated at 2,400shp at emergency mode (used in one engine inoperative situations), it was intended for testing the targeting equipment and armament, and at a later stage it also received a cannon mount.

Test pilot Nikolay Bezdetnov recalled how the initial flight testing had been conducted:

We did the initial flight testing in this order I flew prototype No. 1, used to explore and expand the flight performance, while Zhenya [Laryushin] was flying No. 2, dealing with combat employment where the abilities of performing swift manoeuvring have prevailing significance. Trying to solve the problem with the limited and insufficient for a combat helicopter rate of descent (i.e. vertical speed), he decided to substitute this regime of flight with a steep spiral.

Evgeny Laryushin played an instrumental role in demonstrating the ability of the single-seat helicopter to launch ATGMs at low altitude. This was the chief problem that had been highlighted by MVZ Mil's designer-general Marat Tishtchenko: he claimed that ATGM employment would be impossible for a single-seat helicopter. To refute this claim, the Kamov OKB organised a spectacular experiment.

It installed a mirror on the instrument panel and a forward-facing video camera just behind the pilot flying the V-80. In flight, this camera was able to capture simultaneously the instrument readings, the pilot face (as shown in the mirror) and the terrain in front of the helicopter. Mikheev recalls that when reviewing the recorded tape during the flight, it was possible to see the pilot face (which direction he was looking), hear his voice and monitor the altitude and speed of the helicopter as well as the terrain features in front of it. The pilot voice was recorded and analysed in details to detect any signs of stress in it. The altitude was measured by looking at the helicopter shadow on the ground as a primary reference, as Laryushin flew at only 2m (6ft) above the terrain, just outside Moscow, hiding below trees in NoE flight at 140km/h (76kt). When demonstrating a concealed pass around the forest edge, the helicopter literally rode on a dirt road.

This flight had proven in a clear way, with documentary and visual proofs, that the coaxial, single crewman V-80 could fly at low altitude with the pilot operating in normal-workload conditions. The video footage was then demonstrated at a session of the VVS' Science-Technical Commission, and upon completion its head, Lieutenant General A. Klyagin, addressed the representative of the Science-Research Institute on Aviation and Space Medicine, Colonel V. Davidov. As it became clear later on, Colonl Davidov had desperately tried before the flight demonstration to convince all members of the commission that the single-crewman V-80 could not operate at low altitude.

The so-called factory flight tests of the V-80 continued in 1983, with the first live firings conducted at the Land Forces gunnery range at Smolino. These firings, using V-80-2, were carried out by two VVS test pilots V. Kostin and V. Yudin; they were also slated to fly the Mi-28 at a later phase in order to be able to compare both machines. Yudin flew mostly on the Mi-28, while Kostin had completed the majority of the V-80 test sorties with the use of live ordinance.

The tests at the Smolino range brought various surprises. In one of the sorties, set out to evaluate the search performance of the targeting system, the helicopter had to hover for prolonged periods, with periodic rotations at 180° in order to face the targets. At this moment the target moved across the range and, after rotating with the nose turned back to look at target direction, the pilot had to search for it once again.

Mikheev recalled:

The second prototype, serialled '011' (c/n 800-02), in its initial form lacking cannon mount and without sensor nose. The false windows to simulate a second cockpit proved to be a pretty useful deception measure, as initial Western 'intel' reports on the new Kamov OKB's coaxial helicopter were rather inaccurate. (Kamov OKB)

The second V-80, c/n 800-02, in flight in a late configuration, with the new sensor nose and cannon mount, and sporting a newly applied grey camouflage with a turquoise underside. (Kamov OKB)

After processing the medical parameters of test pilot V. Kostin that were recorded during the sortie, the evaluation team found out a small increase in the heartbeat and breathing rates compared to the same data for V. Yudin who flew the two-seat Mi-28. The medics told us that this is [a] usual occurrence due to the higher workload (mental and physical) of the pilot of the single-seat helicopter. The analysis of the recorded data, however, had shown that the heartbeat and breathing rates had increased only when the pilot turned the nose away from the target; at this moment, as a rule, the workload should be generally low, as no operator tasks have to be performed and the helicopter is controlled by the autopilot. The clarification given by Kostin surprised both the development team and the medical personnel. It turned out that one of the medical sensors put on his body tore off and the graphite powder leaking from it had adversely affected the pilot's comfort. That is why Kostin, when turning away the helicopter nose from the target, got the sensor with his hand and adjusted its position on his body. So, in the event the medical team had to correct its conclusions in favour of the co-axial design.

A sophisticated modelling stand was designed and built at the GosNIIAS (State Scientific-Research Institute of Aviation Systems), where all companies supplying components for the revolutionary new navigation/attack suite were involved, under the overall management of Alla Makogon, the avionics lead designer at the Kamov OKB. This stand was used to study the ATGM employment specifics and had to be approved beforehand by the military and industry authorities. Makogon then headed a team which worked at another stand at the TsIITM (Central Research Institute of Precise Machine-Building), which was designed to evaluate the functionality of the Shkval-V highly-automated TV/laser targeting system.

First round of selection

Meanwhile, the VVS and MAP leaderships pressed the competing design bureaux to accelerate the work on their new attack helicopters. The war in Afghanistan had highlighted the shortcomings of the existing attack helicopters (represented by several Mi-24 *Hind* versions), while the international situation was heating up from day to day after the shooting down of the Korean Air Boeing 747 Flight KAL007 from New York to Seoul via Anchorage by a Soviet Su-15 fighter-interceptor near Sakhalin island on 1 September 1983. The Cold War was in full swing; US President Ronald Reagan had labelled the Soviet Union the 'Evil Empire', while the CIA had initiated a large-scale operation for supplying the armed opposition in Afghanistan with shoulder-launched SAMs and other modern weaponry to be used against the Soviet troops. In this complex and rather tense situation between the superpowers, it was deemed that the conclusions of the preliminary design project, the State Mock-up Review Commission and the results from the factory flight testing of the contenders would be sufficient to seal the fate of the Mi-24's successor.

As Colonel (Retired) Kuznetsov recalled, in October 1983 a joint decision of the VVS CinC, Aviation Marshal Pavel Kutakhiv, and the Minister of Aviation Industry, Ivan Silaev, had called for the organising of a council for the selection of the new attack helicopter to be launched in serial production. This council included representatives of the main research institutes of the VVS and MAP, as well as the management of both helicopter design bureaux. Marat Tishtchenko and Sergey Mikheev presented their reports on the work done and the results that had been achieved so far. During the discussion that followed the reports, the chief of the aerodynamics division of TsAGI, E. Vozhdaev, emphasised the high level of aerodynamic perfection of both experimental helicopters. He also claimed that the V-80 was superior to the Mi-28 in terms of static ceiling and rate of climb. The deputy chief of GosNIIAS, V. Stefanov, highlighted the greater effectiveness of the V-80's Vikhr ATGM and the Mi-28 gun turret. The head of the 4th Directorate of GNIKI (the VVS flight-test centre, based in Akhtubinsk), Major General A. Bezhevets, stated that he would give his preferences to the V-80 because of its performance superiority and easier handling. The head of the 30 TsNII (the main military aviation scientific-research institute of the Soviet MoD), Lieutenant General A. Molokov, noted that the V-80 boasted a superior overall effectiveness/cost ratio an integral criteria that takes into consideration a good many design and operational factors.

All gathered experimental data and design calculations made it obvious that the V-80 had weighty advantages when compared to the Mi-28, and the common opinion of the military representatives would shift to its favour. In this rather difficult situation for him, MVZ Mil's Marat Tishtchenko made a desperate attempt to save his project and rehabilitate the Mi-28, claiming that it would be impossible, due to flight safety considerations, for a single crew member to detect, identify and attack targets at low altitude and employ weapons. This had been confirmed, as Tishtchenko said, by the experience of developing attack helicopters in the USA and also by the Mi-24's combat employment results in Afghanistan.

The next report at the council was made by Colonel G. Kuznetsov as a GNIKI representative. He had noted that the Mi-24P version, armed with a fixed 30mm cannon, proved to be the best attack helicopter type used by the VVS in Afghanistan. He added that according to pilots with combat experience, when flying at ultra-low level, all helicopter handling, search for targets and attack functions (for firing cannon and rockets) would be performed by the pilot alone. In such flight conditions, the WSO could not provide effective assistance to the pilot and could therefore only be considered a ballast load.

Colonel Kuznetsov also highlighted in his report that the aerodynamically symmetrical V-80, boasting a higher power-to-weight ratio and easier handling, could employ its cannon and rockets in a much more effective manner than the Mi-24. When it came to the employment of the Vikhr ATGM, he noted that *GNIKI* specialists had already accumulated a sufficient volume of materials confirming the manufacturer's claimed altitude and speed launch envelope and the missile's long-range launch capability.

Lieutenant General Bezhevets, a Hero of the Soviet Union (decorated with this highest Soviet state award for his combat exploits in Egypt in 1972, flying the MiG-25 single-seat reconnaissance aircraft in missions well inside Israeli airspace), supported Colonel Kuznetsov's arguments, stating that he and V. Kostin (the test pilot who had mastered to perfection the Mi-24 and accumulated good experience on the V-80) had no doubts at all. "Why [could] fighter aircraft, flying at 20–30m (66–99ft) altitude and at a speed of 1,000km/h (540kt), detect and destroy ground targets, while the V-80 could not do the job at speeds up to 300km/h (160kt)? This is nonsense!" he said.

After the reports and speeches, the VVS CinC arrived at the conclusion that the V-80 was the winner in the competition. Aviation Marshal Pavel Kutakhov had such high command authority that his decision was considered a definitive one, without the need of any further discussions and comparative evaluations. In December 1984, after his death, GosNIIAS, TsAGI, 30 TsNII and GNIKI supported the conclusion of the winning selection in the tender, calling for the V-80 to be developed into experimental aircraft for state testing under the in-service designation Ka-50.

It is interesting to note that there were no information leakages to the Western world on the existence of a hotly contested attack

V-80-2 '011' captured on camera while unleashing S-8 80mm rockets in a shallow dive. (Kamov OKB)

The first prototype of the two-seat Mi-28 took to the air for the first time on 10 November 1982. Competitive flight tests held in the 1980s appeared to favour the Kamov OKB's single-seat machine. (MVZ Mil)

helicopter competition in the Soviet Union. MVZ Mil employee Lev I. Chaiko, who defected to the USA in the 1980s, had informed his new US patrons that the Mi-28 was set to become the new main attack helicopter type of the Soviet Army Aviation.

Competition channelled on the second circuit

During the last decade of existence of the Soviet Union, corporate interests had proved stronger than state ones in certain cases; this had clearly been evident during the heated and protracted attack helicopter competition. While the opinion of the legendary Aviation Marshal Pavel Kutakhov was vital within the VVS, the MAP had proceeded

in a completely different manner. Even before the final decision of the tender commission in February 1984, the Minister of Aviation Industry, Ivan Silaev, had signed a decree on the commencement of Mi-28 serial production at the aviation plant in Arsenyev. According to the approved plan, the first serial-production helicopters were to be rolled out just before the celebrations of the 70th anniversary of the Great October Revolution. At the same time, the MAP leadership had intentionally failed to notice the long list of the Mi-28's shortcomings outlined by the military test team, and even the fact that the helicopter had never been submitted for its state testing and evaluation programme (which was to be conducted by the VVS in its GNIKI institute). In fact, the third Mi-28 example, which had undergone substantial design changes to fix some of the shortcomings discovered during the testing of its predecessors, did not enter into final assembly phase before September 1985.

Meanwhile, Aviation Marshal Kutakhov's death in December 1984 represented a strong blow for the Kamov OKB the company lost a keen supporter while the position of its competitor had been strengthened. The MAP leadership then asked the VVS to begin comparative testing of the Mi-28 and V-80, while not formally revoking the tender results set out by the February 1984 decision. It was a somewhat paradoxical situation, as the loser in the tender was touted for entry into serial production, while the winning design had been left without a production plant and even had to prove once again that it outperformed its MVZ Mil rival.

The Kamov OKB troubles in the protracted tender were followed by a tragedy. In 1984, Nikolay Bezdetnov was banned from flight work due to medical reasons, and in this new situation Evgeniy Laryushin was assigned the task to demonstrate manoeuvrability performance, flying the first V-80 prototype. He, in this rather tense situation, had striven to show that the V-80 could do literally everything. On 3 April 1985, during an aerobatics testing sortie, Laryushin ventured beyond the flight envelope limitations and crashed the aircraft; the pilot perished in the wreckage.

Thirty years later, Sergey Mikheev recalled:

Evegeny Ivanich [Laryushin] was a generator of many new combat employment ideas. I remember very well how he had just returned from annual leave and came for a talk with me, presenting his new idea of demonstrating a rapid descent from hover, in order to shorten the time when the helicopter would be exposed to enemy fire (as the rate of descent of all helicopters is limited due to the vortex ring phenomenon). Considering the exceptional manoeuvrability performance of the V-80, he proposed to perform this rapid-descent manoeuvre by lowering the nose to enter into a screw, levelling the machine at 20–30m (44–66ft) above the ground. In our usual practice, all new regimes of flight shall be always modelled by the aerodynamics department and then approved by the methodology council of the flight test station before being experimented in the air. I had no idea that he had decided to try this 'spinning' manoeuvre in the air on the next day … The accident investigation found out that from hover mode the helicopter entered into a flat turn while descending and flying at a forward speed of 40km/h (22kt), pulling a 2-g load. This was an unexplored regime of flight and we lost our friend.

A collision between the blades of the upper and lower rotor had been cited as the chief reason for the disintegration of the rotor system which caused the crash. If the Mi-24 was to repeat the V-80's fatal manoeuvre, this would result in a strike between the rotor blades and the tail boom, but at the time nobody had been willing to think about this. Moreover, some MVZ Mil employees began to distribute misinformation that coaxial helicopters tended to suffer, as a rule, from inherent manoeuvrability problems.

The MAP accident investigation commission, together with the VVS, made a detailed analysis on the causes that had led to the accident. The accident report noted that the main cause was related to the 'human factor'. Nevertheless, Mikheev took a difficult but in this situation necessary decision to increase the separation between the rotor disks by an additional 120mm through extending the height of the rotor column. This design solution was intended to avoid the dangerous convergence of the blades of the upper and bottom rotor

A close-up view of the V-80's sensor nose (belonging to '020', c/n 00-02), sporting the Shkval-V TV/laser day-only targeting system. (Anatoly Demin archive)

disks should the pilot exceed the manoeuvring limitations.

In parallel to the efforts of redesigning the rotor column, the Kamov OKB had accelerated the development of the crew rescue system, which used a lightweight ejection seat. This new system was foreseen by Mikheev during the initial development stage of the Ka-50, and he now considered its prompt introduction as a matter of honour.

According to A. Artunyan, one of the lead designers at the Zvezda company (the developer and manufacturer of the V-80's crew rescue system), the helicopter was initially slated to receive a seat that ejects downwards in the initial stage and then switches to an upwards trajectory while avoiding a hit with the fuselage. Later on, the rescue system, designated as the K-37-800, gradually gained its present form with upwards pilot ejection.

The first experimental ejection conducted on the RD-2500 rocket-driven sled was made on 25 January 1984 at the Faustovo range near Moscow. The follow-on tests, however, revealed some shortcomings, which led to a radical redesign. In its eventual form, the K-37-800 system took the pilot outside the helicopter, dragged by a rocket fired upwards after jettisoning the cockpit roof hatch and the rotor blades; then the main parachute would open upon separation of the seat's backrest. The research and development works on the K-37-800 crew rescue system were completed in 1989, when it was handed over to ground and then state testing. In 1991, the K-37-800 became the first production-standard helicopter aircrew ejection system approved for production.

Meanwhile, the second stage of the Soviet attack helicopter competition gained speed. After the completion of the Mi-28 flight testing programme in April 1985, and the following signing of the flight test report, MVZ Mil's Marat Tishtchenko contacted the GNIKI with a request to receive the V-80's flight test report. In this situation, Mikheev took exactly the same position; in the event, both design bureaux had received the flight test report on the competitor's machine.

The flight performance of the competing machines was then studied in detail by the design teams at the MVZ Mil and Kamov OKB. The MVZ Mil specialists, who analysed the V-80's flight test report, were surprised by the fact that the coaxial helicopter demonstrated

The hard-working V-80-2, '011', seen here retired and resting at Zhulebino site, was used for weapons testing and evaluation. It logged no less than 620 flight hours throughout its long and productive career, launching 100 Vikhr ATGMs and unleashing no less than 9,400 30mm rounds. (Mikhail Lisov)

superior maximum and cruise speeds as well as longer combat radius when loaded with the main armament variant. Before that, the MVZ Mil design team was confident that the high rotor column with two contra-rotating rotor discs would create a sizeable drag, but failed to realise the fact that the V-80 sports a perfect fuselage from an aerodynamic point of view, with low-drag streamlined shapes and retractable undercarriage.

As regarding the flight performance, the V-80 proved clearly superior to its rival. The Mi-28 was additionally handicapped by the shortcomings of its main gearbox its rating allowed the use of only 1,950shp of the power developed by the TV3-117VMA engines, while the V-80's main gearbox was able to absorb the full rating of 2,200shp per engine.

After studying each other's flight test reports, the competitors commenced the preparation of the comparative testing effort, which was set to show which machine would perform better. The first test called for evaluating the ability to detect and destroy armoured targets. It was preformed again at the Smolino gunnery range. The MVZ Mil team, trying to prove the superiority of their two-seat design over the Kamov's single-seater, made an attempt to alter the target placement scheme at the range, but in the event this proved impossible due to financial and technical considerations. Then, again under an MVZ Mil initiative, a virtual forest was introduced at the range: when entering the range, the Mi-28 and V-80 had to initiate a right- or left-hand turn,

overflying an obstacle and then entering into the target search area. This condition was set with the aim of replicating the terrain in the European war theatre, which has lots of rolling hills and forests. But the hidden trick in this condition was that while manoeuvring to fly a NoE profile around the virtual obstacles, the pilots of both helicopters were not able to look at the targets. The Mi-28 WSO, however, who had no problem seeing through the virtual forest, was able to start an unobstructed search for targets scattered at the gunnery range much earlier than the Ka-50's pilot.

After a detailed analysis of this clearly unfavourable situation, Mikheev had to concede the difficult conditions for his helicopter of the comparative evaluation. He realised very well the fact that in case of refusal or publically-voiced doubts, this weakness could be used in favour of the competitor.

In addition, Mikheev had a great deal of confidence that the V-80 could do the job and fare well in this stage of the competition. From the very beginning of the works on the V-80 project, the design team had conducted extensive research on possible ways for reducing the physical and mental workload on the single crew member while flying low-altitude combat missions. There were six modelling stands developed for this wide-ranging research, including one set up at the Kamov OKB. As military medics working in the VVS's aviation medical research institute concluded, the absence of cross-links in the control system of the coaxial helicopter contributed to the ease of handling, while the sophisticated automatic flight control system offered highly automated modes at all sustained regimes of flight, with only 20 percent deflection of the controls (in respect to their maximum travel). This way the pilot was able to control the helicopter together with the autopilot and react to any failures by flying with the autopilot switched on from take-off to landing.

The military specialists dealing with ergonomic issues welcomed the use of the head-up display (HUD) and the helmet-mounted cueing system (HMCS). All the necessary flight, navigation and targeting data could be displayed on the HUD, which was an important consideration for a safe low-altitude flight as the pilot no longer had to look down at the instrument board in the cockpit while searching for targets.

All the switches and controls used during target search and engagement (such as ordinance checks, burst length, rocket firing sequences, etc.) were situated on a panel at the left-hand side, just under the pilot's left hand. Likewise, all switches used in less-demanding regimes of flight were grouped on the right-hand side.

There were also other clever design solutions implemented in order to reduce pilot workload. Upon entering into the target area, he had to input the geographic coordinates of the target into the sophisticated navigation system. Then the helicopter flew towards the destination point in a fully automatic mode, allowing the pilot to concentrate on monitoring the low-altitude flight. The target search commenced at a distance of 8km (4.3nm) from the target's position, well outside the reach of enemy air defence systems and while the pilot had plenty of time. The most complex task in the attack sequence was to keep the targeting mark within the ATGM launch acceptable region for one to three seconds. Then the launched missile continued its guidance towards the target in a fully automatic mode and the helicopter was free to commence defensive manoeuvring (to avoid ground fire) or start searching for another target.

GosNIIAS specialists had arrived at the conclusion that the duration of the phases of flight with a high workload during a combat mission did not exceed one minute, which was immeasurably shorter than the set out limitation of two hours.

Regarding the physical and mental workload, GNIKI, GosNIIAS and the Aviation and Space Medicine Institute concluded that during the most workload-intensive phases of flight, including the autonomous target search and attack, the pilot of the single-seat Ka-50 showed performance no worse than that of the two-seat Mi-28. This was a sign of design success as the concept of the single-seat attack helicopter had demonstrated its viability proving that it was at least equal in overall combat effectiveness to the two-seat competitor.

The comparative tests at the Smolino range commenced on 18 September 1985. The programme included 45 sorties, but the Mi-28 was able to complete only 38 of these (21 of which were considered successful from a testing point of view), while the V-80 completed only 20 (including nine considered as successful). The main problem, leading to the poor success rate of both contenders, had been attributed to the poor reliability of their targeting suites both the production-standard 9K113 on the Mi-28 and the testing-experimental Rubikon-80 installed on the V-80. Nevertheless, the V-80 succeeded in demonstrating the capabilities of its long-range sting, the Vikhr ATGM, which had scored a good hit on an armoured target at a distance of 8km (4.3nm). The Mi-28's ATGM system, in contrast, proved ill-suited to meet the VVS range requirements, which called for 6–8km (3.2–4.3nm), as the Ataka-V missile was only capable of hitting targets at up to 5.3km (2.8nm).

The military test pilots had varying opinions about the new attack helicopter types they flew during the comparative evaluation. Some of them keenly maintained that the Mi-24 should be replaced by a two-seat helicopter with the classical aerodynamic layout, including main and tail rotors. Others, however, were confident that only a revolutionary-concept machine could be superior to the AH-64 Apache, and thus preferred the single-seat, coaxial V-80.

In such a delicate situation, the VVS leadership requested the 30 TsNII scientific-research institute to provide an official conclusion about which new helicopter type should replace the Mi-24. The institute wisely adopted a diplomatic approach in a bid to avoid accusations from the bidders of partial behaviour. The 30 TsNII institute recommended that both types should be launched in serial production. Among the arguments listed to defend this opinion was that a mixture of both helicopters would be optimally adapted to the changing conditions of battlefield operations. The ratio between Mi-28 and Ka-50 production should then be defined on the basis of results in the field testing effort. The better design would become the backbone of the Soviet Army's attack helicopter fleet, while the loser was proposed to be built mainly for export.

Although such a decision could be seen as a bizarre and compromise solution, time showed that the 30 TsNII had adopted a working approach. The dispute, however, was not over. The MAP claimed that the country could not afford to build two attack helicopter types. But it is noteworthy that at the same time, the Soviet Union was building in large numbers not two but three types of MBT and nobody had been over-concerned about this situation. The VVS leadership asked the GNIKI for its views, and thus the comparative evaluation story continued.

The hard work at the Kamov OKB and its suppliers eventually brought good results, especially in the avionics reliability area. The next testing round saw the V-80 amassing 24 successful sorties with 18 Vikhr ATGM launches. The long-range laser beam-riding missile with huge armour-penetrating capabilities made a striking impression on the military specialists involved in the testing effort at the Smolino gunnery range. The missile proved well-suited to defeat the reinforced armour protection of the most modern Western tanks, such as the US M1 Abrams and the German Leopard 2.

Based upon the results of this testing campaign, GNIKI specialists arrived at the conclusion that only the V-80, equipped with the Shkval-V targeting system and armed with the Vikhr long-range ATGM, would be able to engage enemy armour at distances of between 6–8km (3.2–4.3nm), without entering within the reach of the enemy front-line air defence systems operated by NATO countries at the time. The flight experiments also confirmed the possibility of safe employment of the Vikhr ATGM by the V-80 while flying at ultra-low altitude. The helicopter demonstrated that it was capable of performing a flat turn (rotation around the vertical axis) at angular speed equating to the rate of rotation of the Mi-28's gun turret, while retaining a pretty good concentration of hits unleashed by its 30mm cannon.

The V-80's NPPU-80 gun mount with a 30mm 2A42 cannon demonstrated an accuracy (dispersion) of 1.6 mils at 1,000-metre range, which proved to be vastly superior to that of the Mi-28's NPU-28 (also using the 2A42 cannon), which was said to have amounted to 4.6 mils.

In December 1985, the third V-80 prototype (800-03, serialled '012') took to the air in its maiden flight. In October 1986, all the main scientific-research institutes of the Russian MoD (GNIKI, 30 TsNII, NIIERAT, NNIA and KM) submitted their findings. The V-80 was announced as the winner in the competition, getting the highest score of points in the head-to-head race with the Mi-28. It was clearly proved during comparative testing that the V-80 was faster, more agile, better protected and armed, and boasted a better accuracy of delivering unguided ordinance; in short, it was superior to the Mi-28 in most if not all aspects.

The newly appointed VVS CinC, Aviation Marshal Alexander Yefimov, a famous Second World War attack pilot, supported the opinion of his subordinates. In the event, the Central Committee of the Communist Party and the Council of Ministers of the Soviet Union issued joint decree No. 1420, dated 14 December 1987, which called for the further development of the Ka-50 by producing a batch of experimental examples for use in the testing and evaluation effort.

The Soviet Council of Ministers decree No. 1420 on the V-80 selection as the new-generation combat helicopter for the Soviet MoD outlined the further phases of the Ka-50 development effort and also approved an amendment to the technical specification. In reference to the Mi-28, the same document called for further works in order to develop an export derivative; the MVZ Mil was also obliged to utilise the new design solutions already proven on the Mi-28 for upgrading the Mi-24.

It seemed to be a successful conclusion for the Kamov OKB's nine-year-long struggle to win the competition. By this time, taking into consideration the rapidly increasing importance of the Kamov OKB, its chief-designer Sergey Mikheev had at last been promoted to designer-general. It was a long-deserved recognition for the head of

The third V-80 prototype, serialled '012' (c/n 800-03), took to the air for the first time in December 1985. (Anatoly Demin archive)

the design bureau and his hard-working team. In addition, in 1987, another Kamov OKB helicopter type, the civilian-standard Ka-32S, was launched in serial production, while the Ka-126 single-engine light helicopter also made its maiden flight the same year. But the V-80/Ka-50 story had a long way to go in order to be considered a definitive success.

4

BLACK SHARK GROWS AND EVOLVES

Launch into production

The decree of the Central Committee of the Communist Party and the Soviet Council of Ministers No. 1420-355, dated 1987, set out the terms and conditions of the day-capable V-80Sh-1's development completion and its launch into series production at the AAC Progress plant in Arsenyev in Russia's Far East, under the official designation Ka-50. It was set to become the main attack helicopter of the Soviet Armed Forces. The decree put a formal end to the protracted and hotly contested helicopter competition. At the same time, this document had ordered to retain the developed technology base and continue with the development of the Mi-28. The new version, dubbed Mi-28A, as mentioned in the decree, had to be launched in production at the Rostov Helicopter Plant in Rostov on Don in southern Russia, which at the time specialised in the production of the Mi-24's export derivatives. The plant was then required to switch to the production of the Mi-28A destined for export customers. This way the decree of the Central Committee of the Communist Party and the Soviet Council of Ministers had eventually sealed the fate of both competing designs in the keenly contested attack helicopter tender – the V-80Sh-1 was set to be built for the VVS while the Mi-28 was to be offered to foreign customers.

The AAC Progress plant at Arsenyev had been selected as the production site for the Ka-50 thanks to its deep involvement in Mi-24 production and the enormous expertise and experience gathered in the process. The *Hinds* built at the plant were exclusively delivered to the Soviet/Russian military and border protection forces. The first Mi-24 was produced in 1970 while the last example was rolled out at the plant in 1989. A total of 2,443 Mi-24s in at least eight different versions were produced at the Arsenyev plant before switching the complex production process to the much more advanced Ka-50.

The new design required the plant to master the previously unknown composite material production technologies, since the Ka-50 featured extensive use of such materials, used for fabricating the rotor blades and the vast majority of the skin panels.

While the AAC Progress plant worked hard on switching to the Ka-50s and adjusting its fairly complex production process, the Kamov OKB continued building further prototypes for use in the flight testing programme in accordance with decree No. 1420-355.

The fourth flight test example, V-80-4-50, 800-04, serialled '014', was completed in March 1989 at the Kamov OKB's experimental plant, while the fifth example, 800-05, wearing the serial '015', followed suit in April 1990. The latter was also used as the pattern aircraft for the series production. Both of these newly built Ka-50s featured UV-26M chaff/flare dispensers installed in wingtip pods, together with laser warning receivers, while the Rubikon-80 flight/navigation/attack suite was enhanced with equipment for receiving external targeting data. The analogue weapons control systems of earlier prototypes were replaced by a digital one, employing a digital computer, reducing the overall weight. The fifth V-80 was also the first of the type to feature the K-37-800 rocket-based pilot ejection system.

The flight test and evaluation programme continued at a fast pace, with as many as four Ka-50s involved in it between July 1989 and June 1990 used for the developmental testing of the rotor system, flight control system and undercarriage. The third and fifth V-80 examples ('012' and '015') were also utilised in the flight performance evaluation campaign, while the second and fourth examples ('011' and '014') were kept busy with developmental testing of the ordinance selection (there was no prototype wearing the serial '013', as this was considered an unlucky number in the Soviet Union/Russia). These tests also saw the evaluation of the gas-dynamic stability of the engines when firing the gun and launching different types of rockets. Another testing task saw the use of '011' and '014' for exploring the electromagnetic compatibility of on-board equipment.

The first stage of the Ka-50's state testing and evaluation effort, intended to evaluate the flight performance, began in September 1990 by using the fourth and fifth flight test examples, with '014' and '015' flown by military test pilots A. Papay and V. Kostin from the VVS' GNIKI flight-test institute. Both of them had been involved earlier in the helicopter's preliminary testing effort, and were soon afterwards joined by two more military test pilots, N. Kolpakov and V. Pukhvatov.

After that, Alexander Papay devoted the rest of his test pilot career to the Ka-50 and Ka-52, and by late 2014 he was still flying test sorties with Kamov; in 2016 he was not flying anymore but continued working as chief of the flight-test support section of Kamov's flight-test complex.

Papay graduated from the VVS's Syzran Higher Pilot School in 1974 and then saw service as a front-line helicopter pilot with the army aviation branch for six years. In the 1980s, he entered the VVS' Flight Test School and upon graduation in 1981, Papay was appointed to work as a military flight test pilot; he continued flying in this role for 19 years. Papay made his first flight on the Ka-50 on 7 March 1989, and 25 years later he recalled these exciting times: "Immediately after my first Ka-50 flight I realised that there is no other helicopter with such easy handling, able to deploy all kinds of weapons in a pretty simple manner. And I'm still thinking this way."

This flight, in fact, had determined Papay's further career; when he retired from military service in 2000, the skilled pilot went on to work at the Kamov OKB, test-flying different Ka-50 versions. He also lifted off the Ka-31, Ka-60 and Ka-226T prototypes in their maiden flights, as well as the first production-standard Ka-52. In total, Papay flew test sorties in more than 70 fixed- and rotary-wing types, and by late 2014 had accumulated a total of 7,687 flight hours.

The first flights of the VVS test pilots were made at the Kamov OKB's flight test station at Zhulebino on the outskirts of Moscow. After their conversion-to-type training completion, the Ka-50's testing was launched at the gunnery range at Smolino near Moscow, while a small proportion of the flight testing work was conducted at Akhtubinsk in southern Russia, where the VVS's largest flight test centre and gunnery ranges are located.

The volume of the Ka-50's state test and evaluation programme was really huge, with Papay alone amassing 157 sorties and logging 217 flight hours during this effort, including stability evaluation, manoeuvrability performance and navigation system testing. At Akhtubinsk, Papay tested the full ordinance range integrated on the Ka-50. This test phase also included weapons employment in extreme regimes of flight, such as firing the gun and unleashing rockets at pitch angles from -60° to +60° (i.e. nose down to nose up attitude); there are no other attack helicopters in the world cleared to do this. He also fired numerous Vikhr ATGMs. In addition to the self-targeting (performed in the manual mode by the pilot), the Ka-50 was also tested using external targeting data, received via datalink from a Ka-29, as well as performing target search in the automated scanning mode.

Papay recalls his Ka-50 flight testing experience during this stage:

During rocket launches in low visibility conditions, below 3km [1.6nm], I noticed that the TV sight could facilitate target detection at ranges greater than 3km. So I proved that rocket launches in such bad weather conditions could be possible and safe enough. All the live-firing tests were carried out without a single onboard equipment failure. The maintainers worked in a very professional manner and reacted immediately to my post-flight remarks, fixing all the problems. The most memorable moments for me during this testing campaign were experienced during rocket launches and gun firings with pitch up/pitch down angles of 60°. When pitching up the helicopter, the speed decays very fast, while pitching down would cause rapid acceleration in a steep dive. So, the window of opportunity for launching the rockets and firing the gun proved to be very narrow in these conditions and I was under pressure all the time. But the faithful helicopter had never let me down. Since the first flights we had become close friends; I can say that we had been a single organism all the time. In the single-seat helicopter the pilot

The fifth and last V-80 prototype, serialled '015' (c/n 800-05), the first to feature the K-37-800 ejection system. It also saw use in the *Black Shark* movie, made in 1993 in Uzbekistan, and was then employed in various campaigns for testing new mission equipment, wearing the new serial '25'. (OKB Kamov)

A look inside the Ka-50's cockpit, as sported by '015'. (Andrey Zinchuk)

Kamov's veteran test pilot Alexander Papay flew for the first time on the V-80 in the second half of the 1980s, and in 2000 he joined the Kamov OKB; by 2016, Papay was still working for the company as chief of the flight test support section at the Kamov flight test complex. (Author)

and machine are considered to be a single body: the machine, you and nobody else! You trust her and the machine trusts you!

Meanwhile, concurrently with the advance of the flight test effort, technical documentation for a pre-production Ka-50 batch was handed over to the AAC Progress plant in Arsenyev. A decree of the Military-Industrial Commission of the Soviet Council of Ministers dated 1990 called for the construction of a pre-production batch of 12 V-80Sh-1 helicopters; these were to receive the in-service designation Ka-50. In 1991, the first of the AAC Progress-built machines, c/n 00-01, serialled '018', was rolled at the plant and took to the air for the first time on 22 May 1991 in the hands of plant test pilot A. Dovgan.

In January 1992, '018' was handed over to the VVS's State Flight Test Centre, and in February that year commenced flights within the frame of the second stage of the type's comprehensive state testing and evaluation effort, centred on the evaluation of the rotorcraft's overall combat performance; its completion was reported in December 1993.

The protocol on the completion of the Ka-50's state flight testing and evaluation effort was approved by the Russian Air Force CinC, Colonel General Pyotr Deinekin, on 2 December 1993, while approval by the Russian Land Forces CinC, Army General Vladimir Semenov, followed suit on 21 January 1994.

Expanding the mission capabilities

The tactical and technical assignment – a document equivalent to the technical specification used in the Western world for designing and developing a new-generation attack helicopter type, issued by the 30 TsNII in the 1980s, had originally called for the provision of both day- and night-operating capabilities. However, to be capable of operating at night and in bad weather, the new attack helicopter had to be equipped with radar and thermal imaging (also known as infrared night-vision system) or low-light-level television (LLLTV) camera capable of target detection and identification.

The decree calling for the Ka-50's launch in serial production also included a reference to the Military Industrial Commission's assignment, which contained the requirement for round-the-clock operational capability. At the time, the end customer (i.e. VVS) considered that it would be acceptable to have the night targeting equipment housed in pods carried under the stub-wings of the new helicopter.

Taking into consideration the real-world state of development of the Soviet defence electronics and optronic industries in the early 1980s, an initial priority had been given to the incorporation of a LLLTV system intended to be used as the Ka-50's principal night targeting device. The LLLTV technology, in principle, offered some sizeable advantages when compared to thermal imagers for use in the target detection and identification role at night. The first of these is the very nature of the image displayed on the TV screen in front of the pilot; it would be similar to that supplied by the day TV camera, while the image of a similar object delivered by the thermal imaging camera would represent a graphical distribution of the temperature differences between heated terrain (i.e. the background) and the objects present in the scene. The thermal image is displayed in shades of grey or other colours (as used in the screen technology where the image is displayed); that is why its proper interpretation would require the pilot to have certain patterns and skills.

For the Kamov OKB in particular, the LLLTV would enable another advantage, contributing to speeding up the development of their new attack helicopter. The targeting suite of the newly developed Sukhoi Su-25T fixed-wing low-level attack aircraft, which was also equipped with the Shkval automated targeting system, incorporated the Merkuriy night targeting pod. The system was developed by the Moscow Television Science-Research Institute and contained a LLLTV device, based on the VYaZ Gen 1 optronic converter, mated to a silicon intensifier target tube (the so-called EBS vidicon). The optoelectronic converter provides multi-thousand-fold amplification of the ambient night light (the night illumination comes from the night sky, moon, stars, etc.), in order to detect the targets. The Merkuriy had a bulky and heavy design and used two separate lenses – one for the narrow FoV and the other serving the system's wide FoV. The Su-25T's tests with the pod-mounted night targeting system showed that the range guaranteeing stable identification of a tank-type target could extend up to 3km (1.6nm).

On the Ka-50, the bulky Merkuriy system was accommodated in a built-in form inside the forward fuselage, using a circular window protruding on the upper part of the nose. A mock-up of the system was

The first Ka-50 produced at the AAC Progress plant, '018', c/n 00-01, during its roll-out in May 1991. (AAC Progress)

installed on the second V-80 prototype, '011', the while the third one, serialled '012', received a working set of equipment for undergoing a test and evaluation programme.

The tests of the Merkuriy night targeting system proved to be a failure, however, as the system showed a very poor performance. It suffered from insufficient target detection range and low sensibility and resolution; in addition, it was also prone to jamming. As a result, the Merkuriy's follow-on development was shelved and the design team redirected its efforts in integrating a thermal vision targeting system.

The thermal imaging targeting equipment chosen for the V-80 worked in the 8–14 micron wavelength. This is the so-called 'long-wave' band that travels easily through the atmosphere and where the typical ground targets have the maximum of their IR emissions. The long-wave detectors are particularly useful in smoky and dusty battlefields and for seeing through reflective clutter in bright sunshine.

The thermal imager development was awarded to the Science-Research Institute of Applied Physics (NII PF), which managed to develop a working system within a very compressed timeframe. The system had a mercury cadmium telluride (HgCdTe) detector (charge-coupled device or CCD), also referred to as MCT (mer-cad-tel), made of semiconductors that generate a current when exposed to IR light. Cooled to cryogenic temperature, the mechanically scanned detector consisted of a narrow strip along a moving mirror. The technology was then handed over to the NPO Geophizika and Kazan State Institute of Applied Optics for the development of thermal imaging sighting devices that could be suitable for airborne use. The resultant system of the first airborne thermal imager in the Soviet Union had

a rather complicated design, with optical and mechanical scanning of the line detector to form a thermal image of the scanned area. The first experimental example of the system, designated TpSPO-8T, was completed in 1986 and underwent its initial flight tests onboard a Mi-8T flying testbed. The thermal imaging sight was then integrated into the V-80's targeting suite, interfaced to the Ka-50's electro-optical HUD, the PrPNK-80 Rubicon flight/navigation/attack suite and the Shkval-V electro-optical targeting system.

In 1990, the Ka-50's fifth experimental example, serialled '015', was modified with the installation of a mock-up of the Stolb thermal imaging sight, which used the TpSPO-V technology, with a lens and detector integrated with the Shkval-V TV targeting system. The initial flight tests of the Stolb had, however, demonstrated that its design was immature and needed urgent improvements and curing of its teething troubles. The IR detector had to be seriously improved as its performance proved definitely inferior to the Western-made IR target detection devices used on then modern attack helicopters such as the AH-64A Apache.

But this task had been given at the wrong time, as the Soviet Union's ill-fated *Perestroika* (the wide-ranging political and economic reforms undertaken by Soviet leader Mikhail Gorbachev) stalled in 1990 and ended with the inglorious break-up of the Soviet Union into 15 independent states in 1991. The NPO Geophizika was among the first victims of the huge and largely destructive post-Soviet economic and political changes in Russia, a newly-established state proclaimed as the legal successor of the Soviet Union. The former flagship of the Soviet electro-optical research and development branch had eventually collapsed under the pressure of the rapidly unfolding destructive

The third Ka-50 prototype, '012', flew with a mock-up of the Merkuriy NV LLLTV system in the nose, using a large circular port in front of the cockpit. (Kamov OKB)

events that almost ruined the Soviet aerospace and defence industry in the early 1990s.

Nevertheless, the Kamov OKB continued working on the night-capable Ka-50 derivative, and in 1993 presented a project of its attack rotorcraft equipped with a day/night derivative of the Shkval-V sight. Developed by the Krasnogorsk Mechanical Plant (KMZ), it was to use thermal imaging equipment made by NPO Geophizika, but at the time the latter was in a pitiful state and as a result proved unable to supply a working system. The Kamov OKB had to wait for several years to get a suitable new-generation night vision system, this time developed by another domestic company.

There were other prospective projects for enhancing the overall effectiveness of the guided weapons suite that were also abandoned in the early 1990s. One of these concerned, for instance, the automation of the initial targeting provided to the Shkval-V TV/laser targeting system by using an Obzor-800 HMCS, with coverage of 60° left and right in the horizontal plane, 20° down and 65° up. This system was originally intended for faster and easier acquisition and tracking of targets set to be engaged by the helicopter's long-range missiles. The new targeting method called for automatic steering of the helicopter (performed by its automatic flight control system) towards the target designated by the pilot by using the HMCS; then the target was acquired by the narrow FoV of the Shkval-V system for an ATGM launch. This new automated targeting method is said to have resulted in some 30 percent increase in lock-on range and accuracy of target acquisition. After the dissolution of the Soviet Union, however, the TsKB Arsenal design bureau, tasked to develop the Obzor-300 system, remained in the newly independent state of Ukraine and not after long it discontinued its cooperation with the Kamov OKB for integrating the HMCS system on the Ka-50.

Mikheev was also forced to abandon the development of an ATGM launcher unit that could rotate (depress) in the vertical plane due to the lack of funding. Offered by the TsNII TochMASH institute, the new launcher was intended to be used in addition to the existing automatic orientation of the helicopter in the horizontal plane before missile launch (undertaken by the autopilot using steering data derived from the Shkval-V TV/laser targeting system). The rotating launcher for the Vikhr ATGM would allow for automated steering of the missile nose towards the target in the vertical plane, thus shortening the target engagement cycle by 1.4 times.

In January 1993, the Russian MoD signed a contract covering 11 Ka-50s to be delivered within a year, at a conditional price that could be subject to change on an as necessary basis. But the MoD budget had been exhausted soon afterwards, and in May 1993 the contract

scope saw its reduction to only four aircraft. In 1993 and 1994, despite numerous production problems and the sharp increase of the prices of the vendor-supplied parts, the AAC Progress plant eventually managed to complete six helicopters. Four of these (c/n 01-01, 01-02, 01-03 and 01-04) were handed over to the Kamov OKB, while two additional aircraft (c/n 01-05 and 02-01) were delivered to the combat training centre in Torzhok.

In 1995, the AAC Progress plant handed over two more helicopters, but these lacked main gearboxes, black boxes for the control system and HMCSs. Both of these Ka-50s, c/n 02-03 and 02-04, were slated for delivery to the Kamov's experimental plant in Lyubertsi for completion, funded by the company's own funds. The delivery dates for the other helicopter from the 1993 order, however, had slipped several times, as the funds necessary for their completion were allocated by the Russian MoD with a huge delay.

Ka-50 unveiled to the Western world

The previously top-secret Ka-50 was put on an open display soon after the Soviet Union's dissolution. It happened in February 1992, during the large-scale aircraft display at Machulishti air base in Byelorussia (modern Belarus), at a gathering of the representatives of the defence ministries of the former Soviet republics and a group of carefully selected military journalists and photographers. One month later, Sergey Mikheev gave a striking presentation at the London Fighter Helicopter Conference in the UK, where he had also revealed the true designation of the helicopter.

In August that year, the experimental Ka-50, serialled '03' (former '12'), was shown in the air display at the massive *Mosaeroshow*-1992 air show held at Zhukovsky airfield southeast of Moscow. This event had, in fact, marked the formal public unveiling of the type.

The following month, the second production-standard machine, built at the AAC Progress plant and serialled '020' (c/n 01-01), was displayed at the Farnborough SBAC show in the UK. To enhance the striking effect, the helicopter received an overall matt black colour paint scheme, while the fin sported a striking logo representing a lone wolf head and the name 'Werewolf'. In fact, the Ka-50 had already received the NATO reporting name *Hokum*, but Mikheev had never liked it so he decided to give his brainchild a much more attractive name which would better describe its predatory nature.

Until the Farnborough SBAC show, the secretive new Russian attack helicopter was almost unknown in the Western world and was the object of much guesswork and speculation. The US DoD's authoritative *Soviet Military Power 1989*, the annual Pentagon publication, highlighted that the new Soviet combat helicopter (assumed to be designated Ka-41 *Hokum*) was expected to be operational soon. The publication speculated that the type's likely role was air-to-air combat against anti-tank helicopters and slower ground-attack aircraft, and estimated its speed at 350km/h (189kt) – faster than either the Mi-28 *Havok* or US AH-64 Apache, which the Kamov OKB regarded as its real-world competitor.

Jane's All the World's Aircraft 1991–1992 noted, in turn, that the first photograph of the new attack helicopter was published in the West in 1989, with production deliveries expected to begin in 1991. It also guessed that the Kamov OKB designation was Ka-136, while the type's service designation (unconfirmed) was Ka-34. The powerplant was believed to comprise two Klimov TV3-117VK turboshafts, each rated at 2,200shp. At least one prototype, according to the publication, was reported to have side-by-side seating for a two-member crew. The US DoD's *Soviet Military Power 1991* document, however, suggested that the *Hokum* had a definitive tandem two-seat gunship configuration, with raised rear cockpit under continuous glazed canopy. The US

The Ka-50 production line in the AAC Progress plant in the early 1990s. (AAC Progress)

DoD stated that the *Hokum* had not been observed carrying anti-tank guided weapons and that its primary armament of unguided rocket packs, air-to-air missiles and rapid-fire gun suggested suitability for employment as a low-level helicopter intercept system by day and night and in adverse weather. Other combat roles could include countering enemy attacks, preparing for and executing counter-offensives and supporting combined-arms offensives into an opponent's territory. This suggested that the *Hokum* may be used as an escort for amphibious assault Ka-29TB *Helix-B*s based on Soviet Navy aircraft carriers, especially as Kamov military helicopters had always been produced for mainly maritime use. The maximum take-off weight was estimated to be 7,500kg (16,530lb) and the maximum level speed 350km/h (189kt).

For the helicopter's display at the 1992 Farnborough SBAC show, the Kamov OKB prepared a brochure packed with shocking performance data it claimed, for instance, that the Ka-50 could fly at a maximum speed of 350km/h (189kt) and sported a static ceiling of 4,000m (13,120ft). An image in this brochure showed the Ka-50 not only with its usual ordinance options of ATGMs, rockets and UPK-23-250 gun pods, but also armed with weapons resembling the R-73 (AA-11 *Archer*) highly-agile heat-seeking air-to-air missile in addition to the Kh-25 (AS-10 *Karen*) air-to-surface missile and even with torpedoes. The chief idea of these rather bizarre ordinance loads was to get the foreign experts guessing and speculating about the Werewolf's true combat capabilities and purpose.

The Ka-50's debut at the Farnborough SBAC show had created a real sensation as it presented the first opportunity to see the new Russian attack machine up-close. Mikheev recalled, however, that the British authorities had raised certain obstacles, apparently in an effort to spoil the effective display of the cutting-edge Russian combat rotorcraft:

Not long before the beginning of the show I despatched two company representatives, Lev Sverkanov and Vera Popova, to attend a conference in London. Before their travel to the UK, I had advised them to remain in London in order to supervise the Ka-50's re-assembly upon arrival at the Farnborough show ground. At the time I had assumed that the helicopter (transported in partially assembled state by an Il-76 airlifter) would be accompanied by a company team of 16 technicians who would perform all the assembly work at Farnborough. The British Embassy in Moscow, however, had delayed the issuance of their British visas, protracting the process while promising all the time 'that it will be done tomorrow'. In the event, this visa issue had turned into a never-ending story.

Upon my arrival in London from Moscow I took a taxi and went to Farnborough. We arrived there at 5:00 p.m. and were able to enter inside the show ground without problems. I noticed our Ka-50 on the static display, but it lacked rotors and wings, and had a pile of wooden boxes (containing the rotor column and blades) spread around it. All the other aircraft on the display were assembled and ready for the show opening on the next day. It was in the evening and I was shocked to see that our helicopter [was] not ready yet. I immediately walked to the Aviaexport office, the official organiser of the entire Russian aerospace industry display at the show. But there I saw a sad picture – everybody was ready to leave the show ground after the end of the working day. So I had to do something in an urgent manner in order to fix the situation [with the helicopter].

Fortunately, in this moment a bus transporting the Tupolev technical team arrived at the office. They had just completed their work at the aircraft, getting ready to return to their hotel. I, however, decided to seek much-needed assistance from them, so entered into the bus and directly asked: 'Comrades, I have a kind request. My helicopter is not assembled yet. I know you are tired but I would

Sergey Mikheev and Sergey Sikorsky pose for a photo in front of the Ka-50 Werewolf, serialled '020', c/n 01-01, during the type's sensational display at the Farnborough SBAC air show in September 1992. (Sergey Mikheev archive)

This black-painted Ka-52 serialled '024' is, in fact, the former '020' (c/n 01-01), shown at the Farnborough SBAC show in September 1992 and at Paris Air Show in June 1993, which changed its serial in 1995. It is in flight with undercarriage in extended position at the Kamov OKB's flight-test station at Zhulebino, wearing Paris Air Show display serial 'H347'. C/n 01-01 made its last flight on 13 December 2005. (Sergey Nosov archive)

kindly ask you to assist me in assembling the machine.' Perhaps I had looked very convincing; so after mumbling for some time, just to be in order, all of them agreed to provide me the assistance needed.

All the available hands joined to help the Ka-50's frantic re-assembly work at the static display line. Even Mikheev's personal interpreter, Vera Popova, helped the effort as she had managed to find a crane and convince the operator to assist the Russian team assembling the top-notch rotorcraft, as this had been a most-urgent task. All the work on the display site was completed by midnight, with the makeshift assembly team installing the rotor column and rotor blades, joining the wings to the fuselage, suspending the mock weapons and finally removing all surplus materials and boxes from the site.

This, however, was not the end of Mikheev's adventures at the show. As he recalled, on the morning of the next day, he stood alone beside the helicopter when a group of US military officers approached with an apparent intent to start an up-close evaluation of the Ka-50. They were apparently disappointed that the helicopter was not in a disassembled state (as it was the day before), which would allow them to study its design in more detail and identify possible flaws. Instead, the new Russian attack helicopter posed in front of them shining, fully assembled and armed, refusing to reveal its interior secrets. As a partial compensation, the Americans decided to have an interview from Mikheev, who, assisted by Vera Popova, spoke with them for about an hour, explaining why and how this machine would be better than their overpriced and beloved Apache. During the interview, he had revealed some performance figures which had caused a small shock among the US officers. At the end of his presentation, he saw a genuine concern among them, as behind the duty smiles there was an unsaid question: "What if tomorrow we go to war? What if in this war we face a bizarre-looking, single-seat rotorcraft, armed with long-legged weapons. And what about the onboard automation – have the Russians managed to surpass us in the onboard automation area?"

This was definitely not a good day for the US intelligence services at the Farnborough SBAC show ground. A man of Middle Eastern origin (suspected by the Russians of being a US intelligence officer) then approached the helicopter static display in the absence of Mikheev and presenting himself as a Kamov OKB employee, collecting business cards from visitors interested in getting more information about the helicopter. Mikheev recalls these stressful moments with a smile, but at the time the situation at the show ground on the opening day was far from a funny one:

When I arrived at the helicopter in the early morning, a lot of people had gathered on the static display but nobody from our team was present around the Ka-50. I saw an unknown man with [an] Arabic look standing by, replying in English to the questions asked by visitors. I [was] furious and wrote with a marker on paper the following text: 'Please accept our excuses that we will not fly. The Kamov Design Bureau team had not been given British entry visas by the Moscow consulate.' We [hung] this announcement on the helicopter's nose and immediately a TV team saw it, and this way our message was aired.

The Kamov OKB technical team, including the test pilots, arrived two days later, but the flight display had been cancelled. There were too many emotions around the machine at Farnborough and the Russian delegation leadership had not ruled out that possible provocations against the displayed Ka-50 may occur.

The Ka-50's display at Farnborough was a notable event and created a huge noise in the media, which reported that it had stolen the show. The helicopter was also a subject of close examination by the US DoD. *Vertiflite* magazine, the official publication of the American Helicopter Society International, the professional society for the advancement of vertical flight technology and its useful application throughout the world, published an article by Colonel (Retired) Robert McDaniel, president and chief research specialist of the US company Analytical & Engineering Services Inc. Colonel McDaniel was a retired officer of the US Army, veteran of the Second World War, Korea, and Vietnam, and pioneer in the growth of the modern US Army aviation. In his report, he noted that the Ka-50, which was about to reach operational readiness, had been regarded as the most modern helicopter in the world and its potential combat capabilities reflected this status. It was obvious, as Colonel McDaniel noted back in 1992, that the requirements of the Ka-50 had been set out by taking into consideration the combat employment experience of the Mi-24. He also mentioned that it was clear that the Russian designers had been aware of the lessons learned during the Apache design in the 1970s, as that was the most modern and powerful helicopter until the Ka-50's appearance. The planned Apache upgrade and the Comanche development, as well as the Franco-German Tiger, Colonel McDaniel maintained, would reduce the Ka-50's performance supremacy, but there was no confidence at all that the supremacy of this helicopter would be surpassed. It is important to note, as the author emphasised, that the Ka-50's performance, including its single-crew combat effectiveness, had been demonstrated and confirmed in real-world comparative trials pitted against the Mi-28. In turn, the US Army decision to test a single-seat concept under the LHX programme had been based on the results of modelling and analytical research only.

There were also other comments in the West, mostly centred on the Ka-50's supposed weak design points. For instance, soon after the show, authoritative US aerospace and defence magazine *Aviation Week & Space Technology* published an article, based on the observations of pilots and senior executives of US helicopter companies. They were rather sceptical on the night-flying and NoE capability of the Ka-50 after they examined the *Hokum* up-close at Farnborough. While they agreed that the new Russian attack helicopter had some unique design features, they noted 'deficiencies' including extremely limited cockpit visibility and the high workload required by a single pilot operation but they had apparently failed to realise the true extent of the functionality of the, for its time in the 1980s and 1990s, extremely high automation of the Ka-50's onboard systems.

Then Ka-50 '020', accompanied by another machine, wearing the serial '021' (c/n 01-02), was displayed at the Paris Air Show in June 1993, where both *Hokums* conducted display/demonstration flights.

To be named Black Shark

In the event, the name Werewolf, as pioneered at the 1992 Farnborough SBAC show, had proved a short-lived one, failing to stick to the predatory-looking machine. But then the Ka-50 got involved in the movie-making business and as a result gained a new name, which proved to be a long-lived and rather popular one.

Sergey Ptichkin, a well-known Russian military-technology journalist, was the driving force behind an action motion picture showing spectacular combat scenes with the participation of new-generation helicopters, including air-to-air encounters. The idea was inspired by a US movie named *Fire Birds*, which he had watched on video in 1990. Ptichkin's script called for a major motion picture involving a Russian-made new-generation combat helicopter utilised to fight terrorists and the drug mafia. He initially approached the MVZ Mil, proposing the use of the new Mi-28 in a completely new-style

A look at the making of the *Black Shark* movie in Chirchik, Uzbekistan, with Mikheev and pilot Avtukhov in front of the Ka-50 '021'. (Sergey Mikheev archive)

Ka-50 '020' in the early 1990s at Zhulebino flight-test station with the entire range of weaponry then cleared for use in the *Black Shark* film, including free-fall bombs and 23mm gun-pods. It even has a pair of Igla air-to-air missiles suspended under the port outer wing pylon, which had not been cleared for use. (Kamov OKB)

action movie. Ptichkin, however, received the MVZ Mil leadership's firm refusal as the company was reluctant to provide a helicopter for participation in this kind of movie. Furthermore, MVZ Mil bosses had claimed in front of Ptichkin that the Mi-28 didn't need any advertising and was set to enter into Russian military service despite the loss in the competition with the Ka-50. The argument that the movie would be used as a good advertisement of the capabilities of the country's military-industrial complex had also failed to convince Mil MHP's leadership. They had directly and cynically claimed in front of Ptichkin that the money needed to be invested in making the motion picture would be better channelled to the generals and civil officials who would take the decision on commissioning their new helicopter into Russian military service.

Then Ptichkin had no option but to approach the Kamov OKB, where he met Mikheev to propose the same idea. Mikheev, who always had an adventurous spirit, embraced the major motion picture idea with enthusiasm.

The scenario of the motion picture named *Black Shark* (*Chornaya Akula* in Russian) included combat operations of the new attack helicopter in Afghanistan, participating in fictitious missions conducted after the Soviet withdrawal from the country, amid anarchy and the growing powers of drug lords. All the filming was made in the former Soviet republic of Uzbekistan in 1992, where the landscape was very similar to that in neighbouring Afghanistan. It is noteworthy that Mikheev had also taken part in the film – he appeared as himself (a so-called cameo appearance) in the role of designer-general of the brand-new Russian attack helicopter to be used for fighting terrorists and drug smugglers in Afghanistan.

The final scene of the movie called for air combat between the black-painted Ka-50 ('021'), flown by the Kamov OKB test pilot Dmitry Avtukhov, and a Mi-24 with the movie's main villain behind the controls. In this rather spectacular air combat, pitted against another helicopter, the Ka-50 had yet again demonstrated its trademark 'flat' (pedal) turn combat manoeuvre. It enabled the *Black Shark* to fire at the opponent with the nose and cannon pointing at the target perpendicular to the direction of flight – the so-called on-the-beam position.

5

INTO THE 1990s

Black Shark arrives in Torzhok

Upon completing the comprehensive state testing and evaluation effort, the Ka-50 was slated to progress into the so-called field testing and use for training by the initial instructor cadre, tasked to undertake conversion training of pilots from front-line units. Both of these activities had been traditionally carried out at the 344th Combat Training and Aircrew Conversion Centre (abbreviated in Russia as TsBPiPLS), stationed in the small city of Torzhok, some 200km north-west of Moscow. The centre plays an important role in the process of inducting new rotorcraft types into service. Its primary tasks include experimental operation and comprehensive field trials of all new RAA rotorcraft types, training an initial instructor cadre and providing conversion-to-type training of aircrews from the front-line units taking on these new types.

The skilled instructors of the centre regularly visit all the RAA's front-line squadrons to train pilots in advanced combat employment

A production-standard Ka-50 'Yellow 24' (c/n 01-04), operated in the mid-1990s by the Russian Army Aviation's 344th Combat Training and Aircrew Conversion Centre at Torzhok, north-west of Moscow. (Andrey Zinchuk)

A pair of Ka-50s, including '24', c/n 01-04, and production Ka-50 'Yellow 26', c/n 03-02, flying in formation with a Ka-27PS SAR helicopter of the Torzhok combat training centre. (Mikhail Nikolsky)

techniques such as mountain operations and air-to-air combat. The centre also implements and validates various modifications deemed necessary by the aircrews and engineers following their experimental and operational evaluation of the helicopters.

The 344th TsBPiPLS was originally established on 1 November 1979. Its initial structure was based on the 696th Independent Helicopter Regiment (696th OVP), which was later re-designated as the 696th Research Instructor Helicopter Regiment (696th IIVP).

In the 1980s and early 1990s, the 344th TsBPiPLS provided conversion-to-type and advanced training courses to 400–500 pilots and navigators annually. It was also tasked to perform a number of research programmes evaluating the operability, functionality and reliability of new equipment, mission avionics and weapons, as well as conducting various experimental trials aimed at expanding the operational use of the army aviation helicopters.

The first Ka-50 was delivered to the 344th TsBPiPLS on 5 November 1993 – it was V-80Sh-1, c/n 02-01, the first aircraft of the second batch built at the AAC Progress plant. The first pilot from the centre to convert to the new attack machine was its CO, Major General Boris Vorobyov, a well-known Army Aviation pilot with a wealth of combat experience under his belt, gathered during the war in Afghanistan. The lead pilots of the Ka-50 at the 344th TsBPiPLS, Colonel Vasily Khankov and Colonel Sergey Zolotov, were responsible for conducting a huge research programme with the type, including the Ka-50's field trials.

The Ka-50s handed over to the 344th TsBPiPLS sported the standard RAA two-tone green camouflage with a light blue underside, and wore the serial 'Yellow 20'. In 1994 it was followed by three more Black Sharks.

The first Ka-50 conversion-to-type course included a handful of experienced pilots from Torzhok, who were taught to fly and fight the single-seat helicopter, lacking a two-seat training version.

In these cash-strapped post-Soviet times, Kamov supported the operation at Torzhok by despatching two of its best specialists, Evgeny Sudarev and Grigory Yakemenko, who were tasked to resolve in a prompt manner all the technical issues that may arise at Torzhok.

Lieutenant General Evgeny Kashitsyn, then Chief of Staff of the RAA, recalls his first impressions from the Ka-50 he had flown at Torzhok in the mid-1990s: "The first flights confirmed the helicopter's high performance. Our pilots prized the ease of handling and controllability at transient modes during aerobatic manoeuvres. We also appreciated the good stability and accurate stabilisation at the sustained modes of flight. And we even felt that the declared performance had been lower than the actual one."

Experienced combat pilots at Torzhok also tended to say that they had prized highly the automatic stabilisation in the hover, allowing them to fire from ambushes with a rapid pop-out when hiding behind terrain or man-made obstacles. While controlling the hover mode, the pilot had been able to work with ease with the weapons during the sighting and shooting attack phases.

The Ka-50 turned out to be well-suited for the conversion-to-type training of average-skilled pilots with a wealth of experience on conventional-scheme helicopters. But every pilot had to overcome a psychological barrier; in flight, he had to be ready for any abnormal operation of the automated systems and the failures that may occur at any stage of flight in order to take an immediate correct decision to switch to manual control, especially during navigation and combat employment tasks. Due to the lack of a two-seat version with dual controls, in the beginning it was difficult for the instructors to assess the readiness of their trainees for performing the various types of missions. Furthermore, the pilots from Torzhok had to overcome the stereotype that a minimum of two crew members should be available onboard one dealing with the flying and the other with navigation tasks. There were also certain doubts voiced in the beginning regarding the claimed effectiveness of the sophisticated navigation suite and its reliability. But already after the first sorties pilots gave excellent marks

Sergey Mikheev receives the Hero of Russia Golden Star award from Russian President Boris Yeltsin in August 1997. (Sergey Mikheev archive)

to the Ka-50's navigation suite. It was of autonomous type, immune to jamming and could be integrated to other back-up navigation systems for easing the pilot's workload.

Three separate science-research projects were carried out at the 344th TsBPiPLS, centred on the Ka-50's targeting equipment and weapons. The first of them was devoted to the evaluation of the improved Vikhr-1 ATGM and was conducted between 22 November and 20 December 1994. As many as 30 sorties had been flown, with a total flight time of eight hours and 57 minutes. The probability of failure-free operation of the new ATGM demonstrated during the evaluation in Torzhok amounted to 0.99985. This remarkable achievement was reported in 1995, when the ATGM developer and manufacturer, Tula-based KBM, had barely managed to survive, with salaries paid to its employees with a six-month delay.

The pilots in Torzhok also found out that the flight performance of the Ka-50 carrying the Vikhr-1 ATGMs was the same as that of the V-80Sh-1 tested with the earlier Vikhr version. In all 30 test flights amassed under this specific project, the PPrNK-80 Rubikon flight/navigation/attack suite worked flawlessly; there were also no failures reported during the ATGM launches.

By December 1994, the RAA thus received a new-generation anti-tank helicopter, armed with ATGMs capable of defeating all known moving and fixed armoured targets that could be found on the battlefield. The long-range supersonic laser beam-riding missile enabled the Ka-50 to fire and guide the missile undetected by the enemy; this meant that the target could not receive warning in time to enable it to generate smoke screens to disrupt the missile guidance. The firings against tank columns on the move and lined up for attack on the battlefield could be mounted from safe (also known as 'stand-off') distances, beyond the reach of the NATO SAM and AAA systems

providing anti-air cover for NATO tank and mechanised divisions.

Another science-research project named 'Arsenal' was then initiated in 1994 at the 344th TsBPiPLS, aimed at comparing the combat effectiveness of the Ka-50 and Mi-28A. The list of comparative evaluation criteria in this effort included the time for navigation preparation after receiving the attack order, the probability of destruction of single and group targets and the expected losses which would be inflicted by enemy air defence systems. The project saw 140 single-ship and 20 pair sorties, with a total flight time of 180 hours, including attacks against typical armoured targets with rocket, guns and ATGMs. Most of the work was completed by lead pilot S. Zolotov, while the scientific lead of the effort was Colonel A. Rudikh.

In January 1995, the 344th TsBPiPLS commenced the development of the Ka-50's combat tactics. As many as 60 sorties with a total flight time of 100 hours were amassed by three pilots, and the results had been used for writing the Ka-50's combat employment manual that would be used by the front-line units set out to convert to the new machine.

At the same time, the Ka-50 had gained some influential opponents within the highest military circles in Russia, including the RAA CO, Colonel General Vitaly Pavlov. He had shown his hostile attitude towards the Ka-50 programme from the very beginning while openly favouring the losing contender Mi-28A, trying to promote it at every suitable occasion. Colonel General Pavlov maintained an opinion that after the Mi-28A had failed to win the attack helicopter competition, this meant that the competition terms and conditions were set in the wrong way from the start. In a desperate effort to change the situation, he had ordered RAA senor technical specialists to prove that the most suitable way for the recapitalisation of the RAA's struggling attack fleet would be the introduction of an upgraded Mi-24 derivative equipped with a night vision targeting system, armed with the 9M120 Ataka-V ATGM system and featuring a plethora of airframe changes such as non-retractable landing gear and shortened stub-wings. The Mi-24's upgrade effort to Mi-24PN standard was intended to fill the void until the MVZ Mil and Rostvertol could offer a radically-improved Mi-28A version, dubbed Mi-28N, endowed with reasonable night-operating capabilities. The first prototype of the night-capable Mi-28N, OP-1, was built in 1994–1995 and made its maiden flight in November 1996, with its integrated avionics suite still incomplete. However, the second prototype, OP-2, did not take to the air until March 2004. The real advance in the Mi-28N's development effort did not happen until 2003, when the Russian MoD announced that its procurement plans included as many as 50 new-generation attack helicopters to be fielded in front-line service by 2010.

In the event, the efforts of Colonel General Pavlov proved ill-suited to stop the steady progress of the Ka-50 programme in the mid and late 1990s. By a decree signed by Russian President Boris Yeltsin, dated 25 August 1995, the Black Shark was officially commissioned into service with the Russian military. This long-awaited act had resulted in decorating more than 80 Kamov OKB employees with Russian government awards. Two years later, Sergey Mikheev received the highest state award – the long-deserved Gold Star of Hero of Russian Federation.

This happened at MAKS-1997 air show held at Zhukovsky airfield near Moscow, where President Yeltsin met Mikheev in front of the Ka-50 on the static display. Mikheev showed the helicopter and informed President Yeltsin that Major General Boris Vorobyov, a recipient of the Hero of Russia award, would give a spirited display with the Ka-50 later the same day. President Yeltsin, looking thoughtfully at Mikheev, suddenly said: "So, the pilot is a Hero of Russia but the designer is not?" After a short pause, he continued in a tone brooking

no objection: "Please do prepare the documents for decorating him [Mikheev] with the Hero of Russia award!"

At the cocktail reception after the closure of the flight display on the same day, President Yeltsin spontaneously proposed a toast and announced that he had just decided to decorate with the Hero of Russian Federation award Sergey Mikheev and then Russian Air Force CinC, Colonel General Pyotr Deinekin.

Slovakia demo tour

In the mid-1990s, the Kamov OKB took part in a demo tour in Slovakia, where the Ka-50 was seen as having a pretty good chance to be sold. The small East European country was keen to purchase a sizeable quantity of Russian-made weaponry in lieu of writing-off the Russian trade debt, remaining from Soviet times, which amounted to some US$1.7 billion.

In the case of a successful deal, the Black Shark was to get a much-needed launch export customer, which would be used as a catalyst for winning more export orders. By that time, the Kamov OKB had already accumulated some experience in this kind of export business, as the Ka-32 was purchased by various government customers from South Korea in exchange for writing-off Russian trade debt. This proved to be a very successful trade scheme, which eventually saw more than 60 Ka-32s produced and delivered to government operators in South Korea in the 1990s.

The write-off of the Russian trade debt to Slovakia was agreed between the countries in June 1994, and had originally called for the completion of the purchase of Russian-made goods in 1995. The first instalment of weapons agreed in 1994 included six MiG-29 fighters and 24 air-to-air missiles priced at US$176 million. The following year saw another deal for the Igla shoulder-launched SAM, priced at US$87 million. In 1996, Rosvooruzhenie, the leading Russian arms trade

Ka-50 '018' is presented to Slovakian Air Force officers in a hangar at the military airfield at Piestany in October 1996. (Anatoly Klunniy archive)

Yury Gruzevich, deputy director-general of Geophizika-NV, shows the then brand-new Geo-ONV-1 aviator NVG set to high-ranking Slovakian Air Force officers during the Ka-50 demonstration in October 1996. (Anatoly Klunniy archive)

agency at the time, proposed to the Russian government the schedule of the follow-on deliveries to Slovakia, including MiG-29 *Fulcrum* fighters and Su-39 attack aircraft, to take place in 1997, while Ka-50 attack helicopters were to follow suit in 1998. In order to convince the Slovakian government that the Ka-50 purchase would be a worthy and no-risk deal, it was decided to organise a demo tour. The Ka-50 was set to show its combat capabilities at Slovakian gunnery ranges in an effort to win the hearts and minds of the Slovakian military.

The demonstration took place in October 1995, with a VVS-owned Ka-50 '018' self-deploying from Torzhok to Piestany in Slovakia, escorted by a Kamov-owned Ka-32T. The Ka-50 was flown by Sergey Zolotov, an experienced Black Shark pilot from the 344th TsBPiPLS, while the Ka-32T was crewed by pilot Oleg Krivoshein and navigator Pavel Kalinin.

In order to simplify the organisation, the demo tour team decided not to take 30mm rounds and 80mm rockets, as the export formalities of the ammunition would be prohibitive; instead, Mikheev had assumed that such ordinance could be easily found in Slovakia. The ferry flight of the Ka-50 and Ka-32T started at Zhulebino flight test station on 17 October 1995 and was completed without any glitches. The reception in Slovakia was very warm and the Slovak officers were very interested to learn more about the Ka-50, seeing its purchase as a done deal. On 21 October, the Ka-50 flew a familiarisation sortie at the gunnery range, located some 30km (17nm) from the base, and on 22 and 23 October, Zolotov demonstrated accurate gun and rocket firings (using Slovak-supplied ordinance), escorted by the Ka-32T acting as a camera ship, with photographers and video operators onboard.

The demo sorties and firings were judged highly successful and the Slovak officers were very enthusiastic and impatient to take on strength the newest Russian attack helicopter. But as usual, politics

Ka-50 '018' (c/n 00-01) unleashing S-8 80mm rockets from a shallow dive in low-level flight at a gunnery range near Piestany in Slovakie. (Kamov OKB)

had soon spoiled the deal; a combination of Western pressure applied on Slovaks not to buy the Ka-50, together with internal Russian troubles and rivalries. In the event, the deal never materialised and Slovakia instead purchased S-300PMU (SA-10 *Grumble*) long-range surface-to-air systems, with the final settlement of the Russian trade debt reported not before 2013.

The Slovak tour of the Kamov OKB remained consigned to the company's history book as a sales push with a trouble-free ferry flight, also resulting in a series of spectacular Ka-50 photos with the backdrop of a medieval castle in the Tatri Mountains.

Major General Boris Vorobyov (in the centre) was a talented and brave attack helicopter pilot, awarded the Hero of Soviet Union Golden Star for his extraordinary combat exploits in Afghanistan in the 1980s. He was killed in the crash of Ka-50 '22', c/n 01-03, on 17 June 1998. From left to right: three Hero of the Soviet Union recipients involved in inducting in service the Ka-50 – Army Aviation pilots Colonel Kolpakov, Major General Vorobyov and Colonel Novikov. (Kamov OKB)

General Vorobyov's crash

A year after Mikheev's award, tragedy struck at Torzhok, resulting in the death of the famous combat and display pilot, Major General Boris Vorobyov. The tragic event also allowed the Ka-50 opponents within the Russian MoD to inflict almost mortal damage on the otherwise slowly progressing Black Shark programme.

Grigory Yakemenko, team leader of the Kamov OKB's team working in Torzhok, wrote for the company record book:

The personnel of the Torzhok combat training centre [were] inspired by the successful flight operations with the Ka-50. The centre set up in a short time a special programme for flight training of Army Aviation aircrews, used for air display training purposes. It allowed the aerobatics routines to be performed with bank and pitch angles up to 90˚. This display programme also included loops and 360˚ rolls without limitations as the angles in these manoeuvres would exceed 180˚. [At] the end of the programme there was a space allocated for the signature of a Kamov OKB representative but nobody had asked us to ink the document. Major General Vorobyov had well realised that the programme would not be signed in this form by the Kamov OKB, but he had no need of it in another [i.e. amended and restricted] form. It is unclear how and why it had been signed by the Army Aviation Commanding Officer, General V. Pavlov.

The display flights as foreseen by this programme were practiced until the end of August 1997, with General Vorobyov mastering flying the display routine both at day and night. [OnI] the evening of 17 June 1998 he crashed while performing a Ka-50 display training flight. Boris Alekseevich Vorobyov perished in the crash.

The accident investigation commission wrote in its report: "The cause of the crash was an unintentional entry of the Ka-50 into a non-permitted and little-studied regime of flight during complex aerobatics manoeuvrings, exceeding the current flight manual limitations, and beyond the limitations set out for display flights."

According to official data, General Vorobyov had a lengthy interruption in his Ka-50 flights, from September 1997 to 15 May 1998. The fatal flight on 17 May 1998 was only his second after the long pause. The sortie started at 9:55 p.m.. On that day, Vorobyov had completed a Mi-24 flight, then returned to his cottage to take some rest before returning to take part in the second flight shift for the day at the centre. During the pre-flight medical check, the aviation surgeon noted that Vorobyov had a higher heartbeat rate (75 strokes per minute) and blood pressure. The flight data recorder survived the crash intact, and all data was successfully downloaded and analysed. But this did not help to explain General Vorobyov's actions that led to the fatal accident.

Mikheev recalls that General Vorobyov had a love affair with the Ka-50:

A hard-core combat pilot, he found in the helicopter what he had been looking for all his life – a potent and easy to control combat machine. [H]e was irrepressible in his strive to get to the edge of its performance envelope and it was pointless to speak with him to be careful when flying the Ka-50. But I think that he should not be blamed for the crash. Yes, even he committed a mistake, [but] Vorobyov wasn't guilty.

During General Vorobyov's funeral in Torzhok, Mikheev accidentally heard words, spoken by somebody behind him: "And now we will close this helicopter [programme]." The voice belonged to a man he knew well, but Mikheev eventually decided not to turn to face this person.

Second attempt to get night operating capabilities

In the mid-1990s, the Perm-based Urals Optical-Mechanical Plant (UOMZ), which during Soviet times was a serial-production plant within the TsKB Geophizika enterprise, became an independent company. The demand for its traditional products optronic systems for equipping Gen 4 jet fighters rapidly diminished and the company was therefore forced to look elsewhere for new opportunities. Its then director-general, Eduard Yalamov, committed to an initiative to launch the development and production of gyro-stabilised electro-optical systems (payloads), known under the Russian-language abbreviation GOES, similar to the products offered by the world-renowned US company FLIR Systems Inc. In fact, the idea to start dealing with such prospective new technologies originated from Mikheev himself, who saw gyro-stabilised systems on display during the famous Ka-50 debut at the Farnborough SBAC Air Show in September 1992. Yalamov and Mikheev met in London on their way to Farnborough and had a long discussion on the new electro-optical technologies that could be used on attack helicopters, providing vastly expanded target search and track opportunities for round-the-clock operations. Yalamov asked Mikheev for advice on new products, which his newly independent company could develop and produce. Mikheev, in turn, advised his interlocutor to pay special attention to the FLIR Systems products displayed at the show. His advice had eventually been followed by Yalamov, who took the bold step to invest the company's own money in this promising technology area. Now, 25 years later, the UOMZ enjoys the status of the main supplier of gyro-stabilised electro-optical day/night targeting payloads for both the Ka-52 and Mi-35M attack helicopters.

When presenting its GOES product concept, the UOMZ relied upon the support of Mikheev as a future customer and his signature had eventually enabled the company to launch a research and development project. Mikheev gladly accepted the GOES idea and became a keen supporter, seeing the payload as a useful day/night targeting system not only for the Ka-50, but also for some other classes of helicopters.

The family line of GOES systems uses moving ball payloads of several sizes (with diameter of 720, 640, 460 and 360mm), housing four to six different electro-optical modules (sensors) such as a day TV camera, LLLTV camera to provide night vision capability, thermal imager, laser rangefinder/target designator, laser marked spot seeker, laser-beam ATGM guidance system, etc.

The Samshit-50 payload was among the first GOES-type observation/targeting systems, developed by the UOMZ. It was originally intended for installation on the Ka-50 and the then-developed Ka-60R reconnaissance helicopter. A payload with a 640mm diameter, it housed four sensors, each provided with its own window: a laser rangefinder/target designator, TV camera for day operation, Victor thermal imager (supplied by the French company Thomson-CSF) plus an ATGM laser-beam guidance system. The detection range for a tank-sized target provided by the thermal imager was up to 7km (3.7nm), while ATGM targeting by using the laser-beam guidance

system would be possible from ranges of 4.55km (2.42.7nm).

A Samshit-50 payload was installed in early 1997 on the fifth Ka-50 produced at Arsenyev, which was used as a pattern aircraft for the Ka-50's production, wearing the serial '018' (c/n 00-01). The ball payload was mounted in the nose, just above the window used by the Shkval-V sighting system, and had the appearance of a wart. This Black Shark derivative received the new Ka-50Sh designation and lifted off in its first flight in the new guise on 4 March 1997, in the skilled hands of Kamov OKB test pilot Oleg Krivoshein. Soon afterwards, the night-capable helicopter was put on display in front of potential customers at the IDEX-97 defence exhibition in Abu-Dhabi. It remained on the static display, while a production-standard Ka-50 from Torzhok demonstrated cannon and rocket firing as well as ATGM launches.

The Ka-50Sh was also modified with other avionics novelties. It witnessed, for instance, the first attempt to be equipped with on-board radar. The Arbalet radar system, developed by Moscow-based Phazotron-NIIR, used a mast-mounted antenna for 360° scanning in azimuth. This design solution had been inspired by the AH-64D Apache, equipped with the Longbow mast-mounted radar for surface and air target search and tacking, enabling the use of the AGM-114L Hellfire active-radar guided anti-tank missile. However, the initiative to equip the Ka-50Sh with radar for all-weather operations had failed to materialise in the 1990s due to a lack of funding and know-how needed to get the required performance from a small-size mast-mounted radar set.

Another novelty, the Kabris electronic map, developed by then start-up technology company Transas of St Petersburg and integrated into the navigation system, was successfully implemented and tested onboard the Ka-50. The Kabris, using a satellite navigation receiver, replaced the antiquated PA-4-3 positioning system used to provide information by using a moving paper map. It was not a simple navigation system but also represented an integral component of the helicopter's flight/navigation/attack suite. The pilot could select the waypoints of a pre-planned route before take-off directly on the digital map, and then all data needed was fed to the autopilot which could fly the aircraft along the designated route (defined by the set out waypoints), without any involvement of the pilot.

In the late 1990s, the Russian MoD continued to provide a tiny amount of research and development funding to the Kamov OKB each year. This had always happened in a haphazard manner, just before the year-end (and the company was obliged to spend the budget by the end of the year); nevertheless, it allowed some more novelties to find their place on the Ka-50Sh. For example, the helicopter received a new open-architecture flight/navigation suite with multiplex data transfer buses. Developed by the Ramenskoye-based RPKB company, it included three liquid-crystal displays in the cockpit, replacing the traditional electromechanical instruments, in addition to a modified head-up display. The Shkval-V and Samshit-50 targeting systems switched their places the latter was installed on the lower part of the nose, while the former was situated on the top. The Samshit-50 payload, 640mm in diameter, was modified with the more capable Iris thermal imager supplied by French company SAGEM (replacing the Thomson-CSF Victor), in addition to a TV camera, laser rangefinder and laser-beam ATGM guidance unit.

The SAGEM Iris thermal imager used a 288x4 HgCdTe LWIR detector working in the 812 micron wavelength. The system was able to facilitate detection at night of tank- and armoured vehicle-sized targets at ranges of 4–6km (2.2–3.2nm). Later on, a Samshit-50 derivative was mounted on the Ka-52's roof, just behind the cockpit, with coverage of 230° left and right, 25° up and 115° down.

The weapons options of the night-capable Black Shark were to be

General Vorobyov's ill-fated Ka-50 '22' (c/n 01-03) wearing a striking Black Shark-motive paint scheme, flying in formation with '23' (c/n 02-04). (Kamov OKB)

The Samshit-50 sensor ball installed in the nose of Ka-50 '018' in 1997, just above the Shkval-V window. (Anatoly Demin archive)

The Ka-50Sh '018', newly-adorned with two sensor balls on the nose – the GOES-330 is on the bottom, used for targeting purposes, while the TOES-520, facilitating night navigation, is installed on the top. This configuration was displayed at the MAKS-2007 airshow. (Kamov OKB)

expanded with the Kh-25ML laser-guided air-to-surface missile. The modified machine was displayed for the first time in its new guise in June 1999 at a defence exhibition in Nizhny Tagil in Russia, and then at the MAKS-1999 air show. At the static display, the Ka-50Sh also sported the R-73 heat-seeking, highly agile air-to-air missiles, in addition to the 9M39 Igla-V short-range, heat-seeking air-to-air missiles (modified from a shoulder-launched surface-to-air missile system). The Ka-50Sh, however, had never been tested in the air-to-air role and had also never test-launched the two types of missile.

In 1999, the Kamov OKB modified the fourth Ka-50 built at the company's experimental plant, serialled '014', with a two-payload system in the nose. The new GOES-520 payload, 360mm in diameter (used for navigation at night), replaced the Shkval-V day-only targeting system in the top of the nose, while the lower part of the nose housed the GOES-330 payload, 460mm in diameter. The latter included a TV camera for day operations, thermal imager, laser rangefinder and laser-beam ATGM guidance system. It was later replaced by the much larger GOES-640. The new configuration, however, had never been tested in the air due to the acute lack of funding at the time.

NVG story

In parallel with the rolling improvements made to the Ka-50Sh, Kamov commenced work to adapt the cockpit lighting to allow use of a night vision goggle (NVG) set. This kind of night vision device works well in close surroundings, helping crews detecting obstacles in front of the helicopter at ranges in excess of 0.5km (0.27nm) in average night lighting conditions. A helicopter flying at low or ultra-low level at night would have reduced vulnerability to short-range air defences that are reliant upon aiming using line-of-sight, electro-optic and electronic methods.

The introduction of helicopter-borne NVGs was preceded by the launch in production in Russia of Gen 3 optoelectronic converters, suitable for use in pilot NVGs able to see in the 0.75–1.3 micron wavelength that part of the spectrum known as near IR band and present in starlight. In the 1980s, it was found that pilot NVG sets using Gen 2 optoelectronic converters (that are otherwise fully suitable for land vehicles and snipers) were not entirely suitable for airborne use because of flight safety considerations. The reason for that is the insufficient signal/noise ratio that would lower the Gen 2 performance to unacceptable levels. At the same time, US companies ITT and Litton had already mastered the large-scale production of Gen 3 optronic converters without the ion-barrier film, which gave them a notable technology advantage, translated into a tactical advantage when this technology was used by attack helicopter crews. US Army aviators (and their colleagues in most NATO member states) wearing Gen 3 NVGs were able to fly in the dark, search for targets and land on unlit sites on moonless nights, while the Russian army aviation helicopters had to stay on the ground in such conditions. In the best case, Russian aviators could be able to conduct limited operations relying upon external scene illumination by air-dropped illumination bombs, rockets or ground artillery rounds delivering flares descending on parachutes.

Development and production of Gen 3 optoelectronic converters in Russia was launched at the Geophizika-NV, a Moscow-based

Ka-50 '014' (c/n 800-04) shown here in the new nose sensor configuration, with the TOES-521 on the top and the GOES-340 payload on the bottom, was displayed at the MAKS 1999 air show. (Sergey Nosov archive)

Ka-50Sh '018' in flight with the Shkval-V system mounted on top of the nose, while the lower part houses the Samshit-50 multi-sensor observation/targeting turret. (Vadim Pozdnyakov archive)

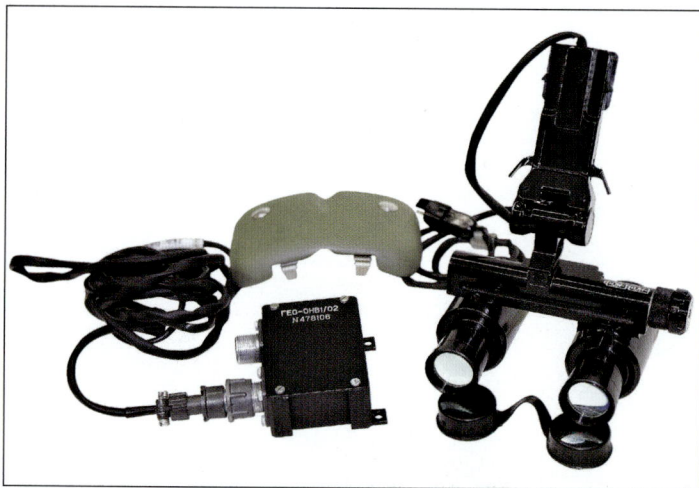

The GEO-ONV-1 NVG set was the first piece of kit of its kind to enter service in Russia, initially on night-capable Mi-8s and Mi-24s, and was then proposed for use by the Ka-50 and Ka-52 aircrews. (Geophizika-NV)

Vera Belikova, the NVG chief-designer at Geophizika-NV, together with Yury Grizevich, deputy director general of the company, responsible for R&D (research and design) activities. (Vadim Pozdnyakov)

privately-owned company, whose management previously worked for the so-called 'Big Geophizika' enterprise (formerly known as the TsKB Geophizika). The small and inventive company, led by director-general Victor Soldatenkov, developed its own technology of applying the ion-barrier film and then managed to launch the mass production of Gen 3 optoelectronic converters (also known as intensifier tubes), used in the Geo-ONV-1 NVG set.

The set, optimised for use by helicopter aircrews, was found to be operationally efficient under starlit conditions, even without a moon. The optoelectronic convertors provide ambient light multi-thousand amplification and the Geo-ONV-1 NVG set had a 40° field of view via a green and white picture. The resulting image is green because this is the colour that the human eye 'accepts best' and is able to discern the most shades of; with this, the NVG set could provide the best picture, despite using only one colour.

Using NVGs, Ka-50 aircrews were made capable of detecting objects reflecting starlight and moonlight, but remained ill-suited to detect features that were matt or non-reflective, or that were too small.

The Geo-ONV-1 NVG set used the dual-image intensifier tube technology ('straight through' tubes), giving a degree of stereo vision and depth perception. It had a single mount on the standard ZSh-7V rotorcraft aircrew protective helmet and a 'flip-up' design.

The new NVG set was initially tested on a Mi-8 helicopter and was then commissioned into service with the Russian Air Force (RuAF) as a useful add-on, suitable for facilitating take-offs and landings from unlit sites as well as low and ultra-low level en-route navigation both single-ship and in formation. Later on, the Ka-50 proved that NVGs, worn by experienced pilots, can be also useful aids for unguided weapons firing at night.

Mikheev had already expressed an interest in this new and promising night-vision technology at an early stage, and on 29 November 1997 he signed a resolution to equip the Ka-50 with an aviator NVG set. The joint development effort of making the interior and exterior lighting NVG compatible and testing the NVGs was supported by two research institutes and the Geophizika-NV company, which provided the Kamov OKB with a Geo-ONV-1 set and evaluated the NVG adaptations of the interior lighting, using green lights only. Without this specific lighting, the NVG image would be affected as any extraneous illumination 'blooms out' the view through the goggles, with even small amounts of light in the red to infrared passband seriously degrading NVG performance.

The fourth Ka-50, serialled '014', was used in the NVG test programme, with Grigory Yekemenko leading the Kamov OKB design team, while the Geophizka-NV was represented by its deputy director-general, Yuriy Gruzevich. The flight testing effort for the NVG-equipped Black Shark was undertaken by VVS test pilots N. Kolpakov and N. Naumov.

The experimental works were required to be completed in a very compressed timeframe, so the Kamov OKB had to provide its technical specification to the sub-contractors within two weeks, while the design drawings were to be approved in late January 1999, and then the cockpit modifications completed within one month. The team had, in fact, failed to meet the original work schedule, while the pilot ejection system proved to be main obstacle for the NVG integration on the Ka-50. The designers found that it would be next to impossible to design a jettisoning device for the NVG set installed on the pilot's ZSh-7V protective helmet in the event of ejection. In addition, the military requirements of the NVG integration required the power supply to be backed-up by a cable and adapter, connected to the helicopter's own electrical system. In the event of ejection, this cable could badly hurt or even kill the pilot. That is why, in June 1997, Yekimenko requested Geophizika-NV's director-general, Victor Soldatenkov, to develop a modified NVG set suitable for use by a helicopter equipped with ejection seat. This, however, proved impossible at that time due to lack of funding; the task was accomplished later, when the NVG set had been modified to equip the crewmen of the Ka-52 two-seater. The development works carried out during the NVG integration on the Ka-52 included a rapidly decoupling device (to snap the power supply cable in the event of ejection) together with a study on the impact forces caused by the NVG set attached to the pilot helmet during the ejection sequence.

Back in the late 1990s, during the underfunded initial testing of the NVG on the Ka-50, the team had to make some compromises to the flight safety requirements in order to kick-start the testing effort. The test flights were performed near Moscow and at the 929th GLITs (VVS flight test centre) in Akhtubinsk. The programme included not only simple flights by also live firings with guided and unguided weapons at night, with pilots wearing NVG sets.

6

BLACK SHARK'S COMBAT DEBUT

Chechnyan war

In late 2000, the Russian press started hinting at the Ka-50's imminent use in war operations in the breakaway republic of Chechnya in the Northern Caucasus. It was the second Chechen war campaign, launched in August 1999, and officially conducted as a large-scale anti-terrorist operation by the Russian Armed Forces. At the outset of the campaign, it was aimed primarily at dislodging illegal Chechen armed groups from their fortified positions in the neighbouring autonomous republic of Dagestan as they occupied a number of cities and villages there with the intent of creating a territory under their control.

The large-scale offensive in what was considered to be Russia's own war on terrorism was launched by the Joint Group of Forces (JGF), running towards the Chechen capital of Grozny from four directions simultaneously, on 1 October 1999; this push eventually led to the seizure of the city in January 2000.

In the summer of 2000, the second phase of the campaign commenced. It was the period when the Chechen armed opposition finally retreated to the mountains in the southern part of the country and switched to effective guerrilla warfare tactics. In such conditions, direct large-scale encounters with large groups of Chechen rebels were rare and RAA helicopters were heavily utilised in a transport and re-supply role, ferrying troops and cargoes into otherwise inaccessible locations in the mountains. The RAA attack assets were used as top cover for ground convoys, 'free hunting' for targets of opportunity and special operations forces (SOF) insertion and extraction.

An event which subsequently received a lot of publicity, in both the Russian and foreign media, was the deployment of two Ka-50s between December 2000 and February 2001. In fact, the idea of establishing a dedicated and self-sufficient combat experimental group can trace its origins back to the mid-1990s, when the Ka-50 completed its state testing and evaluation effort. A decision on setting up an Experimental Combat Group (ECG) was signed on 25 April 1995 by the first deputy minister of defence of the Russian Federation, A. Kokoshkin. Its fleet was planned to include four Ka-50s and four Ka-29s; the latter were to be modified as scouts, capable of performing reconnaissance and targeting missions.

The ECG's main task at the time was to test and evaluate the concept for the employment of combat helicopters as an integrated 'hunter/killer' combat team. The Ka-50 was a novelty in the RAA fleet the first and the only single-seat attack helicopter with coaxial rotor scheme and a very high level of automation of pilotage and combat employment tasks.

The Russian MoD representatives, together with the Kamov OKB, developed a concept for the Ka-50's use in local military conflicts. This was to be conducted by deploying rapid-reaction helicopter groups, armed with precisely guided ordinance and using secure datalinks for command-and-control and sharing targeting data, forming a single command-and-control, reconnaissance and targeting system. After completion of testing, this group was to be integrated into the command-and-control networks of Land Forces and the Air Force, providing continuous exchange of information in real time during air-land operations.

Major General Boris Vorobyov, CO of the 344th TsBPiPLS at the time, was among the principal driving forces behind this idea. At the initial stage, his authority and power, combined with the authority of Kamov's designer general Sergey Mikheev, proved to be enough to get

A Ka-50 devoid of national insignia and serials taking off from Grozni-North in Chechnya. It is armed with two 20-round packs for 80mm rockets and carries two external fuel tanks. (Alexander Artukh)

the ball rolling. In 1995, the Russian Air Force and the Land Force's RAA branch were obliged to provide four Ka-50s and two Ka-29s for the ECG, with two more Ka-29s, taken from the Russian Naval Aviation service, planned to be included in the fleet at a later stage.

The first two Ka-50s, serialled '22' and '24', taken from the first production batch at the AAC Progress plant, were handed over to the Kamov OKB for implementing the necessary minimum of modifications for use in the new role. The first Ka-29 underwent a more serious upgrade, receiving a 2A42 cannon and a secure communication system with data encryption capability. The second Ka-29 also received this system, together with a PrPNK-80 Rubikon flight/navigation/attack system, borrowed from the Ka-50. It was intended to enable the Ka-29 to be used for airborne control and targeting purposes. In an effort to enhance their survivability, both Ka-29s received UV-26M flare dispensers scabbed onto the fuselage sides, as well as engine duct IR suppressor devices. The upgraded Ka-29 got the new designation Ka-29VPNTsU (the Russian abbreviation for Airborne Post for Surveillance, Targeting and Control).

Later on, the Kamov OKB got two more Ka-50s, handed over by the 344th TsBPiPLS, serialled '20' and '21', slated to be brought to the equipment standard implemented onto the first two Black Sharks for the ECG.

However, the idea of establishing the ECG stalled due to lack of funds and other more urgent priorities at the time, as the ongoing war in Chechnya had been drying up the Russian military budget at a very fast rate. In this difficult situation, the Kamov OKB modified the first pair of Ka-50s using its own funds, hoping that it would be compensated at a later stage by the Russian MoD. The company proved unable to fund the modification of the second pair of Ka-50s, and these machines remained idle in the hall of its experimental plant in Lyubertsi, while the first pair of modified Black Sharks and both Ka-29s were handed over to the 344th TsBPiPLS. The modified machines took part in an experimental exercise at the Alabino gunnery range, held from 25 September to 21 October 1997, in an effort to test the effectiveness of their newly integrated mission equipment.

From experimental to strike group

After the crash of 344th TsBPiPLS CO Major General Vorobyov in June 1998, the Ka-50 programme was on the verge of termination and was only saved thanks to the Russian MoD order, dated 29 November 1999, which called for the establishment of the Combat Strike Group (CSG) intended for use in local conflicts.

The Kamov OKB team furnishing field support to the RAA's CSG in Chechnya in front of one of the Black Sharks. In addition to the 80mm rocket packs, it is also armed with Vikhr-1 ATGMs. (Alexey Simonov archive)

At this time, the 344th TsBPiPLS operated only one Ka-50, serialled '24' (c/n 01-04), modified at the Kamov OKB back in 1997. It was decided that the second helicopter for the CSG would be the fifth experimental machine, serialled '25' (c/n 800-05) and used in the 1993 action movie *Black Shark*.

The Kamov OKB commenced the preparation of the two helicopters in a prompt manner, forming a team of technicians and combat employment assistance specialists, including chief designer Vyacheslav Zaritov and test pilot Alexander Papay. Both Ka-50s were further modified, receiving enhanced armour protection and additional mission equipment. The new armour protection features included armoured side windows for the cockpit and armour plating scabbed onto the cockpit floor. The new mission equipment added was represented by the Kabris satellite navigation and moving map system, useful for both ferry flights and combat missions. It enabled the pilot to upload before a sortie the route waypoints and target position, enabling the Ka-50s to arrive at their targets with a circular error amounting to just tens of metres. The helicopters also received digital cockpit video cameras and recorders. The cameras looked through the ILS-31 HUD in a bid to capture the sector in front of the helicopter, together with the information displayed on the HUD.

The work-up of the RAA pilots assigned to the CSG took place between December 1999 and June 2000, in rather difficult training conditions due to chronic shortages of fuel and ammunition. They amassed a total of 28 flight shifts by using two Ka-50s and a Ka-29VPNTsU, amounting to in excess of 150 training sorties (including 125 Ka-50 sorties). These flights were also used to test the functionality of the newly installed mission equipment at various flight regimes, as well as to hone the use of the external targeting method with

correction provided by the Kabris system. The pilots also trained at gunnery ranges, firing the 30mm cannon, 80mm rockets and Vikhr ATGMs. The supply of munitions for the training of the CSG was rather limited, which, in turn, allowed the pilots to only qualify in combat employment in an automatic mode, with the Ka-50's Shkval-V TV/laser targeting system working in the auto-tracking mode. After completion of the training, the RAA command authorities found that the CSG aircrew were combat-ready in day/clear weather conditions in single-ship as well as pair formation; they were also qualified ready for conducting ferry flights in day/bad weather conditions. During the training, they mastered the employment of external targeting received from the Ka-29VPNTsU and from a ground-based automated work station. The Ka-29 aircrew, in turn, was considered combat-ready for providing targeting information to the Ka-50s, while the Black Shark pilots qualified to mount attacks against ground targets by using targeting information fed from the Ka-29VPNTsU.

In December 2000, a directive issued by the Russian Armed Forces General Staff called for the CSG to deploy to the Northern Caucasus region and take part in combat operations in Chechnya. Before commencing the ferry flight, the national insignia and serials of all three helicopters had been painted over.

The CSG personnel included eight pilots and two navigators, in addition to 26 engineers and technicians. There were also two representatives from the RAA Directorate, plus nine Kamov OKB and AAC Progress plant technicians. The combat missions were to be flown only by RAA pilots. The group's technicians had a Mi-24 background, with little or no experience in servicing the Ka-50 and Ka-29.

The ferry flight of the two Ka-50s and the sole Ka-29VPNTsU,

The lone Ka-29VPNTsU resting at Grozni-North airfield. It features the Shkval-V TV/laser targeting system borrowed from the Ka-50, but is devoid of any armament. (Alexander Artukh)

Ground crews prepare S-8 80mm rockets for loading into the B-8V20A rocket packs of the Ka-29VPNTsU. (Alexey Simonov archive)

escorted by a Mi-8, was from Torzhok to Grozny-North airfield in Chechnya, with refuelling stops made at Kaluga, Kursk, Millerovo, Yegorlikskaya and Budennovsk. It took place, however, at the worst time of the year, plagued by the prevailing bad weather. The ferry flight started on 3 December and was completed on 26 December 2000; there were no serious failures reported during the protracted journey.

At Grozny-North, the CSG team had to live and work in Spartan conditions, with the personnel, including the Kamov/AAC Progress team, accommodated in tents with diesel heaters. A damaged heater in the neighbouring tent caused a fire which destroyed the tent housing the Kamov OKB personnel; they were lucky to escape just in time, but all their belongings were consumed by the fire.

Area familiarisation missions were flown from 28–30 December, then familiarisation flying continued on 1 January, while the first combat mission in Chechnya was reported on 6 January 2001.

The Ka-50 pilots flew their local area familiarisation sorties in Mi-24s, then the combat missions were flown in mixed formations, consisting of a pair of Ka-50s and a pair of Mi-24s, or a pair of Ka-50s and the solitary Ka-29.

The Ka-50's most publicised combat mission in Chechnya was the maiden one: supported by a Mi-24, the Black Shark pair attacked a well-camouflaged ammunition depot near the town of Komsomol'skoe. The small, hardened target located in a deep valley was reported as

The entire CSG fleet of two Ka-50s and the sole Ka-29VPNTsU resting on the ramp at Grozni-North airfield. (Alexey Simonov archive)

Kamov lead engineer Alexey Simonov performs maintenance on a TV3-117VMA engine at Grozni-North airfield in Chechnya during the CSG deployment. (Alexey Simonov archive)

An anonymous-looking Ka-50, armed with two 20-round rocket pods, soon after lift-off for another combat mission in Chechnya in January 2001. (Alexey Simonov archive)

having been destroyed by S-8 80-mm rockets launched in a steep dive.

The inclement and rapidly changing weather in the Northern Caucasus region in January 2001 offered challenging flying conditions at ultra-low level, with frequent fogs in the mountain passes when the helicopters had to pass through narrow valleys, but in general this was not considered an obstacle for conducting combat missions in a safe and effective manner.

The Ka-50's coaxial rotor scheme proved more than suitable for flying in such challenging weather and terrain conditions. After the first mission, one of the pilots had enthusiastically said that only coaxial machines should fly combat missions over the rugged mountain terrain in the Northern Caucasus. The lack of a tail rotor made handling the helicopter much easier in side-on wind gusts (i.e. when flying in pulsing crosswind conditions), which could be very dangerous when flying in narrow valleys. The sun-heated walls of these valleys created strong air turbulence; when hitting such turbulent air or when hit by wind gusts, both the Mi-8 and Mi-24 would prove susceptible to veering out of control, which, on some occasions, led to serious accidents.

Combat advantages

The coaxial rotor Ka-50 demonstrated its valuable advantages when flying in mountain conditions, including high manoeuvrability and an exceptional rate of climb. In one of the combat sorties, in an effort to avoid a tall vertical obstacle (high-rising cliffs), the pilot of Ka-50 '24' exceeded all the calculated rate of climb characteristics, with the flight data recorder revealing that the machine (flown by Colonel Alexander Rudikh, CSG CO) had hit a 30m/s (5,900f/m) vertical speed.

The combat operations of the CSG encountered many troubles. The first of these was reported on the very first day of combat work, 6 January 2001, when Ka-50 '25' attacked a target with 80mm rockets at ultra-low altitude. Supported by Mi-24s, it strafed with rockets in a steep dive a well-camouflaged ammunition depot situated near the town of Komsomol'skoe. The small fortified target was destroyed, the mission a success, but after exiting from the attack, the pilot experienced vibration of the helicopter and decided to perform a precautionary landing at Khankala airfield. A visual inspection showed that a blade tip had been damaged by a fragment from an S-8 rocket fired by the helicopter itself. The damaged tip was carefully

removed, then the helicopter made a short ferry flight to return to its base. There it stood idle on the ground for three weeks, awaiting delivery of a new set of rotor blades from Torzhok. The '25' returned to the air on 29 January, and until its re-introduction, the CSG had to fly combat missions with a lone Ka-50 accompanied by the Ka-29VPNTsU.

The CSG was assigned its combat missions from the Combat Control Centre of the Joint Group of Forces in Northern Caucasus. The group received combat orders to destroy targets with known positions – such as camps, hideouts, weapons caches, etc. The majority of these targets were located in difficult-to-access places in the mountains, often in valleys or on hillsides with elevation of up to 1,500m (4,920ft) above sea level. In the last days of their combat tour, the two Ka-50s were tasked to fly free-hunting (search-and-destroy) missions. After the repair of '25', the group resumed flying in its full complement.

As noted by Colonel Rudikh, the Chechen deployment was originally intended to provide material for a research project. One month-long, it was mainly aimed at testing the Ka-50 in conditions close to combat, and also to prove operations with the use of external targeting. Among the main features tested was the Ka-50's secure datalink for sharing targeting information with other helicopters in co-ordinated group operations. In Chechnya, it was used by the Black Shark to receive targeting information from the Ka-29BNPTsU.

Each morning, the CSG received its tasks from the JGF. These usually called for attacking targets in pre-designated kill boxes, situated on the inverse slopes of mountains, otherwise unreachable by field artillery. As Colonel Rudikh claimed, the CSG cleared box by box in the assigned area of operations, with firing results in each sortie recorded on videotape for subsequent analysis.

"I liked very much the digital terrain map [provided by the Kabris system]. It resembled the usual paper map, but the pilot is able to choose any scale suitable and needed. A mark on the moving map shows the helicopter's current position," Colonel Rudikh said.

He also recalled that in the initial combat sorties in Chechnya, the Ka-50 flew in formation with Mi-24s acting as the combat escort crewed by pilots taken from front-line squadrons deployed to the region. They flew as wingmen and were strongly impressed by the Ka-50's never seen before manoeuvrability. In fact, they lacked any idea of the Ka-50's performance and capabilities, which made the Mi-24s ill-suited for escort. Colonel Rudikh noted that after completing the first combat mission, the JGF's aviation head, Colonel Rif Sakhabudtinov, had claimed that it was next to impossible for the Mi-24's crews to provide escort for the Ka-50s. That is why all follow-on Ka-50 combat sorties were flown with escorting Mi-24s piloted by CSG crews, eventually enabling the group from Torzhok to operate in Chechnya as a self-sufficient combat-research unit.

By 14 February 2001, the CSG, together with the escorting Mi-24s, amassed 121 combat sorties, against the 113 originally planned. Seventy-six of these were flown by the CSG machines (logging in excess of 63 flight hours). Ka-50 '24' undertook the most flying in the group, with 36 sorties under its belt, while '25' had 13 and the Ka-29VPNTsU flew 27 more. Each Ka-50 pilot logged 6–10 flight hours in combat, in addition to 1–15 more on the Mi-24. Most of the combat sorties were flown in bad weather, despite the fact that none of the pilots had trained in such conditions during the combat deployment work-up phase in Torzhok.

Rockets were the main type of ordinance used by the CSG helicopters. The two Ka-50s recorded more than 100 S-8 rocket

The Kabris LCD display installed in the Ka-50 cockpit to the right is the original IT-23M CRT TV display of the Shkval-V system. (Andrey Zinchuk)

Colonel Alexander Rudikh, CSG CO, was decorated with the highest Russian state award, the Golden Star of Hero of Russia, for his extraordinary combat exploits during the Chechen war campaign (344th TsBPiPLS)

firings, while the Ka-29VNPTsU added 29 more. Ka-50 '24' reported 43 firings from the cannon, with '25' adding a further 19.

In the event, the pair of Ka-50s logged in excess of 100 firing passes, expending a total of 929 80mm S-8 rockets, as well as 62 more cannon firings expending some 1,600 30mm rounds. The Ka-29VNPTsU logged 29 firings, unleashing 184 rockets.

Only three 9A4172 Vikhr-1 ATGMs were launched, as there were few targets in the CSG's area of operation that would justify expending the expensive guided missiles. All three missiles launched successfully were reported to have found their targets. In a mission conducted on 6 February, two missiles were fired by Ka-50 '24' from a distance of about 3km (1.6nm) at an insurgent camp situated near the village of Tsentroy. One of the Vikhr-1 launches, made from '25', was undertaken without range-finding, but the Rubikon flight/navigation/ attack suite proved able to guide it towards the target and eventually score a direct hit.

The Ka-50 thus received its baptism of fire in Chechnya, 18 years after the type's maiden flight, while in its fifth year of service with the RAA.

CSG lessons learned

Among the main conclusions made from the CSG operations in Chechnya was that the concept of the employment of highly automated flight/navigation/attack suites that could reduce pilot workload had been confirmed at last in real-world combat conditions. The CSG combat experience, summarised in a post-deployment report, showed that its pilots, despite the low number of flight hours logged during the work-up phase, had proved able to quickly adapt to the handling specifics of the coaxial helicopter. The Rubikon flight/navigation/

attack suite enabled the Ka-50 to employ all the weapons in a single attack pass, with a prompt re-targeting. Most of the targets found by the ground reconnaissance teams and slated for attack were situated in difficult-to-access places, which prompted pilots to explore the Ka-50's manoeuvring potential in full.

Flying in inclement weather and over rough terrain, the Ka-50s fired the cannon and rockets at distances of up to 3km (1.6nm) in both automated mode (with the Shkval-V TV/laser targeting system performing automatic target tracking and range-finding) and also in the so-called 'operative' modes. The latter were used in limited-visibility conditions and at short ranges, with all the necessary aiming corrections undertaken manually by the pilot during the firing series based on the miss distance of the first rounds, clearly visible thanks to the tracer rounds used. According to the pilots, the accuracy of the rockets launched in manual mode proved to be a little bit worse than that achieved in the automated attack mode. The post-mission review of the video footage of the firing passes (recorded by the cockpit cameras looking through the HUD) and the analysis of information supplied by SOF reconnaissance teams on the ground confirmed that all the assigned targets had been destroyed.

Another important conclusion drawn from the CSG operations in Chechnya was that the new helicopter showed pretty good reliability in conditions of intense and frequent use. The Kamov OKB team in the field provided only advice to the military technicians, this way refuting the claims that the Ka-50 would need specific and multi-year training of technicians to serve the new helicopter. There were no grounding periods caused by failures.

The joint basing of the Ka-50 and other RAA types in combat conditions had confirmed the Kamov OKB's claim that the RAA's re-equipment with the new helicopter type would not cause a spike in the number of servicing problems when based together with Mi-8s and Mi-24s, using the same ground servicing equipment (GSE). The demonstration of the Ka-50's autonomous basing capabilities, without the need of using GSE, had failed to materialise due to the limited funding provided for the CSG's work-up phase.

The Kabris system, integrating a satellite navigation system and a moving map, had shown itself a very useful navigation aid. The digital moving map enabled pilots to control their position as well as monitoring the position of other helicopters in the group and the targets slated to be attacked. The pilots noted that after a small modification, the Kabris could be used by aircrews from front-line units with average qualification for flying landing approaches in bad weather conditions, without seeing the ground while relying on positional information derived from the new system only.

Despite the limited duration of the experimental combat operation and the inclement weather that precluded the CSG from testing all possible and theoretically justified modes for combat employment of the Ka-50 (including the famous *Voronka* manoeuvre, circling in a flat turn around a target, with the nose pointing at it for firing the cannon all the time), the pilots were more than happy with the Black Shark's demonstrated firepower and manoeuvrability performance in real-world combat conditions. The extensive cockpit armour protection was a welcome factor for boosting pilot morale and confidence while on a combat mission. As Black Shark pilots tended to comment, they had been much more confident sitting into the Ka-50's cockpit than any other helicopter types. The perception of enhanced safety and survivability was added to by the presence of an ejection seat.

The list of Ka-50 design shortcomings revealed during the real-world operations in Chechnya included a need to rearrange the positions of some indicators in the cockpit and the way the information was displayed, as well as to equip it with thermal imagers to enable night search and attack operations. Other recommendations derived from the CSG mission in Chechnya referred to the change of the pumping sequence of the flares from the UV-26M dispenser units and equipping the helicopter with a complete automated self-protection suite. It should be noted that these requirements had been satisfied soon after the return of the group.

The Ka-29VPNTsU was a subject of more pilot comments. For example, the Kabris display in it was placed in front of the navigator, and the pilot had to look at it, distracting from piloting tasks. In addition, the modified Ka-29 proved to be notably heavier, and therefore considerably less manoeuvrable and slower, than the sleek and agile Ka-50. This, in turn, constrained the group operations. At the same time, the Ka-29VPNTsU had accomplished its primary task, to conduct reconnaissance and targeting; it had also been used to provide fire support to the attack helicopters by engaging targets with rockets, fired from its two 80mm packs in addition to the 30mm cannon.

There were also some problems related to the aircrew survivability equipment. The CSG pilots flew their Ka-50 combat sorties in Chechnya wearing lightweight armour vests and armed with the Kashtan sub-machine gun beloved by them because of its convenience of use and accurate fire. The Ka-50's cockpit, however, lacked a suitable place to attach the weapon, while the sealed armoured vest was reported to had spoiled pilot comfort; furthermore, CSG pilots tended to commend that they did not need the vest at all due to the extensively armoured cockpit.

In general, the combat employment results demonstrated in real-world combat conditions during the Chechnya mission by the two Ka-50s and the sole Ka-29 had been judged to be positive. It was also noted in the post-deployment report that after the necessary modification to remove the shortcomings that had been revealed, this kind of dedicated and flexible strike-combat group could significantly enhance the operational effectiveness of the forces employed in local conflicts.

The Army Aviation Directorate recommended the CSG's numerical strength to be expanded to three Ka-50s and one Ka-29, which would necessitate the modification of another Black Shark. The machine selected was the newest one, serialled '26', planned to be delivered by the AAC Progress plant in 2001. The Ka-29 was to be further modified as well, receiving a Samshit-50 day/night targeting system and internal/external lighting compatible with NVGs.

The list of principal requirements raised by the CSG pilots who tested the Ka-50 in real-world combat conditions included a further refinement of the flight control algorithms and developing a simulator for flying the helicopter and employing its weapons. In addition, pilots noted that it would be of vital importance to accelerate the Ka-52's development in order that the two-seater be used as a combat command-and-control machine, replacing the otherwise handicapped Ka-29.

The full satisfaction of RAA demands, however, proved an impossible mission at the time, as the Russian MoD had reportedly failed to provide any additional funding for improving the CSG hardware in the early 2000s. After the factory testing of the Ka-50 simulator, the VVS deputy CinC (responsible for the armament) had stopped the funding, effectively closing the project.

Due to the influence of various adverse factors, the VVS leadership had gradually lost interest in the single-seat Black Shark. The CSG existence was a factor regarded as an obstacle to the concept of a single new-generation attack helicopter type for the RAA, which both the MVZ Mil and Rostvertol promised to develop amidst a large-scale promotion and PR campaign. So the CSG's finale was as expected – an order had been issued to disband the group and all the funding needed for helicopter modifications had been cut.

7
THE KA-52 STORY BEGINS

Birth of the two-seat Alligator

Despite the active countermeasures by competitors from the MVZ Mil and Rostvertol, well-teamed and coordinated with conservative factors within the Russian MoD, the single-seat attack helicopter had proved an effective and affordable combat machine. The Black Shark combat trials in Chechnya had shown that the Kamov OKB's original design concept was a sound one and the company could offer a suitable Mi-24 successor in RAA service. But back in the mid-1980s, when the attack helicopter competition outcome seemed to be sealed, the Soviet military began thinking how to solve the problem of the conversion training of pilots destined to fly the single-seat Ka-50 then slated for large-scale production.

The tactical-technical specification for a Ka-50 derivative, fitted with dual controls and dubbed V-80UB, was originally issued by the VVS back in 1985. The simplest way called for inserting another cockpit in the nose to be used by the instructor pilot, in the same way this design solution had been implemented on the MiG-25PU/RU two-seat jet fighter. The helicopter, however, had some design specifics which made impossible such two-seat stepped-tandem configuration.

As could be expected, Mikheev had a negative opinion on the straightforward reworking of the single-seat Ka-50 into a two-seat training machine. At the same time, however, the Kamov OKB was overloaded with work on more important projects, which is why the V-80UB theme had received secondary importance.

The eventual design configuration, as proposed for the two-seater in the 1980s, included a good many non-standard solutions which would enable the V-80UB to retain its centre of gravity and provide the specification required by the military for field of view for both trainee and instructor pilot in order to grant safety of flight. In addition, the front undercarriage leg lost its retraction mechanism.

The design team built a mock-up of the two-seat machine, but shortly afterwards all work on the project was terminated, even before conducting the Mock-up Commission review. There is no hard information of specific MoD or MAP documents ordering the Kamov OKB to discontinue the design works on the V-80UB theme. Most likely, this decision had been taken during yet another round of the never-ending competition between the V-80 and Mi-28, apparently in an effort to avoid unreasonable spending of funds in case of the commissioning into service of the design proposed by the MVZ Mil.

The closure of the V-80UB theme, however, had a positive effect on the Ka-50's follow-on developments, eventually resulting in the development of the Ka-52, a true reconnaissance-strike platform; it,

The Ka-52 prototype '061' in flight in its early configuration, adorned with the large Samshit-B-1 observation/targeting payload on top of the fuselage, just behind the cockpit, in addition to the mast-mounted fairing for the Arbalet-L air-to-air radar. (Kamov OKB)

A full-scale mock-up of the fuselage of the initial Ka-52 two-seater, with an angular side-by-side cockpit using windows borrowed without changes from the Ka-50. (Kamov OKB)

Nose section mock-up of the proposed Ka-50UB two-seater, intended for conversion and continuation training of the aircrews of the single-seat Ka-50. (Kamov OKB)

however, appeared 10 years later and in another country.

Eight years after the termination of the V-80UB theme, Mikheev attended a meeting where he was asked by the VVS's Armaments Directorate deputy chief, Major General S. Nazarenkov, to design a two-seat Ka-50 derivative. At that time, in 1994, the Ka-50 had already been in serial production in Arsenyev, inducted in service with the Torzhok centre for training of military instructor pilots. But the type had not yet been formally commissioned into Russian military service. At this fateful meeting, Mikheev was hard-pressed by Major General Nazarenkov to start designing a two-seater. The VVS general had openly claimed in front of him that the Ka-50 would not be commissioned into Russian military service without having a two-seat derivative for conversion-to-type training. Mikheev, however, was still unwilling to create an Apache-lookalike coaxial attack helicopter with tandem cockpits.

One of the reasons for walking away from the so-called 'traditional' tandem configuration had been related to the combat experience of the Soviet Army Aviation service in Afghanistan in the 1980s, when there were as many as 14 crashes caused by a lack of information for the WSO that the pilot was dead or badly wounded. Occupying the front cockpit and provided with a simplified set of controls, Mi-24

WSOs proved unable to take over control of the helicopter when needed in sufficient time. At this stage, Mikheev had realised that it would be more suitable to accommodate the two-man crew side-by-side. The shipborne helicopters, where the Kamov OKB had accumulated immense experience and expertise, used this layout and the feedback had always been very positive. Furthermore, the armed Mi-8 versions, often used as makeshift attack helicopters, armed with ATGMs, bombs and rockets, also featured the side-by-side cockpit arrangement for the pilot and navigator that had demonstrated more effective crew interaction than the Mi-24's tandem system.

The main challenge encountered when designing the side-by-side cockpit was to accommodate it within the existing fuselage cross-section. To make it possible, Mikheev proposed to cut the fuselage at frame No. 7 and insert an all-new nose section for two crewmen sitting next to each other – the commander (pilot) on the left-hand side and the WSO in the right-hand seat. Both were to be provided with identical controls. "Well, you wanted a two-seater, so you will have the two-seater. But not exactly the one you had been waiting for!" Mikheev said at the time.

Sergey Nosov, the best exterior designer at the company, was tasked to work on the new layout, proposing an all-new nose section able to be mated to the existing Ka-50 fuselage at frame No. 7. In order to minimise the funding needed for designing and building the new version, which was to run as a company-funded project (albeit with a negligible share of funding contributed by the Russian MoD), Mikheev had advised Nosov to use as many parts as possible borrowed from the single-seater, including the landing gear, ejection seat and flight control system.

The design of the new two-seat nose section proved to be a rather difficult undertaking as the design team had to overcome many obstacles in accommodating the mission equipment into it. The non-standard task demanded non-standard solutions; one of these, for instance, called for using the windows from the single-seater unchanged but turned upside-down to ensure safe ejection conditions for the crew members. There was an adapter added to connect the new nose section with the rest of the fuselage in order to retain the streamlined fuselage shape.

The non-standard idea proposed by Mikheev was enthusiastically embraced by the Russian military, as its leadership supported the

Sergey Mikheev and senior officers from the 30 TsNII research-scientific institute of the Russian MoD in front of the initial Ka-52 full-scale mock-up, which came equipped with a roof-mounted Samshit-B-1 multi-sensor ball. (Sergey Mikheev archive)

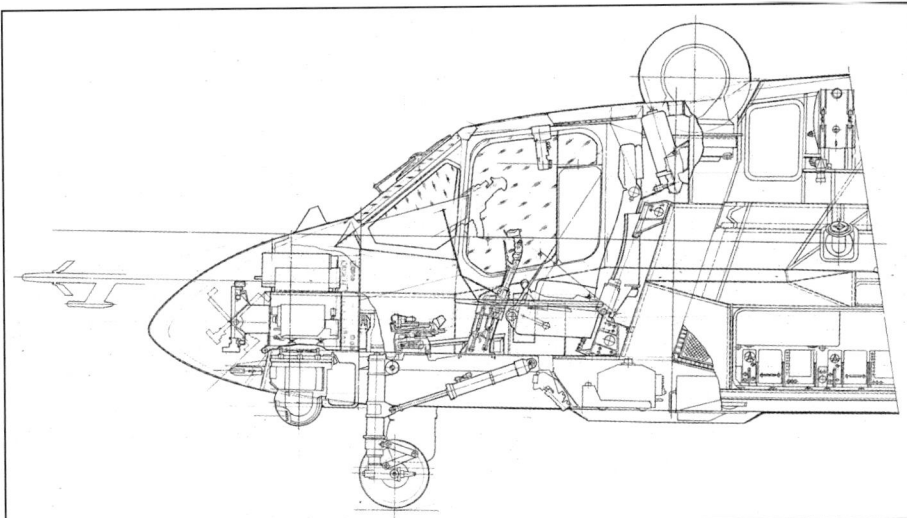

A drawing of the port side nose section of the Ka-52 adorned by two sensor turrets – the main one, used for targeting, installed on top of the fuselage, with the second, used for night time navigation, under the nose. (Kamov OKB)

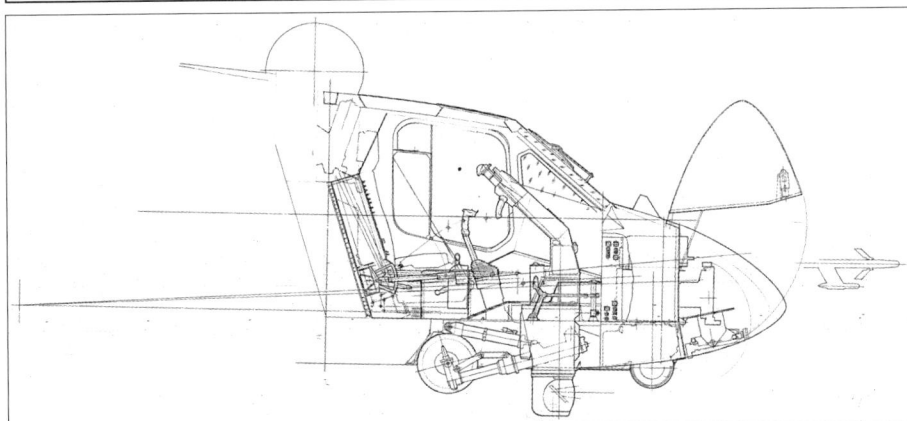

A drawing of the same nose section seen from the starboard side, with the nose undercarriage leg in retracted position. (Kamov OKB)

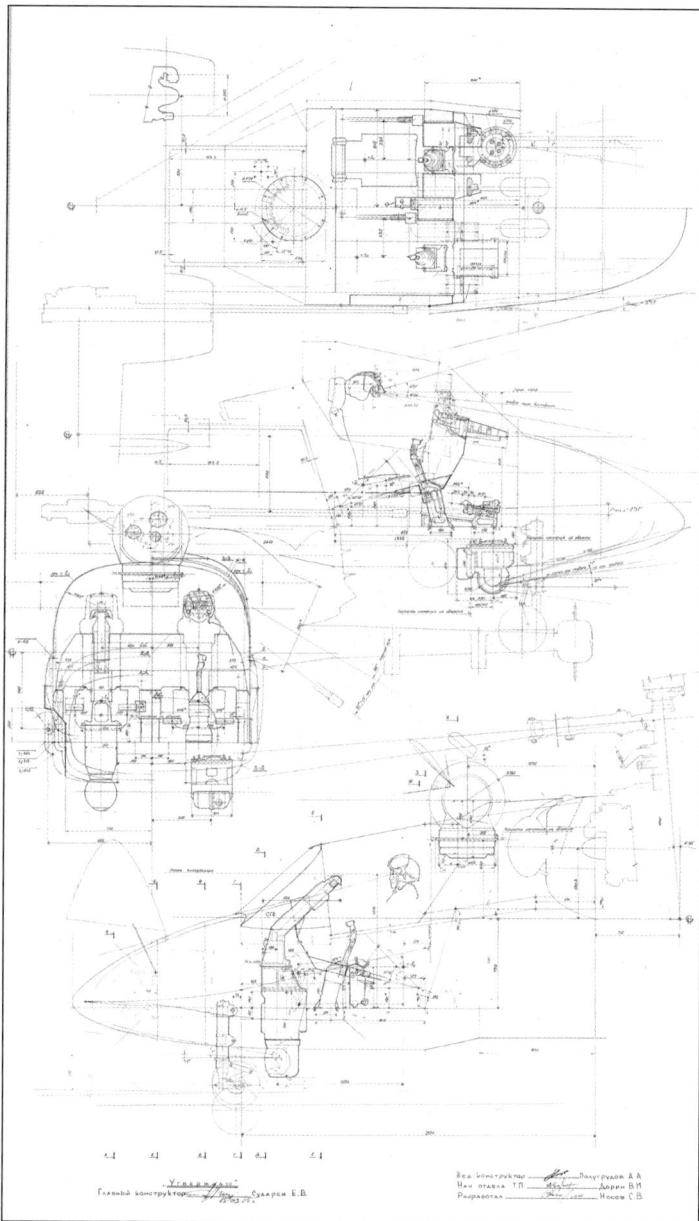

A detailed design drawing of four views of the new nose section of the Ka-52 as built in 1996. (Kamov OKB)

powered by a pair of RD-600 turboshafts, each rated at 975shp.

The development of the Ka-60R enabled Mikheev to offer a two-seat Ka-50 derivative, equipped with the mission suite initially conceived for the Ka-60R, to be used in a wide variety of roles such as battlefield reconnaissance, aerial targeting platform and command-and-control machine. The enlarged nose made it possible to accommodate the new Arbalet airborne radar, proposed by the Moscow-based Phazotron-NIIR company. At the time, radar designers had promised to provide a 'wonder-system', composed of a 360° mast-mounted system, working in the L-band, combined with a Ka-band radar module in the nose, optimised for high resolution surface mapping and small surface target detection. The antenna of the L-band radar was accommodated into the Ka-60's nose, and the Ka-50's two-seater derivative was made capable to use it as well. In addition, the Ka-60 was slated to receive another sophisticated system, the GOES-450 multi-sensor payload for day/night targeting, equipped with a thermal imager, laser rangefinder and laser spot-seeker. Integrating all this new targeting equipment on-board the Ka-50's two-seat derivative would promise to turn it into a unique and fairly potent battlefield machine.

There were no doubts that the Kamov OKB could offer a capable airborne command-and-control platform, as the company had solid experience and expertise in developing helicopters with sophisticated avionics suites for anti-submarine warfare and overwater radar surveillance/over-the-horizon targeting of anti-ship missiles. All of these helicopters of the Ka-25 and Ka-27 family were equipped with sophisticated datalinks for exchange of tactical information, closely resembling the now-modern net-centric warfare concept, as the group submarine search demands the use of highly automated operations and continuous exchange of information between the machines involved in the hunting and killing effort.

The Ka-52 could accommodate a mission commander on-board as the radar-equipped helicopter was tasked with detection of small-size camouflaged targets at extended ranges of 25–30km (13.5–16nm). Then it could attack these or datalink the necessary targeting data to single-seat Ka-50s operating within the same group. The two-seater could also be utilised to provide top cover of the group, as the Arbalet radar was to feature an air-to-air mode, claimed to be capable of detecting air targets at up to 57km (31nm). Then the Ka-52, armed with R-73 heat-seeking air-to-air missiles, could also attack the most dangerous air targets threatening the group.

The VVS approved Mikheev's proposal about the expanded range of possible uses of its two-seat combat helicopter. The 30 TsNII undertook the relevant research and achieved preliminary results confirming the usefulness of Mikheev's novel idea. Then the Russian MoD agreed to provide funding support for the two-seater development, under the same programme, which originally foresaw further developing the Ka-50's operational capabilities.

The two-seat mock-up, built at the Kamov OKB for presentation to the Russian military, however, proved to be too angular and somewhat ugly, failing to inspire anybody, including Mikheev himself. As expected, the Mock-up Review Commission, which evaluated the two-seater's mock-up in September 1994, had also failed to provide enthusiastic comments, and its feedback included a long list of findings of apparent shortcomings in the proposed design. The main target, however, had been achieved, as the military granted their general approval of the layout as proposed by Mikheev. This, in turn, allowed the Kamov OKB to gain time and legal grounds in a bid to begin refining its two-seater's design, turning the 'ugly duckling' into an advanced and better-looking reconnaissance-strike platform.

The two-seater development programme, as expected, had contributed to the Ka-50's commissioning into service with the

concept of having a new two-seat attack machine with a minimal investment on their side. Progress plant's director general, Sergey Bodnya, had also claimed that the high level of commonality between the two versions would allow his company to start with the two-seater's production literally the next day.

At the same time, Mikheev was busy outlining a new concept aimed at expanding the combat employment spectrum of the newly developed two-seater. It was to be able to operate at night and in bad weather. These capabilities had to be developed simultaneously with another helicopter type then taking shape at the Kamov OKB. The Ka-60R Kasatka was conceived in its initial form as a 4-tonne light transport and reconnaissance machine, capable of transporting five or six fully-equipped soldiers. It was originally conceived as the Soviet equivalent of the US Army Bell OH-58D Kiowa Warrior. In its original form, proposed in the mid/late 1980s, the Ka-60 had to be powered by a single turboshaft powerplant, produced at the Omsk Engine Plant, at the time specialised in the production of tank gas turbine engines powering the T-80 MBT. The Soviet military, however, demanded a larger machine, and in 1998 the Kamov OKB began development of the enlarged 6.5-tonne twin-engine design. Dubbed Ka-60, it was

Russian military, which eventually took place on 28 August 1995 as the President of the Russian Federation, Boris Yeltsin, signed the relevant decree.

In the event, Mikheev had enough energy to overcome the resistance of the Russian MoD, which had already expected to field the Mi-28N as the sole new-generation attack helicopter type for the Russian Air Force's Army Aviation branch, to be complemented by newly built Mi-24 derivatives. In April 1996, the Russian Air Force's Main Command approved Amendment No. 3 to the technical specification calling for the development of a day/night attack helicopter based on the Ka-50. Two years later, the architecture of the all-new K-806 avionics suite was approved by the Russian MoD's aviation research-scientific institutes. The technical specification for the K-806 foresaw its use not only on the Ka-52 but also on the Ka-50. At this stage, the design team at the Kamov OKB was not ready and willing to abandon the single-seat Ka-50 after spending such effort and money on its gradual improvement in the 1980s and 1990s.

Alligator v1

The development programme for the two-seated Ka-50 derivative, codenamed Avangard-2, began under the leadership of chief designer Evgeny Sudarev, while the exterior design of the helicopter was made by Sergey Nosov. This time, however, he had the freedom needed to consider new solutions and shapes, walking away from the restriction to get the maximum possible degree of design commonality with the Ka-50's nose section.

The first sketch of the new nose of the two-seat helicopter designated Ka-52 and wearing the internal factory designation V-80Sh2 was approved by Sudarev on 15 March 1995. It featured rounded glazing and a gracious nose able to house the large-size antenna of the Arbalet

The first Ka-52 prototype made its maiden flight on 25 June 1997 in the capable hands of Kamov test pilot Alexander Smirnov and test engineer Dmitry Titov. (Kamov OKB)]

The VIPs gathered at Zhulebino to witness the maiden flight of the Ka-52. Next to Mikheev is the RAA CO, Colonel General Vitaly Pavlov, widely known as one of the biggest opponents of the Ka-50 and Ka-52 within the Russian military. (Kamov OKB)

The initial cockpit layout as proposed for the Ka-52, with a HUD, four CRT displays (two colour and two monochrome), back-up electro-mechanical instruments and even a downwards-looking periscope installed in front of the navigator-operator. (Kamov OKB)

radar under a deep radome, while the Samshit-BM-1 multi-sensor payload was installed on top of the fuselage immediately behind the cockpit. The helicopter featured another payload on the nose offset to port, while a periscope for lower hemisphere view of both pilot and WSO was installed offset to starboard.

Nosov also intended to equip the pilot with a new-style NVG set, featuring optronic converters installed on his helmet side-on, while the image was to be projected on a semi-transparent visor positioned in front of his eyes. Technology issues, related to the parallax phenomenon, however, made this class of so-called collimator NVGs unsuitable for airborne use in Russia at the time.

The Ka-52 prototype was produced by using an existing fuselage of a helicopter originally assembled at the AAC Progress plant in Arsenyev (serialled '21', c/n 01-02), with all modifications and final assembly works performed at the Kamov OKB's experimental plant. This machine was originally handed over by the Russian MoD to the Kamov OKB for experimental works under the original Avangard development programme, and in 1995 it was delivered to the company flight test station in Zhulebino.

It was initially considered that the introduction of the second crew member would not prompt the design bureau to abandon its original concept of a single-seat attack helicopter. Instead, it was claimed that the two-seat concept would provide better opportunities for conducting a range of high-workload combat missions. It would benefit from the concept of four eyes forward to find and engage a variety of targets, with a pretty good field of view forward and sideward granted to both crew members.

In order to speed up the production of the new nose section, it was produced from aluminium alloys and glass-fibre panels, without introducing complex armour protection, while the cockpit glazing used a wooden frame and lacked bullet-proof properties. The weight of the armour protection was simulated by using non-armoured steel plates in the cockpit sides instead of strengthened steel armour plates. In a bid to shorten the design and development effort, the instrument panels for the pilot and WSO were made identical, with the former also provided with an ILS-31 HUD for deployment of unguided weapons and firing the gun.

The aircrew escape scheme was among the problems which necessitated a non-standard design solution. There was no time or funds for additional testing of the ejection system accommodated in the new nose section, so it was decided to simplify the aircrew's escape. In its initial form, it comprised standard crash-resistant seats with parachutes and jettisonable side canopies. Russian MoD representatives initially accepted this solution, but then refused to approve it. Their reason was that at speeds above 200km/h (110kt), it would be impossible to jettison the side canopies because of the airflow pressure.

These considerations forced the design team to start thinking on a new crew escape method. A working idea was proposed by test pilot Alexander Smirnov. He suggested to yaw the helicopter (by hitting the left and then the right pedals) in emergency situations that may be encountered at high speed; this could help to reliably separate the jettisoned movable canopy sections. Smirnov's idea was accepted and the relevant escape procedure was included in the flight manual used during the flight testing of the first prototype. It should be noted that the production-standard Ka-52s eventually received both cockpit armour protection and aircrew ejection seats.

Unsurprisingly, the name 'Alligator' was proposed by Mikheev

Ka-52's first prototype resting next to a pair of Ka-50 single-seaters in Shop No. 7 of Kamov OKB's experimental plant at Lyubertsi in 2007. (Andrey Zinchuk)

himself, who saw a striking resemblance between the appearance of the Ka-52 and the reptile of the same name. Both are able to sit and wait in ambush (the animal down in the mud), then suddenly pop out, catching their prey before returning to their idle condition, well hidden again. The projected performance figures for the two-seat Alligator included a 10,400kg (23,296lb) normal take-off weight, 3,600m (11,800ft) hover ceiling and 520km (280nm) mission range on a full internal fuel load.

The Ka-52 prototype, sporting an overall black paintwork and wearing the inscription 'Alligator' on the fuselage sides, was presented for the first time to the Russian press at the Kamov OKB premises in Lyubertsi on 16 November 1996. The helicopter, displayed in front of the experimental assembly hall, had an all-new ordinance load under the wings, including the Kh-25 air-to-surface missile and R-73 air-to-air missile, in an effort to illustrate the vastly expanded set of roles of the two-seater. It was also equipped with the Samshit-B-1 multi-sensor payload, which featured a French-made thermal imager in addition to a day TV camera and a laser rangefinder/target designator. The all-new shaped nose was equipped with the Rotor day/night observation/targeting system, steering 120° left and right in the horizontal plane. The Rotor featured two sensor windows, one of which served the Thomson-CSF Victor thermal imager.

The wider cockpit provided the advantage of arranging an integrated instrument panel for both crew members, facilitating better interaction between them in a high-workload combat environment. From the very beginning, both seats were provided with identical controls, so that either crew member could fly the Ka-52, giving the helicopter an additional role for conversion and continuation training.

At the Ka-52 presentation, Mikheev informed the gathered journalists that the Alligator was intended to be operated in a raft of new roles such as battlefield reconnaissance, target identification,

distribution and hand-off, working in combined teams with single-seat Ka-50s.

Displaying the Ka-52 in this striking and sophisticated night/all-weather configuration was a deliberate PR exercise undertaken by Mikheev. It proved successful, as the Russian press widely distributed the news, reaching the targeted 'audience', which reacted immediately.

In the event, GK Rosvooruzhenie, Russia's largest arms export company at the time, asked Mikheev to show the new attack helicopter at the Aero-India aerospace and defence exhibition in Bangalore, even before its maiden flight. Well in advance of its maiden flight, the Ka-52 was thus demonstrated to one of its potential customers, upon which Mikheev had relied heavily at the time. In December 1996, the helicopter was put on static display at Aero-India. The interest to the yet-unflown two-seat attack machine was heated by the spirited air display of its single-seat forebear, piloted by Kamov test pilot Vladimir Lavrov.

Maiden flight

The Ka-52 was slated to take to the air in its maiden flight in the skilled hands of Kamov OKB test pilot Alexander Smirnov. At the time he was still a newcomer at the company, starting there in 1995. Smirnov, however, boasted a rich flight-test work experience, with 16 years of test flying with the VVS Flight-Test Institute. He also had pretty good experience in flying both the Ka-50 and Mi-28 during the comparative tests campaigns undertaken by the VVS in the 1980s and early 1990s.

Based on his background, Smirnov was considered well-qualified to take the Ka-52 prototype to the air in its maiden flight. He was joined by flight test engineer Dmitry Titov, who was tasked to monitor the engine parameters at take-off, an important consideration for the new machine, which was heavier by some 500kg (1,100lb) than its single-seat predecessor. The twin-seat configuration downgraded

Another view of the hall of Shop No. 7 of the experimental plant, dated 2007, with three Ka-50s '18', '20' and '014' in addition to the Ka-52's first prototype adorned with the Arbalet-52 radar in the nose. (Andrey Zinchuk)

the flight performance compared to that of the Ka-50, but to "an acceptable extent", as Mikheev noted.

The Ka-52, in this initial configuration, was intended to be used as an airframe aerodynamic prototype. Its new nose section was shorter and wider than that of the Ka-50 and the aerodynamics specialists had some concerns about the adverse effect of the wider nose section, suspecting that it may disturb the airflow feeding the engines. In fact, the airflow behaviour had been predicted by mathematical modelling, only because of the lack of wind tunnel tests due to the shortage of funds and time. The maiden flight had to confirm the theoretical predictions, and it was to be performed with the autopilot switched off.

During the preparation of the Ka-52 for its maiden flight, it was stripped of the Rotor nose-mounted targeting system and received a standard test nose fairing, while the inner starboard underwing pylon was used to house a test instrumentation pod.

The Ka-52 prototype made its maiden flight in hover on 25 July 1997 at the company's flight test station in Zhulebino, in front of a gathered audience including the RAA CO, Colonel General Vitaly Pavlov. During the short flight, Smirnov demonstrated a swift lift-off, followed by hovering at between 2–15 metres. The event entered into the history books as the maiden flight of the first helicopter developed in Russia as an independent country, newly formed after the break-up of the Soviet Union five years previously. The audience then went on to a reception party, but Alexander Smirnov had more work to do. On this date he was also on duty to fly fire-fighting sorties and was scrambled on a Ka-32 to douse grass fires around Moscow with water. As Smirnov later recalled, the behaviour of the Ka-52 in hover flight had been very similar to that theoretically predicted by the Kamov's

renowned chief aerodynamics specialist, Dr Eduard Petrosyan.

The first flight test cycle, including hover flights only, was completed on 13 August 1997 in Zhulebino, and the Ka-52 was then transported by trailer to Chkalovsky airfield east of Moscow for its first forward flight on the circuit around the airfield. After the flight, Smirnov noted that the yaw controllability was neutral (the helicopter movements followed the deflection of the cyclic control stick), but this proved to be contrary to the controllability requirements. The design solution for fixing this flaw called for changing the angle of the fin to provide the required lateral stability of flight. During the second flight testing cycle, the Ka-52 demonstrated a maximum speed of 196km/h (106kt), while the testing programme included low-altitude hovers, turns, and sidewards and rearwards flight at up to 20km/h (11kt). The helicopter also made turns with banks up to 30°. At the completion of the tests, the helicopter conducted a ferry flight back to Zhulebino in order to be prepared for the static display at the MAKS-1997 air show.

Mikheev was keen to bring the new two-seat Ka-50 derivative to the show at Zhukovsky airfield, as this was set to show that despite the many attempts of competitors to suppress the Black Shark and Alligator programmes, the company was alive and kicking, with new developments under its belt. To underpin this idea, the Ka-52, flown of course by Smirnov, flew in close formation with two Ka-50s from the RAA's 344th TsBPiPLS, led by the centre's CO, Major General Vorobyov. As expected, this air display created a striking impression on the spectators.

8

IN THE TWENTY-FIRST CENTURY

Akhtubinsk night attack demonstration

The August 2001 large-scale display of new aircraft at the VVS' Akhtubinsk flight-test centre saw a pair of Ka-50s and the sole Ka-52 demonstrating their day and night attack capabilities, together with other Russian night-capable helicopters.

The composite Kamov/VVS flight test team departed for Akhtubinsk on 29 July. The intensity of the flying in the work-up phase was pretty high, with practice sorties flown from 31 July to 6 August without a break. The Kamov OKB's test team was tasked to convince the MoD leadership, represented at the exercise by the first deputy minister and chief of the General Staff, Army General Anatoly Kvashnin, and the Russian military-industrial complex leadership, represented by the Vice Prime Minister, Ilya Klebanov, that the Russian aerospace and defence industry was well-suited to at last provide aircraft equipped to detect and engage small-size targets at night.

The Ka-50 pilots were equipped with the Geo-ONV-01 NVGs, the first Russian NVG set equipped with Gen 3 optronic converters. Before the exercise, the helicopters were never tested in flight with pilots flying in NVGs. The then new Kamov OKB test pilot, Alexander Papay, had, however, recent experience of using NVGs on the Mi-8 and Mi-24 (he flew both types as a military test pilot), developed in a crash programme in the late 1990s upon a direct instruction issued by Army General Kvashnin.

There were a host of unexpected problems that popped up during the display flights at the gunnery range. Alexander Papay recalls:

I was tasked to demonstrate cannon and rocket firings while flying on NVGs. When I arrived at the gunnery range, the scene was covered by darkness but the NVGs worked as advertised and I was able to see everything. In the moment when I initiated my attack pass towards the assigned target, the Ka-50's electrical system experienced a total failure. Only the NVGs and the weapons system remained operational. So, I was already at the range and had to demonstrate the helicopter. And not only to demonstrate it, but to show its capabilities in the best way possible. So, I performed my attack pass, took the target in sight, launched the rockets and then fired the cannon. All rockets and shells scored hits in the centre of the target. Then, flying visually and looking through the NVGs I managed to safely return back to the airfield.

In this eventful mission, the pilot had a lot of confidence in a successful outcome thanks to the simple-to-control coaxial helicopter.

Papay was then tasked to demonstrate night attacks against a company defensive position and a group of tanks first with 80mm rockets fired from 2.5km (1.35nm), then finishing off the targets with the 30mm cannon. This successful mission, which took a single attack pass, was a clear refutation of the argument raised by Ka-50 opponents that single-seat helicopters could not fight at night.

Test pilot Alexander Simirnov, who had to demonstrate the Vikhr-1 ATGM, was then retargeted, as the originally assigned target, a tank, had already been located by the Ka-50's Shkval-V targeting system. Smirnov, however, managed to break the lock, initiate a new search in a prompt manner, find the newly assigned target, get a lock-on solution and unleash a Vikhr-1 ATGM from a long range to score a direct hit.

In the laser target designation role

In 2002, the Ka-50 took part in another experimental programme, aimed at providing external targeting designation for laser-guided air-to-surface missiles and bombs delivered by fixed-wing aircraft (i.e. external lasing support). The initiative was promoted by Colonel V. Khanokov, deputy chief of the research department at

The laser beam-riding 9A4172K Vikhr-1 guided missile, here test-fired by a Ka-50, has a maximum range of 8km (4.2nm). Its powerful tandem warhead is advertised as capable of penetrating between 800–1,000 mm of reactive armour after dealing with dynamic protection. (Kamov OKB)

Kamov OKB's veteran test pilots Alexander Smirnov (on the left) and Alexander Papay. (Kamov OKB)

Ka-50 'Yellow 24', c/n 01-04, was used for lasing of targets on the battlefield to facilitate deployment of laser-guided missiles and bombs by Su-24M frontal bombers, with the first such sorties reported in 2002. (Andrey Zinchuk)

the RAA's 344th TsBPiPLS, who realised that the Ka-50 could be used as an effective targeting platform, able to conduct battlefield reconnaissance, detection and selection of fixed and moving targets, including camouflaged ones. The main advantage stemming from its use was that the fixed-wing crews delivering laser-guided weapons would spend less time in the target area and would also avoid making repeated attack passes.

For use in the target laser-designation role, the Shkval-V's Prichal laser rangefinder had to be modified for use as designator, capable of establishing laser spots on the targets selected by the pilot to allow the guidance of the Kh-25ML missiles launched by Su-24M bombers. The emitting power of the Prichal was enough to create a good spot on the target to allow missile homing. This was checked for the first time during an experimental exercise in September 2002, held at the Ashuluk gunnery range in southern Russia. Before the exercise, the modified Ka-50, 'Yellow 24', c/n 01-04, saw testing in a firing campaign, together with Su-24M bombers from the Russian Air Force's Lipetsk-based 4th Combat Training and Aircrew Conversion Centre. In this training event, crews of the helicopter and the bomber had to hone the cooperation needed for mounting successful attacks with external targeting and lasing. At the exercise at the Ashuluk range, the Ka-50 achieved three successful target designation set-ups, but the third one is reported to have stalled due to a missile seeker failure.

In March 2005, the research work continued, again at the Ashuluk range, where the modified Ka-50 was tasked once more with providing external targeting to Su-24M bombers, armed with Kh-25ML missiles and KAB-500L laser-guided bombs. A total of 12 munitions were slated to be launched at 12 targets, but this prolonged target designation sequence had threatened to overload the Ka-50's laser rangefinder/target designator due to overheating. The pilot was told to switch off the target designation lasing immediately after the hit of the dropped guided munition, then switch on again for the next attack pass. The plan, however, had been changed at the last moment because the Su-24Ms originally allocated for the experiment were called upon to participate in the Rubezh-2005 exercise in Kirgizstan. In the event, only one pair of bombers was made available for the experiments with the participation of the Ka-50, with each Su-24M armed with two Kh-25MLs and two KAB-500Ls. The pilots were also new, without any prior experience in cooperating with the Ka-50, and they only received one briefing with their Ka-50 colleague before the mission.

The mission then did not go as planned, as the Ka-50 pilot initially failed to detect the first target and lost about 10 minutes in searching for it. After that, due to the lack of coordination with the Su-24M crews, the Ka-50 pilot had to wait too long for a command to switch on the laser rangefinder/designator. Such a command was expected to be issued when the Su-24Ms approached at a distance of 15km (7.8nm), with the launch made from 10km (5.4nm). Instead of the command to switch on the system, Ka-50 pilot Anikin heard the report by the Su-24M crew: "No lock-on established." Anikin then continued with the automatic tracking of the target while waiting for the second attack pass, but the Su-24M crew again reported that the Kh-25ML's missile-seeker failed to achieve lock-on. The exercise chief then ordered the aborting of the mission. The main conclusion made at the post-mission debriefing called for a detailed briefing before each such external targeting sortie, where the Su-24M and Ka-50 crewmen could coordinate their action to the smallest details in order to prevent misunderstandings and establish coordination between the Ka-50's and Su-24M's targeting suites.

The next experimental missile firings, conducted in April 2006, again at the Ashuluk range, proved much more successful, as the Ka-50 pilot easily found its targets and conducted proper tracking and designation, while the Su-24M's Kh-25ML missiles guided as intended at the laser spots and destroyed all designated targets. It was proof that the Ka-50 could be effectively employed in the scouting and target designation role, cooperating with fast jets at the battlefield for deploying laser-guided bombs and missiles.

However, the Ka-50, c/n 01-04, boasting a modified targeting system to play the battlefield scouting and target designation role, was retired in 2010 and then handed over to the Voronezh Military Aviation Institute in May 2011 to be used for ground instruction, together with its modified systems. Afterwards, the VVS was never allocated funds for upgrading the targeting suite of additional Ka-50s, this decision motivated by the prevailing opinion that a single-seat attack helicopter no longer had roles to play within the RAA fleet.

New self-protection suite tested

Another important experimental programme involving the Ka-50 was related to the development and testing of the first Russian-made integrated self-protection suite named Vitebsk. A very advanced piece of kit, intended to provide protection from heat-seeking SAMs, it was designed and developed by NII Ekran of Samara, teamed with several suppliers of hardware. When approached by NII Ekran leadership with the request for cooperation, Sergey Mikheev immediately realised that this would be an add-on of vital importance for enhancing the helicopter's survivability, and agreed to install the system and conduct

A Su-24M bomber toting Kh-25ML laser-guided missiles under the wings. (Andrey Zinchuk)

Ka-50 'Yellow 24' was the only Black Shark with a modified Shkval-V TV/laser targeting system for providing external targeting support (i.e. targeting by means of lasing) to bombers used to knocking-out targets on the battlefield with laser-guided missiles and bombs. (Andrey Zinchuk)

Ka-50 'Yellow 25' (c/n 800-05) was the prototype selected for testing the Vitebsk integrated self-protection suite, here equipped with missile approach warning sensors in the nose and tail, and directional jammer balls or emitting heads (colloquially known as 'Balls of Fate') next to the main undercarriage legs. (Andrey Zinchuk)

A burning flare used to check the operability of the L370-2 missile approach warning sensors of the Vitebsk suite during initial tests of Ka-50 'Yellow 25' in Lyubertsi in early 2004. (Andrey Zinchuk)

The team of Kamov OKB and 5th TsNII specialists ready to test the Vitebsk suite of the Ka-50 in-flight at the Faustovo range near Moscow by deploying captive rounds of heat-seeking shoulder-launched SAMs. (Kamov OKB)

its testing on board the Ka-50.

Initially, NII Ekran specialists insisted on the installation of as many as four missile warning sensors and four active-jammer heads, in order to get reliable coverage. This design solution, however, was judged by the Kamov OKB design team to be too heavy, as analysis had shown that two ball-shaped emitting heads would be sufficient to cover the entire lower hemisphere.

In addition to the L370-2 ultraviolet (UV) missile approach warning sensors (MAWS) and active jammer heads, the Vitebsk self-protection suite also incorporated UV-26M chaff/flare dispensers and L150 laser warning sensors already installed onto the Ka-50's fuselage

sides and tail-end. The MAWS were installed on both sides of the nose and the tail end, while the emitting balls of the L370-5 directional IR jammers were housed immediately behind the main undercarriage wells. The L370 family of directional jammers was developed by the Zelenograd-based Zenith design bureau. These jammers used narrow beams of directed IR energy directed at the approaching heat-seeking missile.

The helicopter chosen for the upgrade with the new-generation self-protection suite was Ka-50, c/n 800-05, serialled 'Yellow 25', used before in the Chechen war campaign and also appearing in the Black Shark movie. The Vitebsk equipment installation works were

The components of the Vitebsk self-protection system as originally conceived for the Ka-50 and Mi-8. (FGUP Ekran)

A pair of wingtip-installed UV-26M countermeasures dispensers for 26mm PPI-26 heat-emitting flares on the Ka-50 '25'. (Andrey Zinchuk)

The emitting head of the L370-5 directional IR jammer. In working position installed on the helicopter, it is facing downwards. (Author)

One of the four L370-2 missile approach warning sensors; this example is installed in the front port fuselage of a Ka-52 two-seater. (Author)

The rearwards-facing L140 Otklik laser warning receiver as installed in the Ka-50's tail tip. (Kamov OKB)

launched in October 2003, and in December that year the helicopter received the complete set. The first tests took place in April 2004 at Kamov OKB's experimental plant in Lyubertsi, aimed at checking the operability of the MAWS by using a burning flare with spectral characteristics close to that of a missile jet plume. The sensors worked as advertised. Then the preliminary testing phase of the self-protection suite was conducted at the Faustovo proving range near Moscow, but this proved a protracted undertaking which took several years to complete. The Ka-50 flew tens of sorties over the range with its self-protection suite switched on to detect simulated threats and emit directed IR energy to disrupt the missile guidance.

The joint state testing of the integrated self-protection suite then followed. It was launched in June 2006 at VVS's Akhtubinsk range, but due to unexpected delays the first test flights were not made until April 2007. This phase was completed in 2009, but the conclusions were somewhat ambiguous. The MAWS proved able to detect missile plumes and issue warning to the pilot in a timely manner. The performance of the directional jammer emitter heads, however, was required to be radically improved. This task was eventually solved

by NII Ekran, and in 2011 the Ka-52 attack helicopter in its latest in-service configuration was approved for the installation of the production-standard Vitebsk-52 suite, already fully tried and tested on the single-seat Ka-50 in the late 2000s.

The concluding phase of the Vitebsk test effort to check the

Ka-50 '25' takes off at Kant air base for another mission in the *Rubezh-2004* exercise, demonstrating precise ground attacks with cannon and rockets at the Edelveis mountain range in demanding hot-and-high operating conditions. (Andrey Zinchuk)

operability of the suite in a real-world situation saw the use of a Mi-8 test-bed. The full-scale test included a number of firings of Igla shoulder-launched, heat-seeking SAMs at the Akthubinsk range in 2011. The real Mi-8, fitted with the L370-5 direction jammer and L370-2 MAWS, was positioned on a hill with its engines running at maximum power and rotors turning. An Igla missile was launched from a distance of 1km (0.54nm), from a side/rear position, which is the most advantageous for SAM firing and guidance on the target. The video released of this test clearly showed that the missile's guidance system was considerably affected by combined use of the active IR jammer and a salvo of heat-emitting PPI-26 flares. As a result, the missile missed the target by some distance, confirming the effectiveness of the Vitebsk system.

Participation in the *Rubezh-2004* exercise

2004 proved to be one of the most important years for the eventual fate of the Ka-50/52 programme. By that time, the Kamov OKB had managed to achieve a marketing breakthrough thanks to its independent participation in the *Rubezh-2004* international exercise in the former Soviet state of Kirgizstan. This happened during the worst crisis times as the company lacked any state orders in the first half of the year and was desperately looking for new businesses. At the same time, it continued the battle with the MVZ Mil to eventually provide the RAA with a new-generation helicopter intended to replace the worn-out Mi-24 fleet. In this battle, the MVZ Mil received great support from Rostvertol, which had de facto become the lead in the marketing effort to sell the new night/all-weather Mi-28N to the Russian military. Rostvertol's prominent director general, Boris Slusar,

had claimed on many occasions that he was committed to get a state order for the Mi-28N production, virtually at any price, because the fate of his plant and several thousand employees would depend on the eventual outcome of this important programme.

In June, the Kamov OKB was approached by P. Kostromin, the representative of Rosoboronexport (Russia's arms export monopolist agency) in Kirgizstan, who asked whether the Ka-50 was going to participate in the large-scale *Rubezh-2004* exercise, involving the former Soviet states participating in the ODKB Treaty (the Organisation of the Collective Security Agreement, whose members are a number of ex-Soviet states, led by Russia). A quick search revealed that the Kamov OKB had never received an invitation to take part in this exercise. The Russian Air Force planned to bring to Kirgizstan its upgraded Su-24M bombers (equipped with the new SVP-24 nav/attack system) and night-capable Mi-24PN attack helicopters. After getting this information, Kostromin promised to ask Kirgizstan's Defence Minister, Eduard Topoev, to send a direct invitation to the Kamov OKB for participation in the exercise, independently from the VVS, since the Russian military had preferred to play the role of an observer.

The company had to borrow money in order to fund its participation in the exercise, which promised to have great marketing significance. The main expenses were related to the logistics of the trip, as the long distance had been viewed as the main obstacle. The company-operated, VVS-owned Ka-50 had to be transported by air from Chkalovsky airfield near Moscow to Kant air base in Kirgizstan. Luckily, the Russian MoD had not banned the participation of the Ka-50 in the exercise in Kirgizstan, with the formal motive 'removal

The Black Shark, in partially disassembled state, is offloaded from a VVS Il-76MD military transport at Kant in July 2004. (Andrey Zinchuk)

Installation of the main gearbox and rotor column in field conditions at Kant. (Andrey Zinchuk)

A rare scene at Kant air base company technicians busy off-loading cases with 30mm rounds from a privately owned VW Passat car in the middle of Kant air base. The ammunition was provided free of charge from the Kirgizstani MoD. (Andrey Zinchuk)

from testing'. Opposition to the Ka-50's showing at *Rubezh-2004* had, however, existed in the form of talks on the sidelines. For instance, the VVS CinC, Colonel General Vladimir Mikhailov, had phoned the defence minister of Kirgizstan, trying to convince him that the Ka-50's participation would be a waste of time. Colonel General Mikhailov also told General Topoev that despite the appearance of the Ka-50 in *Rubezh-2004*, it would never be accepted in squadron service in Russia.

In the meantime, all the preparations at the Kamov OKB were completed in a smooth manner, and the Ka-50 (c/n 800-05, serialled '25') had been brought to Chkalovsky airfield in a partially disassembled state to be loaded inside a VVS Il-76MD military transport aircraft (serialled RA-78840), operated by the 223th Flight Detachment (a commercial arm of the Russian Air Force's Military Transport Aviation branch), leased out for the period of the Kirgizstan expedition. The Kamov OKB team sent on the mission to Kant numbered 22, including two photographers and one interpreter; expedition head was Evgeniy Sudarev, the company head of the Ka-50 programme. The team got a budget of US$24,000 in cash, a huge amount for that time, needed to cover all the expenses that would be incurred in Kirgizstan, related to accommodation, transportation, fuelling, purchasing various services at Kant and solving any other issues that may arise.

The first issue arose at the Russian customs office at Chkalovskiy airfield, as the customs paperwork had not yet been completed and the team leader had to speak with the State Customs Committee, which would authorise the travel and solve the paperwork problems. This proved to be a success thanks to the recognisable Black Shark brand of the Kamov OKB, as the action movie with the same name had gained wide popularity in Russia and the Ka-50 was a well-known machine. The night flight to Kant was uneventful, and on the next day

the helicopter was unloaded from the Il-76MD's cargo compartment and reassembled in a prompt manner.

The next issue was related to the lack of an APA truck-mounted ground power unit (which was originally expected to be supplied free of charge by the VVS), so the Kamov OKB team had to rent one from the Kant airfield support units of the Kirgizstan Air Force and pay for the fuel. At the same time the fuel for the helicopter was purchased from a local supplier, which proved to be even cheaper than that offered by the VVS. Another issue was related to ordinance availability, as the Russian military base at Kant had refused to provide the Kamov OKB with any ordinance. The company once again had to approach the Kirgizstani hosts, this time asking for 30mm rounds for the 2A42 cannon. The reply was positive, but due to the lack of any other suitable vehicles, the ammunition cases loaded with the 30mm rounds provided free of charge by the Kirgizstan military had to be transported from the military depot to the helicopter in a privately owned VW Passat car.

The first check flight at Kant after the completion of the reassembly works was conducted by the Kamov OKB chief test pilot, Alexander Papay. Yuriy Timofeev was the second company test pilot included in the team, who also flew sorties during the exercise.

The next day saw the general rehearsal of the main *Rubezh-2004* phase, held at the Edelveis high-altitude gunnery range in Issak-Kull district, some 250km (135nm) from Kant. In addition to the attack passes, the Ka-50 was also slated to display its spectacular aerobatics capabilities in front of the high-ranking audience, performing in the skilled hands of Papay.

During the attack passes at the general rehearsal, the Ka-50 demonstrated once again the high accuracy of the 30mm cannon, delivering all shells within the same area. But this accuracy would not be particularly noticeable for the high-ranking audience, as the burst

Kamov technicians prepare 80mm S-8 rockets for loading on the Ka-50 at Kant. The rockets were provided free of charge by the Russian Air Force and ferried from the depot to the airfield by the mini-buses originally rented by the company for personnel transportation between Kant and Bishkek, seen in the background. (Andrey Zinchuk)

The ground crews meet test pilot Alexander Papay (in the middle with the light grey suit) immediately after a flight at the Edelveis range. (Andrey Zinchuk)

Ka-50 '25' departs Kant for a sortie at the Edelveis range. (Andrey Zinchuk)

A Ka-50 performs an attack pass at the Edelveis
mountain gunnery range. (Mikhail Lisov)

of tracers ended, as a rule, in a single spot. The hits scored lacked the smoke and fire effects otherwise needed for stunning high-ranking spectators, in the way that had been shown by the Mi-24PN pair firing 80mm rockets, with hits dispersed over a wide area.

The next day, the Kamov OKB team at last received the go-ahead from the VVS to receive 80mm S-8 rockets held in stock at the Russian military base at Kant airfield. There was no special truck provided to transport the cases laden with rockets from the depot to the apron, so these had to be loaded in the two mini-buses used for transporting the team; each of these buses accommodated four cases on the floor, between the seat rows.

The Ka-50 was thus fully armed with rockets and cannon rounds for the exercise. The Vikhr-1 ATGM was not used as it was expensive and there were no worthy targets to demonstrate its unsurpassed armour-penetrating capabilities. Furthermore, the Vikhr-1's launch would not be so interesting for the gathered VIPs, as it had to be made 8km (4.3nm) from the targets. At this distance nobody could see the streaking missile at supersonic speed, while the fire and smoke effect of the hit would be also unimpressive.

In general, the exercise saw use of 23 aircraft, including RuAF Su-25s, Su-24Ms, Mi-24PNs, Kazakhstani Air Force Su-27s, Kirgizstani Air Force Mi-8MTs and even a single RuAF A-50 airborne early warning and control platform used to provide overall radar control over the range.

The exercise scenario called for the Ka-52 providing air cover for the operation of a Kirgizstan special forces assault landing team delivered by a Mi-8MT helicopter, with no shooting, conducting dry attack passes only. Then the helicopter had to give an aerobatics display fully loaded with rockets and cannon rounds, at an altitude of 1,800m (5,900ft) above sea level and at ambient air temperatures

Ground crews meet test pilot Yuriy Timofeev after landing at Kant. (Andrey Zinchuk)

reaching 35°C. After that, the Black Shark was slated to show its teeth, 'cleared hot' for attacking targets situated on a hill slope before returning back to Kant.

The Ka-50 performed as expected on the VIP day of the exercise, impressing the gathered high-ranking spectators from Russia, Kirgizstan and other ex-Soviet states, including the defence ministers of four of these states. Russian Defence Minister Sergey Ivanov, who had never seen such an aerobatics display, was suitably impressed by the Ka-50's demonstration. This was enough to justify the Kamov OKB's efforts and expenses spent to take part in the *Rubezh-2004* exercise. Both the impressive aerobatics routine and sniper attacks demonstrated by Papay had proved that after a decade of decay and disintegration of the Russian military machine and defence industry, there was still something kept in reserve to show and further develop into a fully operational new-generation weapons system.

In August 2004, soon after the end of *Rubezh-2004*, a VVS commission was tasked to check the possibility of completing the Ka-50 airframes staying idle at the AAC Progress plant. It found that there was a technical possibility to produce as many as nine Ka-50s, using four almost complete airframes in addition to five more that had to be completed (c/n 03-03, 03-04, 03-05, 04-01 and 04-05).

Ka-50 proposed for fighter role

While the Ka-52 was tested at the gunnery range for firing rockets and cannon, Mikheev had to solve another important issue. The Russian military was more than happy to see the development of the two-seat Ka-52, but had rapidly begun losing any interest in the single-seat Black Shark. The inertia in thinking could not be stopped, as even the best of the military officers who came after Major General Vorobyov's

crash had voiced their doubts on the viability of the single-seat attack helicopter concept. Many years later, the new CO of the Torzhok centre, Colonel Andrey Popov, who had already mastered flying the Alligator, asked Mikheev: "But why not make a fighter on the Ka-50's base?" He could hardly have realised that Mikheev had already promoted the idea of developing a specialised fighter derivative of the Black Shark in September 2006, describing it in detail in a letter to the Chief of the General Staff of the Russian Armed Forces, Army General Yuriy Baluevsky. In this letter, Mikheev noted that it could not be ruled out that terrorists would try mounting attacks from the air against critical infrastructure in Russian territory (such as power stations, dams, bridges and communication nodes) in the foreseeable future by using hijacked fixed-wing aircraft and helicopters. To prevent such incidents, the air defences of all sensitive areas should be considerably strengthened, including the introduction of suitably equipped helicopters for air-to-air combat.

These helicopter-interceptors would be useful for rapid-reaction defence against non-traditional air threats that could be difficult to be engaged by traditional ground-based air defence systems due to technical reasons or where the use of ground-based missiles and artillery may be ineffective. In his letter, Mikheev proposed to deploy the single-seat Ka-50 in a fighter-interceptor role, as the fast and agile helicopter proved well-capable of engaging slow-flying air targets. In the newly proposed interceptor configuration, the Black Shark would be equipped with production-standard and well-tested systems such as the Kopyo air-intercept radar developed by the Moscow-based Phazotron-NIIR and an electro-optical search and targeting system made by the Geophizika-ART company, similar to that installed on the Su-27 fighter.

The Ka-50's fighter-interceptor version would be armed with R-77 active radar-guided missiles and Igla heat-seeking missiles, in addition to the new Hermes-A long-range guided missile system, in development at that time by the Tula-based KBP design bureau. The Black Shark in its new guise was intended to retain the powerful and trusty 30mm cannon. It was advertised by Mikheev as an effective system to counter low-speed/low-altitude air threats such as UAVs, light airplanes and helicopters, para-sailing and motorised hang gliders that could be used for terrorist attacks from the air.

The letter also noted that the new targeting suite of the Black Shark had an open architecture design, enabling the helicopter to be integrated into the existing command-and-control network deployed by the Russian Air Force's national air defence system. This, in turn, would enable a prompt scrambling to intercept an approaching target as early as possible, shortening the reaction time in the face of detected air threats.

Another important consideration highlighted by Mikheev in his letter referred to the fact that the Ka-50 could be able to be integrated with an A-50 airborne early warning and control aircraft, with the Ka-31 airborne early warning helicopter for receiving targeting information from them.

Unfortunately, the letter to Army General Baluevsky remained

A computer-generated image of the Black Shark's fighter-helicopter derivative, designated Ka-50I. (Kamov OKB)

unanswered and the Ka-50's fighter-interceptor derivative never materialised. The arrival of the two-seat Ka-52 and its rapidly progressing test and evaluation effort had finally sealed the fate of the single-seat Ka-50.

In the meantime, 10 years later, the worldwide proliferation of small- and medium-size unmanned air vehicles (UAVs) started to be viewed as a growing threat, still without adequate countermeasures; hence the helicopter role in anti-UAV operations is going to become more and more important in the late 2010s and early/mid-2020s.

9
INTERNATIONAL MARKETING EFFORTS

Turkey ATAK competition

In the early/mid-1990s, Russia's attack helicopter programmes had been hit by moribund national finances. To compensate for this, the Kamov OKB, under the leadership of its designer general Sergey Mikheev, had become very proactive, promoting the Ka-52 in several big international attack helicopter competitions.

The two-seat Ka-50-2 Erdogan was offered by a joint venture of Kamov and Israel Aircraft Industries (IAI), and had been ranked as the second choice to meet the Turkish Army requirement in the so-called ATAK tender, only behind the Bell Helicopter AH-1Z King Cobra.

The tender for 145 attack helicopters, the majority of which were to be locally-built at Turkish Aerospace Industry (TAI), and with a significant proportion of locally produced components, was launched by the Turkish MoD in April 1997.

Earlier that year, Mikheev visited Turkey and asked high-ranking government officials about the real chances for his company to compete in the expected huge tender for new-generation attack helicopters. The Turkish reply was not encouraging, so Mikheev had to think how to position the company as an acceptable bidder by using a non-standard commercial approach of teaming with a politically acceptable partner. This idea had been explored for the first time in June that year, during the Paris Air Show, where he had a meeting with the IAI's head, Moshe Keret. Mikheev suggested the two companies join forces to submit a bid in the expected Turkish mega-tender. The reply from Keret was positive and the next step in the process called for getting a green light from the authorities in Moscow. In accordance with Russian legislation, the prime mover from the Russian side in such a competition had to be Rosvooruzhenie (the biggest state-owned arms export company, rebranded in 2000 as Rosoboronexport), while Kamov had to act as the main subcontractor.

By that time, IAI had accumulated a wealth of useful experience in work on the upgrades of Soviet/Russian legacy military air platforms such as the MiG-21 fighter (for a number of African states such as Uganda and Ethiopia) and the Mi-25 attack helicopter (for the Indian Air Force). It also boasted a pretty good commercial position in Turkey, where the Israeli company acted as the main avionics integrator of the F-4 and F-5 upgrades; this entailed good relations with the high-ranking decision-makers in Ankara to provide a significant marketing assistance. Furthermore, IAI agreed to participate in the ATAK tender as a risk-sharing partner, covering a proportion of the expenses related to the bid preparation and demonstrations to be held for the Turkish military during the competition.

The negotiations for division of responsibilities and risks among the partners in the Turkish project proved to be a long and painful undertaking. IAI insisted on taking on the project's avionics integration, in addition to the logistic support and after-sales servicing. Mikheev, however, had no idea why IAI would be willing to take on this activity but in general was not ready to give concessions, so he eventually retained this business for Kamov. The eventual agreement on the division of responsibilities in the ATAK tender called for the IAI submitting the bid, while the helicopter, armed with the 2A42 cannon, had to be provided by the Kamov OKB. The new avionics suite was to be developed by the IAI Lahav division, which had also been tasked to integrate its own systems into the Russian-made vehicle. IAI had also insisted the integration activities of the new avionics suite be carried out in Israel, followed by testing, including rocket, cannon and missile test firings.

After the completion of the bid in December 1997 and January 1998, and its submission by IAI, the next step in the tender called for the in-flight evaluation of the Ka-52 by the Turkish military. It was to be performed at Kubinka military airfield near Moscow, where

Sergey Mikheev and IAI's head, Moshe Keret (to the right), at the signature of the teaming agreement for a joint bid for the ATAK tender. (Sergey Mikheev archive)

The Kamov OKB team at work during the preparation of the ATAK bid in the IAI Lahav premises at Tel Aviv's Ben Gurion Airport. (Kamov OKB)

Turkish Army pilots flew the machine in April 1998; IAI had also asked its pilots to be allowed to fly demo rides. Alexander Smirnov was the Kamov OKB test pilot nominated to fly with Turkish and Israeli pilots, showing them the capabilities of the Alligator. In total, four Turkish pilots got the chance to try the Ka-52 in the air, together with Leon Parag, IAI's chief test pilot.

IAI then requested more flight tests for the avionics development, in order to collect complete data on the Ka-52's handling performance. The Kamov OKB agreed with this condition, and a special evaluation programme was drafted and launched on 14 September 1998. In October, IAI's Leon Parag underwent a short flight training course, preparing him for a solo flight in the Ka-52. It was conducted at Lukhovitsy airfield south of Moscow, and in one of these training flights Parag hit the performance limits while trying to explore the Ka-52's capabilities at extreme regimes of flight. Understandingly, Mikheev was not happy with this rather aggressive handling behaviour, which could cause accidents, and he threatened to stop the training flights if Parag continues this carefree style of flying.

In November that year, Kamov began adapting the Ka-52's cockpit lighting for NVG use as the Turkish ATAK tender requested that the new-generation combat helicopter should be capable of day and night operations, with NVG sets worn by both crew members. At that time, however, the Kamov OKB lacked any NVG integration and operating experience.

In an effort to compensate for this shortcoming, test pilots Smirnov and Krivoshein were sent to Israel in May 1999 to undergo a short NVG training course, flying the Bell 206, with Leon Parag acting as their instructor, while employing Gen 2 NVGs. This was an invaluable experience which was later utilised to the full extent, in an effort to make the Alligator night-capable to meet the Russian MoD specification for an all-weather/night-capable attack rotorcraft.

The second phase of the ATAK tender was launched in July 1999, calling for a detailed evaluation of the helicopters offered by the bidders in night sorties and deploying various types of armament. The Ka-52's sole prototype was despatched to Turkey for participation in this evaluation phase, piloted by the two newly NVG-qualified company test pilots, Smirnov and Krivoshein; team leader was chief-designer Evgeny Sudarev. Together with the Ka-52, the Kamov OKB despatched a Ka-50, intended to be used for weapons demonstrations (by using the cannon, rockets and the Vikhr-1 ATGM), piloted by Colonel V. Zolotov from the 344th TsBPiPLS; Kamov test pilot Yury Timofeev was used as a back-up in this phase.

The Alligator was used to a full extent to demonstrate to the Turkish tender committee the new avionics suite. It was equipped with two different suites – the first of these was Russian-made, used for targeting, while IAI supplied the second, with LCD displays replacing the conventional instruments, which was used for flight/navigation purposes.

The Ka-52 was also demonstrated flying on NVGs using Israeli-supplied Gen 2 sets. IAI's Leon Parag requested to fly the NVG demo sorties with Turkish pilots occupying the Ka-52's right-hand seat. Initially, the Russians were not willing to allow this, fearing the loss of the only Ka-52 prototype, but IAI then offered to insure the helicopter for US$400 million in the event of complete loss. Only then was Parag allowed to fly the Alligator in the demo sorties, providing night familiarisation rides for Turkish Army Aviation pilots. It is noteworthy that Parag, having immense experience in flying many different types of combat helicopters, had also expressed an opinion that the side-by-side cockpit was better than the stepped tandem arrangement.

The flight and weapons demonstrations were carried out successfully, and the Turkish tender organisers said that they were happy with the results, especially with the superior performance, the Ka-52's trademark. Thus, after the completion of the second phase of the tender, the Kamov/IAI offer was considered to have the best chance of success in the tender.

Then, suddenly, the Turkish authorities raised a set of additional requirements to the Russian/Israeli consortium offering the coaxial attack machine. The most serious of these called for the introduction of an all-new cockpit configuration, with the pilot and operator accommodated in a tandem cockpit, something that was not in the original ATAK tender technical specification. The tandem cockpit, introduced by Bell for the Huey Cobra attack helicopter back in the 1960s, was widely regarded as a standard layout for attack helicopters, and now the Kamov OKB was forced to swiftly redesign its two-seater, offering the new Ka-50-2 Erdogan derivative.

Additional requirements called for the integration of a GIAT 621 20mm cannon, using the NATO-standard 20mm round, while the B8V20 rocket packs were to be replaced by NATO-standard 70mm ones. The maximum take-off weight was 11,300kg (24,904lb), normal take-off weight 9,800kg (21,600lb), maximum speed 310km/h (167kt), hover ceiling OGE (Out of Ground Effect) 4,000m (13,123ft) and range on internal fuel 520km (280nm).

Tandem layout

There was little time to meet the newly raised Turkish requirements, but Mikheev remained calm, promising the new derivative after only

IAI test pilot Leon Parag in the right-hand seat of the Ka-52's cockpit after a training flight. Next to him is the Kamov OKB test pilot Yuriy Timofeev. (Kamov OKB)

three months, displaying it at the IDEF defence exhibition that was planned to be held in Ankara in July 1999.

The new tandem cockpit proposed for the ATAK tender had its front seat just in front and slightly lower relative to the standard position on the Ka-50, while the second seat was installed to the rear and slightly higher. Externally, the new nose section resembled a glazed balcony, with the armour protection of the crew members sacrificed in an effort to obtain better visibility and meet the additional tender requirements.

The new gun was installed under the fuselage, meeting the Turkish requirements, with 360° coverage of the turret in the horizontal plane. It was mounted on a retractable platform, stowed to the right when on the ground; while in the air, in combat position, the gun was lowered beneath the fuselage, able to traverse through 360° in order to fire in any direction. The turret was installed under the mid-fuselage, at the same location where the 2A42 was installed on the original Ka-50, in order to get low dispersion of rounds when firing and reduce the recoil influence on the firing accuracy otherwise plaguing the nose-installed guns of the Apache, Tigre, Mangusta and Rooivalk. The gun was provided with 700 rounds.

The Turkish-requested Gator derivative, dubbed Ka-50-2, was to be armed with up to 12 Vikhr-1 missiles or 16 Rafael NT-D advanced ATGMs. The NATO-standard rocket pods were suspended under the stub-wing pylons. For use against air targets, the Ka-50-2 was to receive an additional armament consisting of four US-made Stinger or Russian-made R-73 air-to-air missiles.

The IAI flexible modular avionics suite was designed with open architecture, including two MDP (R-3081) central processors and two Mil Std 1553B data exchange busses (one serving the fire control system and the other intended to meet the needs of the flight/navigation suite). Both crew members were provided with Hands On Collective and Stick (HOCAS) controls.

For the integration of the new and still-secret Israeli-made Rafael NT-D ATGM, IAI had only provided Kamov with the interfaces, which were to be connected to the targeting suite. This way the missile could be exported directly to Turkey, without the need for the integration works to be performed in Russia.

The Ka-50-2's avionics suite included mainly Israeli-supplied systems such as the NAVFLIR observation-search turret (with thermal imager) and the gyro-stabilised HMOSP (Helicopter Multi-mission Optronic Stabilised Payload system) turret containing a TV camera and thermal imager in addition to a laser rangefinder and laser-beam missile control device. This nose-mounted sensor payload was to provide the crew with tactical target acquisition, which included detection, range finding and tracking in day/night and adverse weather conditions.

The crew members were provided with the IHS (Integrated Helmet System) helmet-mounted cueing and display system that projects flight and weapon data, as well as the FLIR (Forward Looking Infrared) image onto the pilot visor. The IHS can also slave the HMSOP to the pilot's or WSO's line of sight for easier and faster tracking of targets intended to be engaged with the GIAT 621 cannon.

The instrument panel was dominated by four MFCD multifunctional LCD displays – two for the pilot and two for the WSO. The Erdogan was also set to receive inertial and satellite navigation systems in addition to a TACAN tactical navigation system, three UHV/VHF and one HF radio. The integrated self-protection suite was to include radar and laser warning receivers, UV missile approach warning sensors and countermeasures dispensers. The ATGM selection included 12 Vikhr-1 or 16 NT-D missiles.

In June 2000, the Turkish Government officially announced that it had selected US company Bell Helicopter (offering the AH-1Z King Cobra) as the preferred bidder in the tender and would enter into negotiations to sign a contract. The Ka-50-2 was nominated as the forerunner in the competition.

The first attack helicopter tender, however, was abandoned in May 2004 over disagreements between the Turkish Government and Bell Helicopter on the extent of industrial cooperation and technology transfer, which made it impossible for the parties to sign a contract. During the protracted and eventually fruitless negotiations with Bell Helicopter, the Turkish side had used the fact that the Ka-50-2 was nominated as the forerunner in an effort to apply additional pressure on the US company to agree with the terms and conditions of the contract. In the event, the US Government banned the transfer of some sensitive computer hardware and software technologies, and shortly afterwards the negotiations had been discontinued.

In this changed situation, Kamov and the Russian government continued offering a lucrative technology transfer should the Ka-50-2 be selected by the Turkish Government, including know-how for the upgrade and permission for its export to other countries as well as organising avionics production in Turkey.

In December 2000, the Russian government continued the sales push, offering a radical price reduction as part of the project that was to be implemented in lieu of writing off the Soviet foreign trade debt to Turkey. In addition, Russia had offered a big offset programme, with proposals for establishing export-oriented helicopter production, while the total price of the programme was less than that offered by the US companies. This meant that Turkey would be able to produce the Ka-52 in a unique configuration and also undertake its upgrades and exports to other countries; a list of 20 such countries had been agreed between Turkey and Russia. In addition, the Turkish defence electronics industry was offered the opportunity to produce elements of the helicopter's avionics suite, including the mission computer and other sub-systems. Furthermore, Kamov and FGUP Rosoboronexport (the new Russian arms export agency created through merging Rosvooruzhenie and Promexport in 2000) developed three variants for implementation of the ATAK programme which would allow reduction of the total costs by between 30–40 percent. In June 2003, Moscow also announced that it was ready to offer a price reduction of 10 percent in the event of contract signature.

In June 2003, the Russian-Israeli team went even further, offering an additional discount of US$10 million should the Ka-50-2 be selected. There were also hints that, on 15 October 2003, the Undersecretary of Defence Industry (SSM), the government's senior procurement decision-making official, Ali Ercan, had taken a motivated decision to sign the contract with the Russian bidder, but a month and a half later he was fired from the government. Then on 14 May 2004, the ATAK tender was cancelled altogether; this news was publicly distributed to the press in a written statement after a four-hour meeting of the Executive Committee of the Turkish SSM that co-production of 50 attack helicopters would not proceed.

ATAK-2 tender

The second Turkish attack helicopter tender, ATAK-2, launched in August 2004, saw the Kamov OKB participating alone with the Ka-52 this time, under the umbrella of Russia's state arms export monopolist, Rosoboronexport, which once again acted as the main bidder. The new Turkish programme called for the delivery of 50 aircraft within five years, with 41 more options, while its budget amounted to US$2.7 billion. This time, in addition to the conditions calling for local production in Turkey and unconditional transfer of technologies and licenses, the customer also required written guarantees issued by the countries of the bidders that there would be no political obstacles to export. The new tender conditions had also obliged the bidders to use as much as possible locally made systems, and be responsible for their integration. The initial offer submission was set at 11 June 2005.

After a careful evaluation of the tender requirements, Kamov and Rosoboronexport managements had decided to bid, but this time without Israeli assistance, as this would not provide added value in the new situation. By this time, the Kamov/Rosoboronexport team was also participating in the South Korean attack helicopter tender with the Ka-52, and had already accumulated valuable expertise and experience in making comprehensive bids on the international arms market.

To make a competitive enough bid for the ATAK-2, the Russian team did a huge amount of preparatory work to reduce the price of the first 50 helicopters, and expressed its readiness to satisfy the Ankara request to be authorised to sell the helicopter to other countries. The offset programme included the license production of the Vikhr-1

The Ka-50-2 Erdogan full-scale mock-up, here armed with an R-73 air-to-air missile on the outermost starboard pylon in addition to a pair of Vikhr-1 ATGMs on the outermost port pylons. UPK-23-250 gun-pods are suspended on the middle pylons, with B8V-20 rocket packs on the innermost ones. (Andrey Zinchuk)

A close-up view of the Ka-50-2's retractable turret with a GIAT 621 20mm cannon with 700 rounds, shown in stowed position to the right. (Kamov OKB)

A computer-generated image of one of the configurations proposed for the tandem-cockpit Ka-50-2, armed with a nose-mounted 20mm turret and optronic observation/targeting payload on the top. (Kamov OKB)

ATGM. In the event of winning the tender, the first 12 helicopters were to be delivered within 41 months of contract signature, and the entire quantity of 50 machines (38 of which would be built by the Turkish aerospace industry) were promised to be delivered within 79 months.

According to Mikheev, the Russian team committed to provide some unprecedented concessions, made in order to win the tender. For the first time in the world, one baseline helicopter was offered to a demanding customer in not one or two but three different configurations, including a single-seat, two-seater with side-by-side seating and another two-seater derivative provided with tandem cockpit arrangement. All three machines retained the high flight performance of the baseline design, unmatched by the competing designs participating in the tender. The high degree of design commonality was a significant feature, common for the three proposed versions. Mikheev noted:

Each crew member of these two-seat derivatives can control the machine without restrictions. This enables the helicopter or group commander to be able during the operation to communicate with the other helicopters and a ground command post. The cockpit ergonomics is optimal for controlling a group of attack helicopters and deploying the entire arsenal.

The other bidders in the ATAK-2 tender included AgustaWestland (offering the AW129 Mangusta), Eurocopter (offering the Tiger) and Denel (offering the Rooivalk). US helicopter manufacturers Boeing and Bell Helicopter refrained from participation in the tender because of the impossibility of receiving preliminary export licenses from US Government, which was among the prime requirements of the Turkish MoD.

The new offer was submitted to the Turkish tender committee in autumn 2004. In November that year, a Turkish evaluation team visited Russia. It toured the Kamov's new flight-test complex in Chkalovsky, east of Moscow, where it was given a static display and air demonstration of the sole Ka-52 Alligator prototype, reviewed the Ka-50-2 Erdogan mock-up and attended a detailed technical presentation. Turkish company Vestel was also included in the programme, as it had been intended to act as a local technology partner in the Ka-50-2 project.

Exchange of visits were held throughout 2005, and in spring of 2006 a high-ranking Turkish delegation visited Moscow once again, led by Murat Bayar, the SSM head. A total of 42 Turkish experts took part in this visit, including the Army Aviation Chief, Brigadier General Tamer Hadjioglu. The delegation visited the Kamov and Rosoboroexport premises in Moscow, in addition to the Transas and Krasniy Oktyabr companies in St Petersburg. Turkish test pilots were slated to fly the Ka-52 in a variety of testing and evaluation missions, including weapons deployment. Live firings with 30mm cannon and 80mm rockets were organised at the shooting range of the RAA's Torzhok training centre north of Moscow, where the Turkish team sent five pilots and nine engineers to participate in the evaluation programme.

For these live firings from the Ka-52, Kamov had to count exclusively on the skills of test pilot Alexander Papay, as the helicopter still lacked an operational targeting suite at the time. Papay had to rely on a simple cross, painted with a marker onto the ILS-31 head-up display, used for aiming during attack passes for firing the cannon and rockets. This was not a new task for Papay, who had accumulated a lot of gunnery experience in both automated and manual targeting modes flying the single-seat Ka-50. This time he also managed to score accurate hits despite the non-existent sighting equipment onboard the Ka-52. During the attack passes with a Turkish pilot occupying the right-hand seat, the rest of the Turkish team was accommodated in an escorting Mi-8 to evaluate the accuracy of firing and get an idea of the Ka-52's combat manoeuvrability.

The flight demonstrations were conducted in excellent fashion and the Turkish pilots were impressed by the Ka-52's performance. They were disappointed to some extent, however, by the lack of possibility of test-firing the Vikhr-1 ATGM. To avoid explaining that there was a problem with the supply of missiles, Kamov officials told the Turkish team that the future customised Ka-52 would be armed with an ATGM system as selected by the customer. In this case, missile firing tests should be conducted only after the completion of the integration works.

After a detailed analysis of the behaviour of members of the Turkish evaluation team, as Kamov OKB veterans tended to recall later on, it had been evident that the ATAK-2 tender outcome had been predetermined long before April 2006, chiefly due to political reasons. The potential customer was not interested in the Russian Alligator as its future main army attack helicopter; instead, the Turkish intention was to learn as much as possible about the strengths and weaknesses of the new-generation helicopter of a possible enemy. There were several members of the Turkish team, formally presented as pilots-engineers working for SSM, but suspected of having been sent on an intelligence-gathering mission. Most of the Turkish questions forwarded to the Russian team had referred not to the helicopter itself, the organisation

The Ka-50-2 Erodogan mock-up on display, together with the Ka-52 prototype and a production-standard Ka-50. (Kamov OKB)

The Ka-52's first prototype taking-off for firing of the 30mm cannon during the evaluation campaign held by the Turkish military test team at the Torzhok combat training centre in May 2006. All the gun and rocket firings were performed by Alexander Papay, aiming via a simple cross painted on the HUD as the helicopter had lacked any targeting equipment at the time. (Andrey Zinchuk)

Turkish Army Aviation Chief, Brigadier General Tamer Hadjioglu, enters the Ka-52 cockpit for a familiarisation ride at Kamov OKB's flight-test complex at Chkalovsky near Moscow in the spring of 2006. (Mikhail Lisov)

Sergey Mikheev greets SSM head Murat Bayar after his flight in the Ka-52 at Kamov's newly built flight-test complex at Chkalovsky east of Moscow. (Kamov OKB)

Murat Bayar, the SSM head, sitting in the right-hand seat of the Ka-52 for a demo ride in 2006 at Chkalovsky. (Mikhail Lisov)

The Ka-52's first prototype ready to lift-off with a Turkish pilot in the right-hand seat during the weapons evaluation undertaken by a Turkish test team in April/May 2006 at the Torzhok combat training centre north-east of Moscow. (Andrey Zinchuk)

of its after-sale servicing or its serial production; instead, the questions asked for more information about the OKB Kamov's shareholders and subcontractors. It became clear that the Turks were interested not in the machine, but in collecting as much information as possible on the real state of Russia's aerospace and defence industry. Nevertheless, members of the Russian team tried not to pay too much attention to such details during the visits.

In the event, too much effort was wasted in participating in the tender but no results were achieved. The outcome of the tender, announced on 22 June 2006 by Turkish Defence Minister Vecdi Gönül after a Defence Executive Committee meeting, called for shortlisting Denel of South Africa and AgustaWestland of Italy. Gönül added that they were the lowest bidders and both met Turkey's requirements. There was no reasonable explanation given why the Ka-52 had not been included in the shortlist. The Russian attack rotorcraft was actually in a completely different class from the Mangusta offered by AgustaWestland and Denel's Rooivalk, boasting much better overall flight performance, much more powerful weaponry and incomparably more extensive armour protection. At the time of shortlisting the bidders in the ATAK-2 tender, the Ka-52 was the only design that had been tested in real-world combat.

Shortly afterwards, the T-129 attack helicopter offered by AgustaWestland was selected as the winner in the ATAK-2 tender, with a contract signed in September 2007.

Lessons learned

After the ATAK and ATAK-2 tenders, a lot of questions had been raised in Russia, with detractors spreading innuendo about both the Kamov OKB and Mikheev himself. There were even claims that

Mikheev had sold out to the Jewish people when he had decided to collaborate with the IAI for the ATAK tender back in 1997.

Recalling those stormy days, Mikheev is convinced that the company participation in both ATAK and ATAK-2 could be seen as exercises that proved highly useful for the Kamov OKB. The company gained much-needed international experience in terms of NATO requirements, and learned the specifics of participating in international tenders and bids preparation, conducting new-style presentations and holding meetings with international partners and customers. During the ATAK tender, a potential customer raised, for the first time, the requirement to change the avionics system, and the Kamov OKB had to implement a project with open-architecture avionics that would allow fast and easy changes of the system while adding new Western-made digital systems. Also for the first time in Russia, a helicopter design bureau had managed to adopt Western avionics design standards that were widespread around the world.

The biggest benefit derived from the ATAK and ATAK-2 tenders was perhaps related to the design of the Ka-52's definitive avionics suite. Tested in the air and launched in production in the late 2000s, it traces its origins from the offers made in the Turkish tenders. "Experience is gained in specific work cases and cannot be obtained in idle speculation," said Mikheev.

Korean attack helicopter tender

Kamov and Rosoboronexport also submitted an offer for a Ka-52 derivative for the Korean AH-X tender for attack helicopters, launched in March 2000. The other contenders were US rotorcraft manufacturers Boeing, offering the AH-64D Apache Longbow, and Bell Helicopter, with the AH-1Z Cobra, while European and South

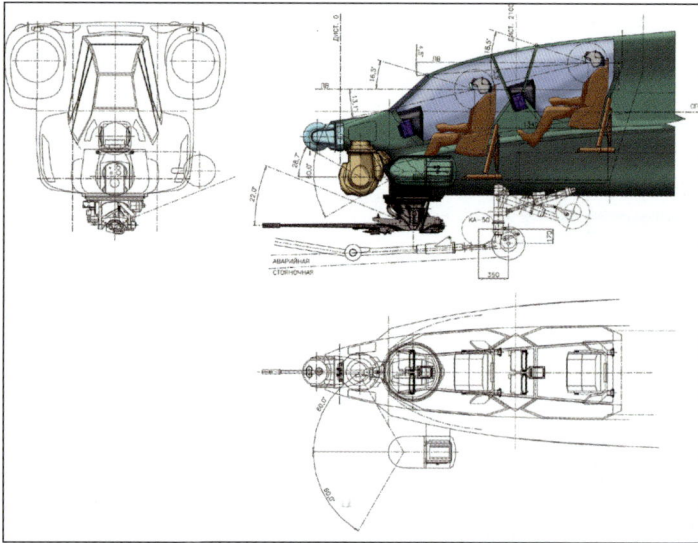

A detailed nose section drawing of the proposed Ka-50 two-seat tandem version for the South Korean tender. The coverage of the Thales Topowl helmet-mounted cueing and display systems for both crewmen is also shown. (Kamov OKB)

A 3-D drawing of the Ka-50's two-seat version proposed for the Korean attack helicopter tender. The helicopter is armed with a GIAT 621 20mm cannon in an undernose turret. (Kamov OKB)

African helicopter manufacturers refrained from competition for the project. The Rosoboronexport/Kamov team offered the Ka-52K version (K denoting Korean), equipped with avionics supplied from Israeli, French, UK and Belgian companies.

The Korean attack helicopter project originally included the procurement of 34–40 attack helicopters after 2004, at a cost of about US$1.6 billion. The minimum operation requirements called for twin-engine helicopters capable of flying at speeds of over 240km/h (130kt). The first stage of the competition set to evaluate the performance of the contenders was passed with success in 2000 as the Ka-52 demonstrated its best features. At the second stage, in April 2001, a Korean team visited Russia to evaluate the production facilities, with three pilots tasked to test in flight the Ka-52, conducting weapons employment sorties, including rocket and cannon firings.

In November 2001, however, South Korea terminated the ambitious AH-X project and eventually decided to develop and produce its local KMH (Korean Multi-Purpose Helicopter) project, teamed with a foreign partner.

10
KA-52's DEVELOPMENT CONTINUES

New avionics suite

The two-seat Ka-52 inherited the baseline avionics system, originally developed in the mid-1990s for the Ka-31 airborne early warning helicopter, optimised for operation from ship decks. It was designed and developed jointly by the Kamov OKB and the Ramenskoye-based RPKB company, based on Baget-series mission computers, MFI multi-functional displays, MFPU multi-function control and display panels and other electronic systems supplied by RPKB. The ultimate design of the Ka-31's avionics suite was frozen in 1998. For the avionics suite of its two-seat attack helicopter, Kamov acted as the primary integrator of the PrPNK-52 flight/navigation/attack suite, while RPKB had to act as the principal supplier of the new electronic systems; this role was then expanded to cover the Ka-50, Ka-60U and the new-generation AEW helicopter. The agreement between RPKB and Kamov was inked in February 1999, and after that the document was blessed by the Russian Deputy Defence Minister (Chief of Armaments of the Russian Federation Armed Forces), Colonel General Anatoly Sitnov, one of the main driving forces for the development of new-generation weapons systems in the late 1990s and early 2000s.

The concept approved by Colonel General Sitnov called for the K-806 avionics suite to be used for the so-called aircrew intellectual support role during all phases of flight. Its 2-D and 3-D maps were required to facilitate terrain-following low-level flight based on digital map elevation data and altitude data (height above ground level) derived from the helicopter's own sensors. The K-806 introduced for the first time in the Russian avionics branch information exchange between the avionics systems by using the GOST 26765.52-87 protocol, a Russian carbon copy of the widespread Western standard Mil Std 1553B.

The processing-management system, representing the core of the PrPNK-52 avionics suite, was also set to be used on the new derivatives of the Ka-50 as well as on the newly developed Ka-31SV and Ka-60U special-mission helicopters. It processed the raw data fed by the nav/flight suite (comprising inertial gyro reference system, automated direction finder, Doppler radar and other components) and managed the operation of the onboard radios, targeting system and self-protection aids. The flight, navigation and general system status and targeting data could be displayed in front of the crew on colour multi-function displays.

Experienced instructors from the 344th TsBPiPLS and officers from the RAA command insisted on having a fully-rated pilot in the Ka-52's right-hand seat, while the 929nd GLITs recommended that the helicopter's WSO should have a navigator background (as the crew is composed on the Mi-28N), without any pilot training.

The new avionics system was developed using funding received from the development of the Ka-31 AEW helicopter ordered by the

Indian Navy, in addition to the Russian MoD budget that had been allocated for Ka-60 development. The latter was the first to test the operation of the Baget-53, a fourth-generation mission computer using open architecture; it also featured the most powerful digital processor manufactured at the time in Russia.

The Ka-60 programme, however, ran into trouble after the Russian MoD implemented drastic cuts in its research and development budget, so Mikheev was eventually forced to use the results of integrating the new-generation avionics suite on other helicopter platforms. He chose Ka-50, c/n 01-04, and it became the first Russian helicopter boasting an open-architecture avionics suite.

The radar of the Ka-52 was developed in parallel to the new flight/navigation/attack suite. Based on the architecture of the Kopyo, a centimetric-wavelength radar system developed by the Moscow-based Phazotron-NIIR as a private venture for the Indian MiG-21 upgrade, the Ka-52's radar, initially named Myech-U, was required to boast better performance than that of the AN/APG-87 Longbow radar equipping the AH-64D Apache Longbow. In its initial form, it was a set made of two different radar modules, working in different frequency bands. The main radar, featuring a slotted array antenna 500mm in diameter (dubbed Arbalet-Ka), was intended to grant the superiority to the AN/APG-78 in terms of range and resolution performance. The large antenna, needed to achieve the required range and resolution performance, was possible to be installed only in the Ka-52's volumous nose. It looked to the front and worked in the millimetre-wavelength (Ka-band) in order to provide the needed high resolution and contrast when used for detection of fixed surface targets on the surrounding terrain background. As Mikhhev recalls, the initial military requirements called for detection range against a tank-size target of up to 12km (6.5nm), combined with a high precision in determining the target's angular coordinates.

The other radar module (dubbed Arbalet-L) installed on the rotor mast and housed in a small fairing was intended to operate in the L-band. It was to be used for detection of tactical combat aircraft or helicopters at 1215km (6.58nm) range, and also for issuing warnings on incoming shoulder-launched missiles in a 360° sector around the helicopter, seen at up to 5km (2.2nm) distance.

The Ka-52 was also intended to feature a helmet-mounted targeting and display system. Initially it was decided to use the Sura system, originally designed for MiG-29 and Su-27 fighters. It was slated for use

The Ka-52 prototype in ultra-low-level flight over water while toting a bizarre mix of weaponry, just for display purposes. Its arsenal includes as many as 12 Vikhr-1 ATGMs, one 20-round pack of 80mm rockets and one R-73 air-to-air missile. (Alexey Mikheev)

The Ka-60 Kasatka was initially conceived as a battlefield reconnaissance and targeting helicopter, equipped with the same mission avionics suite as that designed for the Ka-52. (Author)

Sergey Mikheev shows the Ka-52's FH-01 Arbalet-52 radar, which uses a conventional parabolic reflector antenna. (Kamov OKB)

Sergey Mikheev and RPKB head Givi Dzhangkagava discuss Ka-52 avionics integration details. (Sergey Mikheev archive)

on the Ka-50 as well, and test pilot Papay recalls that he had flown the Black Shark wearing the Sura. As Kamov flight test station personnel recall, only two helmet-mounted targeting sets based on the Sura (dubbed Obzor-800) had been produced for testing and evaluation purposes on the Ka-50.

Papay also said that in general he had liked the Sura system, but was not able to provide a definitive opinion if this would be really needed on a combat helicopter. The Ka-50 was not intended to be used in air-to-air combats, while the ATGMs utilised laser-beam guidance, necessitating automatic target tracking. The Sura helmet-mounted targeting system was most useful in air-to-air combat, allowing the pilot to cue the seekers of its air-to-air missiles towards the selected targets, obviating the need to point its nose toward these.

Based on the experience with the Sura, the Ryazan-based GRPZ company commenced work on a much more sophisticated system, with a visor in front of the pilot's eyes displaying synthetic images of the outside world, supplied by TV and IR cameras, combined with flight/navigation and targeting display symbols. The resultant system, however, turned out to be too heavy when installed on the already considered heavy ZSH-7V protective helmet. Its weight was 1.8kg (4lb), plus at least 0.5kg (1.1lb) added by the NVGs installed on it and the associated counterweight, thus causing serious strain on the pilot's neck in two-hour long missions. In the event, it was decided that it did not make sense to make such a sophisticated helmet-mounted targeting and display system on the ZSh-7V's base. Another issue with the system was related to its positioning accuracy including determining the position of the pilot's head in a coordinate system referenced to the air vehicle, which had to be recalculated at a very fast rate (in milliseconds) all the time, in accordance with the helicopter's attitude (angles of bank, pitch and yaw). As a consequence, the Ka-50 had never received an operational helmet-mounted targeting and display system; the same is still true for its successor, the Ka-52.

The pilot's workplace in the upgraded Ka-52 cockpit, featuring colour multi-function displays and an ILS-31 HUD. (Andrey Zinchuk)

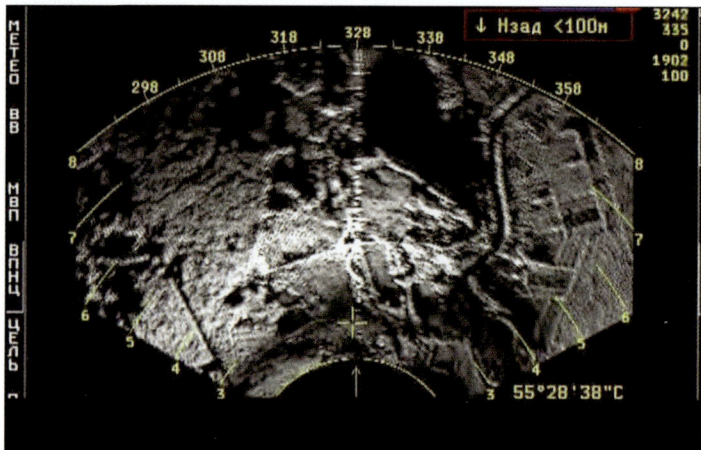

The radar display in the ground target search mode. (Phazotron NIIR)

A derivative of the Sura-K HMCS, dubbed Obzor-800, was adapted for use by the Ka-50 pilot but was never used on the Ka-52. (KP SPS Arsenal)

The Ka-52 prototype with a mock-up of the mast-mounted Arbalet-L radar antenna, originally intended for an air-to-air role. It also comes equipped with a Samshit-B-1 targeting payload mounted on the roof and a TOES-520 turret under the nose, used for navigation at night. (Author)

A prototype of a new-generation helmet-mounted sighting and display system proposed by GRPZ in the early 2000s. (Kamov OKB)

In the 2010s, GRPZ resumed works on a new-generation aircrew helmet-mounted cueing and display system (HMCDS). The specification of the system was a fairly complex one as it was set to provide the pilot with graphical information on the regimes of flight and the engine operation, as well as projecting a video image supplied by external sources; in addition, the HMCDS was required to display the line of sight allowing off-boresight target designation and cueing of the GOES-451 payload simply by turning the pilot's head towards the intended target.

When designing the HMCDS, the GRPZ design team carefully studied the Western experience in this area, where two principal systems had been put in widespread use. The first of these were NVGs featuring an integrated display system (such as the Israeli ANVIS system) while the second used images, supplied by external sensors, including thermal imagers, that were projected onto the pilot's visor (such as the US-made IHADSS, used on the AH-64 Apache), together with the flight/navigation information and targeting/aiming symbols. The latter, however, proved next to impossible to be implemented in a system based on the existing ZSh-7V aircrew helmet worn by Ka-52 pilots. Geophizika-NV designed a NVG set with built-in flight information display shown for the first time at the MAKS-2011 aerospace exhibition, but it had failed to attract any specific interest among the Russian military experts responsible for the new-generation attack helicopter mission suite; in turn, army aviators had expressed a big interest in the new-style 'smart' NVG set.

In the event, GRPZ designers selected the variant with projection of the information fed from external cameras for display onto the pilot's visor. They also decided to use an electro-optical head positioning system in order to track the angular coordinates of the line of sight. This system proved to be less prone to jamming than the electro-magnetic one. The optical part of the HMCDS was of binocular type, with a 40° field of view in the horizontal and 30° in the vertical plane. The pilot could rotate his head within 180°, and the system's error in determining the angular coordinates amounted to tens of angular seconds.

GRPZ designed a test and evaluation bench, allowing the HMCDS to be integrated with the GOES-451 payload. In order to offer a lightweight system, as the pilot would not be able to use heavy headgear for prolonged periods of time, the designers decided not to use the ZSh-7V and instead introduced a new-generation lightweight protective helmet developed by the Zvezda company. The development of the complex HMCDS, however, proved to be a very protracted process and there was no information when it would be completed, tested and eventually cleared for use on the Ka-52.

Another helmet-mounted cueing system was proposed by the Elektroavtomatika company of St Petersburg as a much simpler and affordable solution. Named NSTs-T, its design was based on that of the proven Sura-K system used on the Su-27/30 series of jet fighters. It used IR sensors for head movement tracking and positioning, together with micro accelerometers built in the ZSh-7 helmet.

The new avionics suite also included a multi-channel video recording system for post-mission debriefing (to analyse pilot actions in flight) and recording of onboard system failures, developed by the

The cockpit of '061' in late configuration, adorned with the new-standard K-806 avionics suite, including multi-functional displays for the pilot in the left-hand seat and the WSO in the right-hand one. Both of them have full flight controls. (Andrey Zinchuk)

Elsi company of Velikiy Novgorod.

A wide-band datalink system named Briz was developed by the RTI company, able to provide exchange of high-resolution video information at distances of up to 100km (54nm). This system was intended to link the two-seat Ka-52 with other Ka-52s and Ka-50s, as well as with ground command-and-control posts, AEW (airborne early warning) and surface surveillance helicopters over the battlefield. The datalink would enable the two-seat Ka-52 to be employed as the commander's machine in group operations, able to provide targeting information for the single-seat Ka-50s included in its tactical group. The idea of using the Ka-52 in conjunction with Ka-50s was raised by Mikheev himself.

ATGM troubles

In the mid-1990s, the Ka-50's and Ka-52's development suffered a serious blow caused by the decision of KBP's designer general, Arkadiy Shipunov, to discontinue Vikhr-1 ATGM production. The last batch of missiles was produced in Tula in the mid-1990s, and the entire production documentation was handed over to the Izhevsk-based Izhmech plant, where serial production was launched later in the decade. The two platforms using the long-range anti-armour missile, the Su-25T and Ka-50, had failed to be launched into mass production. In addition, the plant experienced serious financial difficulties, and despite reaching 90 percent readiness to launch ATGM production, it had eventually cancelled all such efforts.

At the same time, Arkadiy Shipunov offered a follow-on missile, the Hermes-A, based on the proven missile design used in the Tula-based Instrument Design Bureau's (KBP's) Pantsir hybrid SAM/AAM

system. It was to be able to knock out ground targets at a range of up to 24km (13nm), but the development was considered to be a protracted and rather expensive undertaking. Shupunov made an attempt to sell the Hermes-A to Libya's Colonel Muamar Gadhafi, who initially expressed keen interest, but in the event the sides failed to seal an agreement over the development and sale of the new long-range missile intended to be launched from the Ka-52. The Hermes-A ATGM was even fire-tested on the Ka-52, with live launches conducted in 2003.

In the meantime, the Kamov OKB had to search for a new missile for the Alligator offered to the RAA. The only available option was to call KBM of Kolomna, the developer of the 9M120 Ataka-V ATGM system installed on the Mi-28 and its follow-on derivative Mi-28N. The Ataka-V was deemed suitable for the Ka-52, but it used heavy and bulky guidance equipment that had to be integrated onto the helicopter. This was seen in the late 1990s as an insurmountable obstacle, threatening to leave both the Ka-50 and Ka-52 without a 'long sting'.

Fortunately, in the early 2000s, Russia's all-powerful Federal Security Service (better known under its Russian-language abbreviation FSB) funded the development of a laser-beam riding version of the missile to be used by the Shturm-V ATGM system, known as the 9M120-1. This derivative of the proven anti-tank missile was fully acceptable for Mikheev, as the design bureau had accumulated great experience of integrating its older version (with semi-active radio-beam command guidance) on the Ka-29 shipborne assault helicopter. This new missile, latter dubbed Ataka-1, was also considered suitable for integration on the Ka-52. In addition, KBM offered a helicopter-borne version of the 9M39 Igla shoulder-launched surface-to-air missile for the Alligator,

A picture derived from the thermal imager of the Ka-52's GOES-451 payload. (via author)

The Hermes-A ATGM has been designed by Tula-based KBP as the next-generation guided missile for all occasions and may be proposed for inclusion into the Ka-52's arsenal in the early 2020s. (Author)

housed in the Strelets twin-round launch module.

End of the Ka-50 development

The numerous on-board systems conceived in the joint project with RPKB added weight and complexity, and the design team began to question if the pilot of the single-seat Ka-50 could cope with the workload of the expanded set of missions, most of which were to be flown at night. In the beginning, the Ka-50 was conceived as a narrowly specialised anti-tank helicopter, but in the 1990s its anti-tank capabilities were considered to be slightly inadequate while lacking sufficient capability to seek and destroy small-size targets. The Russian analogue of the OH-58D Kiowa Warrior had never been developed, as the Ka-60 programme stalled due to lack of a suitable engine and was eventually terminated. The new Ka-31SV battlefield reconnaissance helicopter, in turn, featured a very sophisticated mission suite and was deemed unsuitable for performing the targeting role supporting battlefield attack helicopter operations.

In this situation, the Russian MoD pushed and pushed again for Mikheev to abandon the single-seat helicopter concept and instead concentrate on a suitably equipped two-seat machine. The development of the Ka-52 received funding from the MoD, albeit scant, while the Ka-50 got none; at the same time, Mikheev had yet to prove his concept of a two-seat attack helicopter equipped with a sophisticated targeting suite including powerful radar.

The long-time competition entered a new phase in the early 2000s, but this time the opposing camp was under the leadership of Boris Slusar, director-general of Rostvertol. The MVZ Mil was still recovering from a pitiful state after ill-fated privatisation attempts which saw a proportion of its shares acquired by its US competitor, Sikorsky. Slusar had powerful tools in his hands and was committed to bringing the night-capable Mi-28N into production in an effort to secure the future of his plant, which employed over 5,000 workers. He had never hidden the fact that he was determined to fight by any means available in a bid to achieve his goal at a time when the Russian defence budget was not big enough to support two independent, funding-intensive development and production programmes for new-generation attack helicopters.

In this rather complicated situation of increasingly cut-throat competition between the Mi-28N and Ka-50/52, it was deemed that only one helicopter type would be purchased by the Russian MoD, while the loser would be allowed to wither and die. However, both Mikheev and the new management of the AAC Progress plant in Arsenyev were not ready to surrender without a fight.

Light at the end of the tunnel

The Russian MoD funding allocated for research and development activities at the Kamov OKB in 2002 accounted for the equivalent of a mere US$9.32 million (equating to about 300 million roubles). This was an increase by 70 percent compared to 2001, but the amount proved hardly enough to cover even half of the expenses of the design bureau and its experimental plant.

In August 2003, VVS CinC, Colonel General Vladimir Mikhailov announced that the service had decided to continue with its new-generation attack helicopter procurement drive. This was no shock, apart from the fact that he said not one but two different types would be added to the RAA inventory at the same time. Colonel General Mikhailov said at a press-conference that that the VVS had eventually selected both the Mi-28N and Ka-52 for fielding into front-line service. But at that moment Russia's attack helicopter procurement policy was viewed as mismanaged, underfunded and overlong, so many saw this announcement as just another hastily organised and

The KBM Ataka-1 ATGM's integration on the Ka-52 was a forced measure undertaken in a crash programme in the late 2000s due to the unavailability of the Vikhr-1 at the time. (via author)

executed PR exercise.

In mid-2004, however, the interest in the Ka-50/52 programme sparked once again after the successful combat demonstration of the single-seater at the *Rubezh-2004* exercise in Kirgizstan. Russian Defence Minister Sergey Ivanov saw with his own eyes the effective attack operations, as the Ka-50, flown by Alexander Papay, had managed to repeatedly score accurate hits with rockets and cannon on small targets at a mountainous shooting range in pretty difficult hot-and-high conditions; at the same time, the upgraded Mi-24PNs demonstrated disappointingly low accuracy.

The interest expressed by the Russian defence minister gave hopes to the Kamov leadership that the Black Shark programme might be resurrected in the foreseeable future. In the second half of 2004, the company submitted a proposal for upgrading the Ka-50; the research and development works under this project were to amount to only 443 million roubles (equating to about US$15 million). Moreover, the company was requesting only a quarter of the amount to be allocated in 2005, but in the event it received a negative reply from the Russian MoD.

The Ka-52 programme had also failed to attract any increased interest within the Russian MoD, with a mere amount of five million roubles (US$166,000) allocated for funding of the development and testing work in 2005. The message coming from the Russian MoD at the time was a clear one – nobody there was interested in using the company's services, at least inside the attack helicopter domain.

Facing this pretty grim situation, Mikheev, together with the newly appointed director general of the AAC Progress plant, Yury Denisenko, committed to take an unusual marketing approach. They invited selected high-ranking representatives of the General Staff, the VVS Main Command and the Financial Inspection of the Russian MoD for presentations in Lyubertsi and Arsenyev. The main purpose of the invitation for these large-scale presentations was to show the MoD officials the enormous amount of work that had been done by the design bureau and production plant in developing, testing and launching into production the Ka-50 and Ka-52, and then to discuss the follow-on steps.

Both the design bureau and the plant had a lot to show in 2005. The Ka-52 had just completed the first stage of its state testing and evaluation effort, intended to explore its flight performance and strength characteristics. In 2004, the Alligator flew for the first time equipped with the Arbalet-52 radar, which provided a detailed surface picture and confirmed the designer's expectations in terms of detection performance. The times between overhauls (TBO) of the main gearbox and the retirement life of the rotor blades were also confirmed – 900 and 2,000 flight hours respectively. A sizeable proportion of the testing and development work was conducted by using the company's own money, thanks to royalties obtained from the sale of Ka-31 AEW helicopters to India and the continuing commercial sales of the Ka-32A11BC heavylift workhorse to export customers worldwide.

Then a letter, summarising all the achievements of the Ka-50 and Ka-52 programmes, was sent to the chairman of the Military-Scientific Committee of the General Staff, General Valery Volodin. He was among the biggest opponents of the Kamov coaxial attack helicopters and had recently outlined eight points intended to prove that the Ka-50 and Ka-52 should be called 'armed' instead of 'attack' helicopters. General Volodin focussed all the power of his attacks onto the two-seater, as he already considered the Ka-50 to be a dead programme. He claimed, for instance, that the Ka-52 had no armoured cockpit glazing, the fuselage had an excessively large cross-section and therefore a large radar cross-section, and the crew members sat side-by-side instead of in tandem, which was the arrangement used by all 'true' attack helicopters, etc. Furthermore, he had noted that the Ka-52 lacked a transport cabin and thus could not be used for rescuing crews of downed helicopters on the battlefield.

Some of the accusations voiced by General Volodin could be refuted with ease – the Ka-52 prototype was built in a prompt manner by using an existing Ka-50 fuselage, while the technical specification issued by the Russian military had never contained any detailed requirements in terms of armour protection. But at the time, Mikheev never got the chance to defend his two-seat brainchild, as he was not invited to working sessions of the Military-Scientific Committee, chaired by General Volodin. The claim that the Ka-52 lacked transport capability could be seen as a particularly strange one, as there is no single modern attack rotorcraft type with such a capability around the world. In the event, Mikheev's and Denisenko's official letter addressed to General Volodin had been ignored.

The hostile attitude of the MoD's leadership had at last motivated Mikheev to commence an aggressive direct marketing campaign, arranging face-to-face meetings with important military decision-makers in an effort to explain the real situation with the Ka-50/52 programmes and convince them to grant their support for the completion of the development and testing effort.

The breakthrough came at one of the air shows abroad in 2005, where Mikheev, sitting at the Rosoboronexport stand, noticed the Russian Deputy Defence Minister and armaments chief of the Russian Federation Armed Forces, Army General Alexey Moskovsky, passing by. Mikheev jumped from his seat to intercept the deputy minister, offering to give him a short briefing on the state of the Ka-50/52 programmes. A small private room at the back of the stand was selected for this improvised and rather short briefing. Mikheev told Moskovsky: "Alexey Mikhailovich, we need to develop a Ka-52 version for supporting the *Spetsnaz* (special operation forces) of the Main Intelligence Directorate [of the Russian General Staff]." General Moskovsky immediately agreed with Mikheev and promised to initiate the first steps to move the programme forward. It was a turning

The Ka-50's development was gradually closed at the Kamov OKB in the early 2000s as no funding had been allocated from the Russian MoD. (Andrey Zinchuk)

point for the Ka-50/52 programme revival, as General Moskovsky, a powerful decision-maker, kept his promise and eventually got the ball rolling in the Russian MoD.

The impromptu meeting between General Moskovsky and Mikheev had a weighty impact on the Ka-52's fate in the second half of the 2000s. The director general of the AAC Progress plant, Yury Denisenko, had also managed to show that his plant was alive and kicking, and could easily launch the new helicopter in serial production. By 2005, the crisis at the AAC Progress plant was over and the profits from deliveries of Moskit anti-ship missiles to export customers were invested in the modernisation of the helicopter production line.

In the meantime, Denisenko had also initiated a campaign to win the hearts and souls of the pilots and technicians from the Torzhok training centre. He promised to restore the serviceability of the grounded Ka-50s operated by the centre. He kept his promises and hence, in 2006–2007, two of the Torzhok-based Black Sharks were brought back into serviceable condition.

In the protracted fight for survival of the Ka-50/52 family, Mikheev also used the capabilities of the Russian press to the full extent. He managed to organise a highly successful and well-orchestrated PR campaign, involving a plethora of influential Russian defence journalists, such as Viktor Litovkin and Sergey Ptichkin (at that time working as a reporter for the authoritative *Rossiiskaya Gazeta* daily newspaper). Both of them passionately promoted and defended the coaxial attack helicopter family in their reports. Even the editor in chief of *Krasnaya Zvezda* (*Red Star*, the official Russian MoD newspaper) invited Mikheev for a lengthy interview. The newly established TV channel *Russia Today* also had an interview from him, where Mikheev presented and promoted his coaxial attack helicopter concept. This

wide-scale and fruitful media campaign was waged virtually free of charge.

In the event, the multi-front struggle to continue with the development of the Ka-50/52 family line proved successful, largely thanks to the charisma and stamina of Sergey Mikheev, combined with the never-ending activity of Yury Denisenko and his adviser, Major Genetal (Retired) Yakim Yanakov, in addition to the personal support of the Russian Defence Minister, Sergey Ivanov, and the huge experience and wisdom of his deputy, Alexey Moskovsky. The eventual outcome of this huge collective effort was positive, and in mid-2005, Ivanov signed the long-awaited decree for the resumption of the Ka-50's serial production, together with acceleration of the Ka-52's development works. To make it happen in a compressed timeframe, three existing Ka-50 fuselages were earmarked to be converted into Ka-52s, slated for use in the type's comprehensive developmental test programme. The Ka-52's development budget allocated in 2005 accounted for 80 million roubles (equivalent to about US$2.6 million at the time), still a very small proportion compared to the actual needs.

Competitor's team creating new troubles

In the meantime, the competitor's supporters continued their wide-ranging offensive against the Kamov OKB, claiming that the Ka-50's upper and lower rotor blades were prone to striking each other. During 2002, however, the company aerodynamics specialists, together with test pilots, undertook an in-depth research of the blade behaviour at critical regimes of flight. Using special equipment to monitor the deflection of the blade tips, they found that even during the worst-case manoeuvres in the horizontal plane, the minimum distance between the tips of the lower and upper blades was 66cm. When performing inclined loops in the vertical plane, this distance

Sergey Mikheev and Army General Alexey Moskovsky, a keen supporter of the Ka-52 programme who had been able at last to get the ball rolling in the difficult mid-2000s. As a result, the Alligator completed the testing programme at the end of the decade, which, in turn, paved the way for its serial production and entry into service with the Russian air arm. (Sergey Mikheev archive)

could reduce to 63cm, which was judged as being safe enough and satisfied the combat employment conditions. The test flights within the frame of this research programme were performed by Kamov test pilot V. Lavrov, and the flight test report bore the signatures not only of the members of the Kamov OKB team, but also of VVS State Flight Test Centre representatives who were involved in the test effort. With this, the prescribed measures taken in a bid to fix the shortcomings identified during the investigation of the 17 June 1998 Ka-50 crash at Torzhok had been completed in full.

In the summer of 2005, during a conference at the celebration of the 55th anniversary of the Syzran Higher Air Force Pilot School, the former Russian Army Aviation CO, Colonel General Vitaly Pavolov, speaking about the Black Shark, mentioned that it did not make sense for an attack aircraft to be armour-protected like an infantry fighting vehicle. This was an apparent suggestion that the Ka-50 was considered overweight due to its extensive armour protection.

At the same event, however, two Ka-50s from the Torzhok centre gave a spirited air display during the airshow devoted to the celebration, held at Syzran-Troekurovka airfield. On the way back home, one of the Black Sharks suffered from an incident which proved yet again the high reliability of Kamov's trademark coaxial rotor scheme. The wingman's machine lost its rudder in cruise flight, which separated from its hinges and fell to the ground. This fact was noticed by the rearmost helicopter in the group, while the pilot of the unlucky helicopter, Major A. Menyailo, had failed to spot the rudder loss at all as there were no changes in the controllability and stability of his aircraft. When warned by the group leader about the incident, he decided to continue the flight to the nearest airfield instead of performing an immediate forced landing because the helicopter had remained fully controllable all the time. In peacetime, the flight manual prohibits continuing the flight with a rudder missing, but this would be perfectly possible in wartime conditions. The damaged helicopter, lacking its rudder, was then ferried to Torzhok by Kamov OKB test pilot Alexander Smirnov in an uneventful flight.

The competitor's supporters had also claimed that the Ka-50's design would lack enough battlefield survivability. This claim had been repeated by the Russian Air Force CinC, Colonel General Vladimir Mikhailov (who was among the biggest Mi-28N supporters) in March 2006, during a meeting with foreign defence attaches. He emphasised that the coaxial rotor scheme, as a rule, suffered from some serious inherent shortcomings; for instance, if the rotor was damaged in combat, the helicopter could not return home. Then, just before the of visit a high-ranking Libyan military delegation keenly interested in the Ka-52, Colonel General Mikhailov had claimed in an interview for *Rossiiskaya Gazeta* newspaper, without being backed by any valid arguments, that the Black Shark's design had more shortcomings than, for instance, the Mi-28N. He had blatantly ignored the well-known fact that a Ka-50 returned to base during the war in Chechnya with a damaged rotor system. When asked to comment on this hostile claim, Mikheev said that the shortcomings of both helicopters should be compared at the test ranges, but nobody within the Russian military had been willing to do that at the time.

Alligator learns to shoot

The restarting of Ka-50 production in Arsenyev had no negative influence on the Ka-52's development. The two-seat derivative of the

Yury Denisenko and Sergey Mikheev talk to the press after the first flight of the first production-standard Ka-52 in Arsenyev on 29 October 2008. (Sergey Mikheev archive)

Ka-52's first prototype shooting its 30mm cannon on the ground in late 2005. (Kamov OKB)

Ka-52 '061' shooting with the 2A42 cannon at a ground target in a shallow dive, using the slow rate-of-fire mode. (Kamov OKB)

Black Shark reached a stage where it had to be tested firing the cannon and rockets initially on the ground (to check firing safety) and then in flight (to check engine resistance to powder-gas ingestion). This testing was intended to be complete before the demonstration of the helicopter to a high-ranking Turkish delegation. The helicopter lacked targeting equipment, so aiming had to be carried out in the manual mode only, with the main purpose of these firings to check the engine gas-dynamic stability when ingesting powder gases from the firing cannon.

The testing trials were performed at the shooting range of the Torzhok combat training centre in autumn 2005. There were no doubts in the Kamov team that the trials would be successful, thanks to the high design commonality with the Ka-50, but the VVS had strict requirements to duly test the helicopter's weaponry by following a careful step-by-step approach, first on the ground and then in the air.

The first trials were carried out on the ground, with the helicopter set up on uneven ground, with a slight bank angle, but this was deemed acceptable for the initial shooting trials. At this stage, a problem had been encountered with the munitions supply, since the Torzhok logistic servicemen provided ammunition for the Mi-24P's GSh-30-2 cannon, which featured a different detonator design (using electrical rather than mechanical activation) than that used in the rounds of the 2A42. This had caused frequent stoppages during the initial cannon

[In the early and mid-2000s, the production tempo of the Ka-50 at the AAC Progress plant in Arsenyev was very slow because of scant funding provided by the Russian MoD. As many as seven partially assembled helicopters are here gathering dust and waiting for better times. Three of these were completed in 2008–2009, while the rest were re-worked into two-seat Ka-52s. (AAC Progress)

Ka-52 '061', sporting a new nose configuration, with a single large payload (most likely a GOES-451 or its derivative) and lacking the nose-mounted radar. The aircraft also sports a new two-tone grey camouflage scheme. While this photo is dated 2010, the configuration had been introduced two years earlier. (Dmitry Pichugin)

live firing testing. In the event, Kamov's ordinance specialists found this discrepancy and ordered the right type of munitions for the remainder of the firing trials.

The first 2A42 firings in the air from the Ka-52 caused an unusual incident as a civilian Mi-8 was flying in the shooting direction, at the edge of the range, transporting a gas pipeline repair team. The Mi-8 crew and passengers proved to be the wrong place and in the wrong time, inside a military installation without a prior notice and authorisation. So they were lucky to escape the projectiles unleashed by the Alligator that passed by at a close distance; after this the scared Mi-8 crew immediately flew the helicopter away.

Ka-52 increases its potential

The stiff resistance of the VVS leadership to embrace the single-seat Ka-50 and their preference expressed towards the two-seat Ka-52 eventually prompted Mikheev to accelerate Alligator development work by implementing all the new technical features proven on the latest Black Shark derivatives except the Kabris moving map device. The two-seater received the new and more powerful VK-2500-01 turboshaft developed jointly by Klimov in St Petersburg and Motor-Sich in Zaporozhye, Ukraine. Compared to its predecessor TV3-117VMA, the new engine featured an increased power rating in one engine inoperative (OEI) situations, up to 2,700shp, while the take-off rating was upped to 2,400shp. Its service life was extended to 6,000 flight hours, with TBO set at 2,000 hours. Main performance-boosting novelties implemented in the VK-2500 design are said to have been centred on an all-new turbine section as well as a BARK-78 digital control and monitoring unit. The engine weighs 300kg (660lb) and is described as being capable of maintaining its maximum power rating at ambient air temperatures of up to 45°C.

The extra power derived from the VK-2500-01 had compensated for the performance degradation caused by the increased maximum take-off weight of the Ka-52 in the production-standard configuration – it proved to be some 600kg (1,344lb) higher than that of the single-seat Ka-50. Thanks to the increased OEI rating, the new engine also provided a significant power margin during operations at high altitude and extreme heat.

The Ka-52's definitive avionics suite was designed in accordance to the concept approved by Army General Anatoly Sitnov back in 1999. Named Argument-52, it featured open architecture and used many novelties which were conceived for the first time by the design team during the participation in the Turkish tender, where the Ka-50-02 Erdogan version was proposed, equipped entirely with Western-sourced, all-digital, open-architecture avionics systems.

From the very beginning, the Ka-52 was conceived as an all-weather, day/night reconnaissance-strike helicopter. Its all-weather capability was facilitated mainly by the Arbalet-52 radar, while the night attack was facilitated by the combination of the GOES-451 optronic payload and the GEO-ONV1-01K NVG sets for both crew members, using a battery pack as the counterweight. This version of the NVG set featured a rapidly de-coupling device for the power cord, useful in case of aircrew ejection.

The Arbalet-52 radar system was also changed after design analysis had shown that the installation of the second antenna on the rotor mast, in the way this solution had been implemented on the AH-64D Apache Longbow, could cause huge vibration issues, with associated costs and time penalties. In addition, the antenna would incur a weight increase and avoiding its installation on the mast made it possible to trade the weight savings for getting better armour protection or additional ordinance. In the event, the Phazotron-NIIR proposed to install all the radar equipment in the fuselage, saving weight and lowering vibration levels, which, in turn, would increase the reliability of the radar components.

In its eventual production form, the nose-mounted Arbalet-52 was capable of delivering a radar picture of the underlying surface, with options to scale it up or down and select sectors of interest for detection and tracking of ground, sea and air targets. The radar was able to deliver highly accurate positional information and discriminate the targets against the surrounding background. It was also able to provide missile warning (in respect to SAMs launched against the helicopter head-on and side-on) and facilitate attack runs against ground and sea targets using the cannon and rockets, as well as cueing the optronic payload towards the target selected by the crew. Maximum tank-size target detection range reached 15km (8.1nm).

The technical specification for the day/night optronic targeting system for the Ka-52 was approved in April 1999 and then forwarded to the developer, the Perm-based UOMZ company. It represented a large and bulky payload, 640mm in diameter, then designated as the GOES-640, incorporating a Russian-made Modul-Avia thermal imager, TV camera with a 14x magnification (zoom), laser rangefinder/designator with range up to 20km (11.4nm), laser-beam ATGM guidance system and laser-marked spot seeker. The payload was also to include the Okhotnik multi-channel image enhancement system. The development of the GOES-640, however, was considerably delayed and as a temporary solution the less-sophisticated GOES-451 had been adopted, but not long after it became the permanent optronic payload installed on the production-standard Ka-52.

The optronic payload was eventually positioned under the nose, as this could provide the best spatial coverage compared to the other alternatives tried before, such as on top of the fuselage behind the cockpit. In its in-production form, the bulky and heavy GOES-451 ball, developed and manufactured by the UOMZ, was installed immediately behind the huge radome covering the Arbalet-52's antenna.

To the left of the GOES-451, on the development helicopters another smaller turret was installed: the UOMZ TOES-520, housing a TV camera and thermal imager (non-stabilised), useful for navigation purposes at night. This system, however, had not been installed on the production-standard Alligators as this functionality had been added into the latest GOES-451 version.

The improved fire control system allowed automatic employment modes for the cannon, rockets (80mm S-8 rockets fired from B-8V20A packs), Ataka-1 and Vikhr-1 ATGMs, as well as the Igla air-to-air missiles fired from twin-round Strelets launchers. In the manual mode, used in case of failure of the central processor of the fire control system, it was made capable of providing cannon and rocket firing.

11

SYSTEM DEVELOPMENT AND TESTING COMPLETION

Launch into production

The first Ka-52 prototype was used to test large numbers of various novelties implemented post-2005, intended for use in the production-standard Alligators. In order to accelerate the development works, the Russian MoD authorised the use of incomplete Ka-50 fuselages stored at the AAC Progress plant in Arsenyev. Three of these, gathering dust in the assembly hall since the mid-1990s, were set out to be completed as Ka-50s while another two were slated to be converted into two-seaters. In fact, the first fuselage derived from the third production series, c/n 03-01, had been used to build the first production-standard Ka-52, while the remaining three (c/n 03-03, 03-04 and 03-05) were completed as Ka-50s and handed over to the 344th TsBPiPLS in Torzhok in 2008–2009. These were the last Black Sharks ever produced. In total, the Ka-50 was built in five experimental and 13 production-standard examples, one of which was later converted into the Ka-52 Alligator first prototype, while another was re-worked as the Ka-50-2 Erdogan mock-up. By 2008, the total flight time amassed by the Ka-50s and the lone Ka-52 prototype amounted to in excess of 5,000 hours.

The first Ka-52 to be built at the AAC Progress plant (referred to as the second Ka-52 prototype), serialled '062' and wearing the new c/n 00-02, took to the air for the first time on 27 June 2008 in the skilled hands of Alexander Papay and Yury Timofeev. On 28 October that year, another Kamov test pilot, Vitaly Lebedev, lifted off in Arsenyev the second two-seat machine produced there, serialled '063' (c/n 00-03); it was considered to be the first pre-production Ka-52, also built

by using an incomplete Ka-50 fuselage.

The Ka-52's state testing effort was formally launched at the 929th GLITs on 6 September 2008, with two aircraft '061' and '062' which had successfully passed through the preliminary tests. In accordance with the approved test plan, these two machines amassed 77 flights until December that year. The preliminary conclusion issued by the test team had clearly noted that the upgraded Ka-52 combat helicopter was able to perform in a full scope the tasks set out by the VVS CinC for the V-80Sh2. The 'Notes and recommendations' chapter of the flight test report lacked the designer's nightmare the so-called List No. 1 of shortcomings that should be rectified before commencement of the aircraft's production.

On 26 December 2008, Sergey Mikheev received the long-awaited news that the Russian Federation Government had issued a decree on the launch of the Ka-52's serial production; the document had been signed by Prime Minister Vladimir Putin. The plant in Arsenyev was ready and willing to take on the challenge, rolling out the first production-standard three-aircraft batch in 2009 (c/n 01-01, 01-02 and 01-03), still utilising a great many parts and assemblies such as fuselages, rotor systems and main gearboxes originally built for nine Ka-50s in the mid-1990s.

The five Ka-52s manufactured in 2008–2009 took an active part in the state testing and evaluation effort, completed in full in 2011. Later on, together with the heavily utilised first prototype, these machines participated in a wide range of follow-on flight test and evaluation initiatives, the main one of which was the development and testing

Ka-50 'Yellow 27' (c/n 03-04) was among the three last Black Sharks manufactured at the AAC Progress plant in 2008–2009. It performed its last flight in Torzhok on 29 October 2012. Now the entire Ka-50 fleet at the centre is held in long-term storage. (Dmitry Pichugin)

Ka-50 'Yelow 24' (c/n 01-04) was retired in 2010, and then in May 2011 was handed over to the Voronezh Higher Air Force Institute for use in a ground instruction role. (Dmitry Pichugin)

The second Ka-52 (c/n 00-02), wearing the serial '062', was flown for the first time in June 2008. It was built at the AAC Progress plant for use in the completion of the joint state test programme. (AAC Progress)]

effort of the new design features to be used in the shipborne Ka-52K derivative.

One of these helicopters, c/n 01-02, serialled '52', was lost in a test sortie on 29 October 2013, flown by pilot Yury Timofeev and navigator Vladimir Yurtaev during the development testing of systems intended for use in the Ka-52K (while testing the operation of the new air condition unit). The helicopter burst into flames following a hard landing at Kamov's flight test station in Zhulebino with a failed flight control system; the crew members were lucky to escape at the last possible moment, albeit with some injures. The subsequent investigation held by the Ministry of Industry and Commerce found that the accident was caused by a fractured link of the collective pitch control for the upper rotor disc; the failure had occurred due to a manufacturing defect. The defective part was manufactured in the early 2000s at a plant near Moscow. The main cause of the manufacturing defect was, in turn, attributed to gross negligence of the employees tasked with part fabrication and subsequent quality control.

Luckily, the substantial strength reserves of the defective part that were originally set out by the Kamov designers had helped to avoid fatalities. The accident investigation commission found that the process of a gradual failure of the part, caused by the manufacturing defect, took enough time for the crew to realise that there was a serious mechanical problem with the rotor control system and initiate immediate descent, succeeding in returning to the base and almost completing the landing before the rod disintegration. From the date of installation on the helicopter to the accident date, the defective part had worked in a normal mode for four years. In the case of correct

Ka-50 'Yellow 28', c/n 03-05, was among the last three Black Sharks produced, delivered to the Torzhok centre in 2009; this example made the type's last flight in front-line service on 8 November 2012. (Andrey Zinchuk)

fabrication, its fatigue life, as demonstrated by additional analysis made at Kamov, could exceed 300,000 hours.

Ka-52 '062' during engine tests before its first flight, with test pilots Papay and Timofeev in the cockpit. (AAC Progress)

Kamov test pilots Papay and Timofeev posing with AAC Progress personnel and managers after the first flight of the second Ka-52 prototype '062' (c/n 00-02) on 27 June 2008. (AAC Progress)

The Alligator final assembly line of the AAC Progress plant, with three helicopters in the final completion stage. (AAC Progress)

The third Ka-52, c/n 00-03, serialled '063', during its final assembly. This was the first pre-production Alligator built, which lifted off for the first time in October 2008. (AAC Progress)

Ka-52 '063' and one of the last production Ka-50s, sitting together at the AAC Progress plant's flight-test station on 29 October 2008. (AAC Progress)

Ka-52 '063' during one of its initial flights in Arsenyev, devoid of any sensor balls that were installed later on when the type joined the state testing and evaluation effort. (AAC Progress)

Ka-52 '063', equipped only with the TOES-520 sensor turret, with a Ka-27PS belonging to the RAA Torzhok combat training centre in a flypast formation over Moscow in May 2010. (Dmitry Pichugin)

Ka-52 '063', wearing a display livery that resembles an alligator's skin colour pattern, undergoing rotor and systems checks before a display sortie at the 2013 Paris Air Show. (Author)

The cockpit of '063', which sports some differences to the definitive production-standard layout. (Author)

The third pre-production Ka-52, '53' (01-03), in flight over Moscow in May 2010. (Mikhail Nikolsky)

Two of the three pre-production aircraft built in 2009, '52' (c/n 01-02) and '53' (c/n 01-03), in close formation flight in 2010. While '52' is devoid of the Vitebsk-52 self-protection system, it is armed with six Ataka-1 ATGMs under the port wing outer pylon. (Kamov OKB)

Pre-production Ka-52 '52' (c/n 01-02) crashed on landing at the Kamov OKB flight-test station at Zhulebino in Moscow on 29 October 2013; luckily, both crew members managed to escape the aircraft at the last moment and then continued their flight test careers. (via Author)

CHAPTER 12

IN RAA SERVICE

Alligator taken on strength by the Torzhok centre

The first four production-standard Alligators for the RAA were completed at the AAC Progress plant in the second half of 2010, and in December that year these machines, serialled '92' to '95', were transported by air to Tver-Migalovo in a partially disassembled state by Il-76MD transports, and then on-board Mi-26 heavy-lift helicopters for a short trip to their new home. On 28 December 2010, the four Ka-50s were officially handed over to the RAA's 344th TsBPiPLS at Torzhok, where they had to undergo field trials and were put in use for training an initial instructor cadre. New round-the-clock combat tactics, techniques and procedures were also developed by the centre's skilled instructor-research pilots.

Some six months later, the RAA's first front-line unit to be equipped with the new attack rotorcraft, the 575th Air Base (Army Aviation) at Chernigovka in Russia's Far East, took on strength its initial Ka-52 batch.

In 2011, the economic situation in Russia began to improve to a level that at last allowed the Ministry of Defence to place large-scale/long-term orders for new weapons systems, with delivery extended until 2020. The consequences of the 2008 economic crisis had been largely overcome, with oil and gas prices experiencing a steady growth, which, in turn, had resulted in an increasing stream of revenue derived from the export sales of hydrocarbon fuels that could be spent for funding large-scale defence procurement projects.

This rather favourable economic situation in Russia in the early 2010s had a pronounced positive impact on the Ka-52's production rates and its commissioning in service with the Russian military. On 3 September 2011, VVS CinC Colonel General Alexander Zelin signed an eagerly anticipated decree No. 337, 'Ref: Experimental operation of the Ka-52 combat helicopters'. This document referred to the initial operation of the Alligator with the VVS (Army Aviation branch), including the evaluation of its fight, technical, tactical, combat, maintenance support and ergonomic performance in real-world operation in front-line units. In addition, the experimental operation had also been intended for the development of tactical/combat employment manuals that would take into consideration the new capabilities of the Ka-52's sophisticated day/night targeting suite.

The main base for conducting the experimental operation was set up at the 344th TsBPiPLS in Torzhok. The new type was assigned to the 3rd Instructor-Research Helicopter Squadron (IRHS) of the centre, which at the time was equipped with Ka-50s and Mi-24Ps, and also had a handful of Ka-27PS search and rescue helicopters. Four more Alligators, this time featuring the full-standard avionics configuration including radars and full-scale self-protection suites were added to the fleet in early 2012.

The aircrews and engineers from the 344th TsBPiPLS's research and development department have done a great job since early 2011 in developing and evaluating new combat employment tactics, techniques and procedures in a bid to maximise the combat capabilities of the Ka-52, boasting an all-new day/night sensor suite.

The first and so far only Ka-52 crash in military service took place at the Torzhok centre, on 12 March 2012. A crew composed of pilot Lieutenant Colonel Dmitry Rakushin and his WSO, Lieutenant Mikhail Fedorov, crashed a Ka-52 during a routine night training sortie in limited visibility conditions. The helicopter, serialled '99' (c/n 05-04), inadvertently entered into a zone with intense snowfall and was destroyed in the controlled crash-landing. Radio contact with the helicopter was lost at 2104, and the search organised by 344th TsBPiPLS rescue teams proved fruitless; the Ka-52's wreckage was eventually found the next morning, with the crew members dead inside.

The accident investigation revealed that Lieutenant Colonel Rakushin, the 3rd IRHS CO, had insufficient proficiency in instrument flying on the Ka-52. All his prior pilot experience was accumulated on the Mi-24, including combat sorties flown in Chechnya. He converted to the Ka-52 when he was appointed as CO of the 3rd IRHS in 2011, and had only limited flying experience in it while retaining habits inherited from other classic-scheme rotorcraft. According to experienced helicopter pilots from the 344th TsBPiPLS, in the rather stressful conditions, flying in zero-visibility due to the intense snowfall,

The side-by-side seating arrangement is highly-appreciated by RAA pilots with a Mi-24 background who converted to the Ka-52, because communication and coordination between the Gator crew members are now much easier and faster. (Andrey Zinchuk)

An anonymous early production Alligator of the first four-aircraft batch, devoid of serial, lifting-off in early 2011, soon after delivery to the Torzhok combat training centre. (Dmitry Pichugin)

From 2011 the four initial production-standard Alligators of the 344th TsBPiPLS (one of these shown in flight), complemented in early 2012 by four more full-configuration machines, were used for training an initial instructor cadre, which in turn began training the crews of the Alligator-equipped front-line attack squadrons, stationed at RAA bases in Chernigovka, Korennovsk, Ostrov, Dzhankoi and Khabarovsk. (Mikhail Lisov)

The pre-production and production-standard Alligators introduced additional armour screens scabbed onto the canopy glazing to protect the pilot and the ejection seat booster from small-arms fire and high-speed missile warhead fragments. (Andrey Zinchuk)

A camouflaged Ka-52, 'Yellow 93' (c/n 03-03), taxiing in to the parking and servicing area of its home airfield at Torzhok. (Author)

With no tail rotor, the coaxial rotor Ka-52 also needs no tail boom and associated transmission components extending beyond the main rotor's diameter. This is a very important flight safety and combat survivability factor. (Author)

This Ka-52, serialled 'Yellow 91', (c/n 04-05), sporting the definitive production-standard configuration with the Vitebsk-52 self-protection suite and Arbalet-52 radar, was delivered to the Russian Army Aviation combat training centre at Torzhok in January 2012. (Author)

The remains of Ka-52 'Yellow 99', (c/n 05-04), which crashed near its home base of Torzhok on 12 March 2012. (via author)

Rakushin had acted as instructed in the past on the Mi-24, looking in the same way at the instruments and handling the machine exactly in the same manner. The Mi-24, however, has a linear relationship between the pitch down attitude and the speed – the bigger the pitch down angle, the greater the speed. The Ka-52, however, features a different set-up, with a non-linear relationship – in the fatal flight, it initially pitched up, entered into a climb out and its speed reduced to zero; then the helicopter entered into a dive, with an increasing bank angle, gathering speed and eventually colliding with the ground. Most probably, the pilot had lost his altitude awareness (falling into spatial disorientation), but was still trying to find the landing site in intense snowfall conditions and sharply reduced visibility. In this rather stressful emergency situation, however, he had proved ill-suited to switch to instrument flying and level the helicopter, which was flying with increasing pitch and bank angles towards the ground. Until the very end, the pilot had continued trying to see the landing site through the snow, losing control over the flight regime. The WSO was unable to assist due to his very limited experience, and just before the collision with the ground he had shouted: "Commander altitude!" That was the last that was heard from them.

Delivery to front-line units

The coaxial rotor Ka-52 Alligator is set to become the most numerous attack helicopter type within the RAA fleet. A successful and capable combat rotorcraft design, it completed its extensive test and evaluation effort in the definitive production configuration in November 2011; this achievement had finally opened the doors for its service-wide introduction. As a result, two separate Ka-52 batches are believed to have been ordered by the Russian MoD (in addition to a 12-strong initial batch) in an effort to replace the majority of the RAA's obsolete attack rotorcraft fleet and set up all-new attack squadrons. The first contract, dating from October 2008, covered the production of 36 units, with the final examples taken on strength in 2012. The second order, dating to 31 August 2011, foresaw the delivery of as many as 146 Ka-52s, slated to be taken on strength by the RAA between 2013 and 2020.

In 2011, 12 Ka-52s were produced, followed by 24 more in 2012. The price of the Ka-52s manufactured in 2012 is reported to have been 810 million roubles, equating to around US$25 million at the then exchange rates. Fourteen more Ka-52s were produced in 2013, ten in 2014 and up to 16 in 2015 (including four Ka-52Ks for testing and evaluation purposes).

As of March 2016, five front-line Army Aviation squadrons were equipped with the Ka-52 and as many as 69 pre-production and production-standard examples were reported to have been delivered.

The Alligator had originally been slated to equip one attack squadron in most of the RAA independent helicopter regiments and brigades. The type would thus be eventually operated by 10–12 front-line squadrons, each of them with a fleet of 16–22 aircraft.

The first front-line squadron to take the new attack type was included in the structure of the then 575th Aviation Base (Army Aviation), stationed at Chernigovka airfield in Russia's Far East (in the eastern Military District), only 80km (44nm) away from the AAC Progress plant. The air base took on strength its first four initial-configuration Ka-52s in May 2011, and by the year-end its fleet amounted to 12 examples in the initial-production configuration, lacking the radar and self-protection suite. Four more full-configuration machines were received in 2012, and another four followed suit in 2013. The first regular training flights of the squadron were conducted in June 2011, with the deputy base CO, Major Andrey Volkov, having the distinction to be the first aircrew commander to take the Ka-52 to the air, with First Lieutenant Sergey Kolesnikov acting as his WSO.

The choice of Chernigovka as the first front-line operator of the new type had been determined by its proximity to the production

The Ka-52's 40mm-thick triplex windshield is designed to withstand hits of armour-piercing rounds up to 12.7mm calibre. (Author)

The Ka-52 with a full combat load can hover out of ground effect at 4,000m (13,120ft). The coaxial scheme is not sensitive at all to the wind direction at landing, while conventional helicopters have to land into the wind. (Andrey Zinchuk)

By early 2016, the 'Gator soldiered on shoulder-to-shoulder with the Mi-28N in one training centre, two front-line regiments and one army aviation brigade. (Andrey Zinchuk)

This pair of Ka-52s is assigned to the attack squadron of the 319th OVP stationed at Chernigovka in Russia's Far East. The Alligators serving with this regiment wear yellow serials. (Russian MoD)

On 26 December 2008, the VVS CinC, Colonel General Alexander Zelin (shown in the Ka-52 cockpit), signed the long-delayed preliminary report on the completion of the first stage of the Ka-52's state flight testing and evaluation. Note the white rocket booster of the K-37-800M ejection seat used to drag the pilot out of the aircraft. (AAC Progress)

plant. It is exactly the same approach that made the 575th Air Base predecessor, the 319th Independent Helicopter Regiment, the first Soviet Air Force unit to be equipped with then brand-new Mi-24A armoured attack helicopter in 1972. This proximity, in turn, enables them to solve in a prompt manner any technical problems that may arise (mostly represented by the type's teething troubles and the need to implement certain modifications) by using factory warranty teams despatched to the air base. If the problems turn out to be more serious, then the affected helicopter can be easily taken back to the plant by ground transport for repairs or modifications as needed. During the latest round of Russian military reforms, in December 2015, the 575th Air Base (Army Aviation) was transformed into the 319th Independent Helicopter Regiment (319th OVP), returning to the unit organisational structure and number plate it had until December 2009.

The Ka-52 has been highly praised by RAA aircrew for its easy handling, excess power and lack of performance degradation, even when flying in demanding hot-and-high conditions. System reliability has also reportedly been improved by far. "It flies nicely and looks menacing," claims Russian Flight Test-Research Institute pilot Mikhail Pavlenko. This is perhaps the shortest but also a rather adequate summary of the very nature of the coaxial rotor, two-seat Alligator.

The second RAA front-line unit to field in service the Alligator was the 393rd Aviation Base (Army Aviation), stationed at Korennovsk airfield in the southern part of Russia, in the Southern Military District. It welcomed its first machines in February 2013, and by April that year its fleet grew to 16 Ka-52s wearing red serials. It is interesting to note that the 393rd Air Base had fielded an eclectic mixture of all three new Russian attack rotorcraft types: Mi-28N, Mi-35M and Ka-52 equipping two squadrons. In December 2015, the Korennovsk-based army aviation unit was transformed into the 55th OVP.

The next front-line unit to take on strength the Ka-52 was the newly established 15th Army Aviation Brigade (15th BAA), stationed at Ostrov airfield in Pskov Oblast, assigned to the Western Military District (not far from the border with Estonia). As many as 12 helicopters were delivered in early 2014, equipping one attack squadron, while in early 2015 the unit also took on strength at least four Alligators formerly operated by the Korennovsk-based, Ka-52-equipped squadron. The Ostrov-operated helicopters wear white serials.

The fourth Alligator operator within the RuASF was the 39th VAP (Helicopter Aviation Regiment), newly established in late 2014 and stationed at Dzhankoi airfield in the Crimean peninsula (a territory annexed by the Russian Federation in April 2014), again in the Southern Military District. It took about a dozen Ka-52s that were previously operated by the 393rd Air Base (Army Aviation). These Alligators were handed over to the 39th VAP in late 2014 to equip one of its two attack squadrons. The Dzhankoi-operated helicopters wear blue serials.

The fifth RAA squadron to take on strength the new type was the newly-formed attack squadron of 573rd Air Base (Army Aviation), stationed at Khabarovsk-Bolshoy airfield in the Eastern Military District. By mid-2015, it had a fleet of 12 Ka-52s that commenced regular training operations in June 2015. Eight more were taken on strength in December that year, bringing the total fleet to 20 units. In December 2015, the 573rd Air Base (Army Aviation) was transformed into the 825th OVP.

In 2013, when the RAA operated a fleet of 36 Ka-52s, the annual

As many as 20 Ka-52s were built in 2012, including four for the 575th Air Base (Army Aviation) at Chernigovka and 16 more for the 393rd Air Base (Army Aviation) at Korennovsk. One of these, 'Red 46' (c/n 06-05), is shown. Ka-52's acquisition price in 2012 was 810.47 million roubles, then equating to US$24.56 million. (Andrey Zinchuk)

The first Alligator destined for the 825th OVP, known until December 2015 as the 537th Air Base. The machines of the attack squadron of this regiment wear blue serials. (Russian MoD)

A group of 10 Ka-52s belonging to the attack squadron of the 319th IRH seen lined-up at a forward operating base in Russia's Far East during a field exercise. (Yury Smityuk)

The Ka-52 is known as a very precise platform for delivering S-8 80mm rockets, fired from 20-round packs. Here, a salvo has just been unleashed from a Torzhok-based Ka-52 in a shallow dive. (Andrey Zinchuk)

The KTE-52 is a fixed full-mission simulator for the Alligator, developed by the TsNTU Dinamika company, with the first example delivered to the RAA in 2011. (TsNTU Dinamika)

flight time per helicopter was 59 hours, while for the first six months of 2014 it amounted to 34 hours (amassed by a total of 46 helicopters in operation at the time). In early 2015, the availability rate used to show the percentage of airworthy fleet was hovering at 83 percent.

In July 2015, the Russian Helicopters holding company released for public use a company presentation containing a wealth of technical data on the Ka-52's initial operation with the RAA. According to the document, by 1 September 2014, three RAA front-line and one training squadrons operated a total fleet of 58 helicopters, while in January 2015, 10 more machines were added. The fleet was distributed as follows: 344th TsBPiPLS training centre in Torzhok, eight; 575th AB (AA) in Chernigovka, 22; 393rd AB (AA) in Korennovsk, 16; and 15th BAA in Ostrov, 12. By January 2015, the Ka-52 was introduced with a fourth front-line squadron, operated by the 573rd AB in Khabarovsk, which took 10 newly built machines, plus two of the Chernigovka-based Ka-52s. In early 2015, the Ka-52 fleet of the Korennovsk-based squadron was redistributed to two other bases, complementing the fleet of the Alligator-equipped attack squadron of the 15th BAA in Ostrov and equipping one squadron of the 39th VAP in Dzhankoi. In 2016, the Korennovsk-based regiment took on strength a batch of a dozen new factory-made Ka-52s to replace the 2013-delivered examples that had been handed over to the Ostrov- and Dzhankoy-based units but the actual deliveries did not take place until December.

Well-suited for mountainous operations

As Kamov's test pilot Alexander Tcherdnichenko boasted in 2013, the Ka-52 is simple to control, and pilots who have never flown coaxial helicopters before tend to like the Alligator. They feel pretty comfortable as they understand that the coaxial Ka-52 is easy to control and has a fair response to control inputs.

"We have a working avionics suite fully meeting the requirements of the Russian military," Kamov OKB's veteran pilot Papay told this author in April 2010. Designer-general Sergey Mikheev added that he thinks the Ka-52-equipped front-line units should specialise in mountain operations due to the useful features of the two counter-rotating, three-blade coaxial rotors, which contribute to the helicopter's compact appearance, stability in flight and high agility.

The Ka-52's flight control system is considerably simplified and more reliable compared to that of conventional helicopters, thanks to the lack of a tail rotor. The six rotor blades also reduce vibrations because they mutually suppress their oscillations.

"The pilots who flew the helicopter are convinced that the coaxial rotors sport weighty advantages," claimed Mikheev. "Most if not all of the armed conflicts are happening, as a rule, in hot and high environments and the Ka-52 is more than fit for facing this tough reality."

Another advantage for fighting in mountains, which is more of a psychological factor, is that crew members have a good chance of survival thanks to the ejection seats when operating over rugged terrain, there are few chances of finding a suitable spot for an emergency landing of a damaged helicopter. This is confirmed by Tcherdnichenko, who says:

The most unique feature of this helicopter is the ejection system, which had never been used on any other aircraft before. It is designed to drag the pilot out of almost any emergency situation whether the helicopter is set on fire or shot down or even if it disintegrates in mid-air. The pilot does not have to think about opening the escape hatch without his parachute getting caught on something inside the cockpit. One move [pulling out the ejection seat handles] and he is ejected outside the aircraft. The system has a wide range of use: a pilot could bail out in almost every position, even when almost on the ground.

Availability and reliability data

According to the Russian Helicopters-released presentation, by 20 August 2014, 11 out of 46 warranted RAA Ka-52 with warranties of two years after the hand-over were reported as being in unserviceable condition, which means that the serviceability rate of these helicopters was kept at 76 percent.

The total flying time amassed in 2012 by 16 helicopters in warranty was 487 hours, while in 2013 the total time logged by 32 helicopters grew to 1,888 hours. During the first six months of 2014, the fleet of 46 Ka-52s amassed 1,559 hours. The mean time between failures (MTBF), valid for those helicopters still kept in warranty, in 2012 amounted to 6.54 hours, and in 2013 to 7.3 hours, while during the first six months of 2014 it increased to 7.53 hours.

The experimental operation of the Ka-52 was launched by the VVS CinC order dated 3 September 2011, with two subsequent supplements issued on 28 March 2013 and 5 November 2014. The main aim of the experimental operation effort was to evaluate the Ka-52's tactical-technical, flight, maintenance, ergonomic and combat performance in real-world operational conditions in the air force units. It was also intended to work out the combat employment methods and related flight manuals, and evaluate the overall combat effectiveness of the new attack helicopter. The total flight time amassed during

In order to be able to cope with the expanded mission set in the post-Cold War era, the Alligator has received a sophisticated sensor and data exchange suite, as well as a variety of new air-to-surface and air-to-air missiles. (Yury Gruzevich)

The Ka-52's coaxial layout has a superior aerodynamic performance, resulting in faster and tighter turning, which is an important consideration when operating in mountain conditions and during air combat against other helicopters. (Author)

the experimental operation of the type, completed in April 2015, amounted to 11,172 hours.

The general conclusions, as outlined in the report dedicated to the completion of the Ka-52's experimental operation, are that the overall performance demonstrated during the real-world operation (in front-line and training units) met Russian MoD requirements. This means that the Ka-52 can be operated in air force units within the scope of its intended combat tasks, while taking into consideration the operating limitations set out in the rotorcraft flight manual. The combat employment of the weaponry was possible and safe in both the main and back-up modes, in tested conditions, while the avionics was judged as operable, enabling the Ka-52 in general to perform its assigned combat tasks. Based on these conclusions, the report recommended that the Ka-52 attack helicopter should be commissioned in service with the Russian Federation's Armed Forces.

In late October 2015, the RAA Ka-52 fleet at last received the long-awaited Vikhr-1 ATGMs. The production contract for 1,972 missiles, signed in mid-2013, amounted to 13 billion roubles (equating to about US$419 million at the time of signature). It was awarded by the Russian MoD to the Izhevsk-based Kalashnikov concern (created by merging the two ordinance manufacturing businesses based in the city of Izhevsk-Izmekh and Izhmash). The manufacturer, however, experienced serious difficulties in setting up a smoothly working production line for the new missile, which, in turn, created a number of unwelcome quality issues. As a result, Kalashnikov reportedly failed to meet the original delivery schedule for completion of all deliveries until the end of 2015.

In July 2015, Yury Borisov, Russia's deputy defence minister, responsible for the procurement of new weaponry, acknowledged in front of the Russian press that the Kalashnikov concern had

The Ka-52 aircrews from Korennovsk, Dzhankoi, Torzhok and Chernigovka demonstrated excellent performance in both editions of the Aviadarts-series of gunnery competitions held in the summer of 2015. (Andrey Zinchuk)

reportedly failed to meet its contractual commitments to deliver the ordered numbers of Vikhr-1 ATGMs due to numerous technical issues encountered during the production process. In October the same year, Borisov announced that the faults were at last fixed and the technical documentation had been modified in order to allow Kalashnikov to start producing missiles that are compliant to the quality requirements imposed by the Russian MoD in the contract. The revised delivery schedule, agreed with the Russian MoD, called for the contract completion in spring 2016.

Aviadarts, the proving test of a successful concept

The Alligator fleet had demonstrated an outstanding performance at the Aviadarts series of popular gunnery competitions organised by the Russian air arm, taking first place in a head-to-head competition with the other RAA attack types.

The first event was organised in 2013 under the auspices of newly appointed Defence Minister Sergey Shoigu, the second edition followed in 2014 this time with national and international phases and the intensity reached its peak in 2015, again with national and international phases.

In general, Aviadarts competitions are conceived as multi-stage combat employment events, chiefly intended to select the best aircrews in each separate air branch of the RuASF, who have to demonstrate a balance of skills in all major combat training elements. As a rule, the initial (or so-called pre-qualification) stage of the competition is conducted within the four military districts in Russia and was intended to down-select the best-prepared aircrews for participation in the two follow-on stages. The set of exams in this stage includes checks of the physical fitness and tactical knowledge of the competing aircrews, as well as a gunnery competition within each regiment and air base.

According to the Russian Air Force CinC, Colonel General Vladimir Bondarev, who had been the principal driving force behind the Aviadarts series, the contest is conceived not as a traditional military exercise but as a pure gunnery competition to judge the aircrew skill-sets in accurate firing of aircraft guns and rockets, as well as precise delivery of bombs and air-dropped cargo from low-level flight. Participants are expected to demonstrate a combination of their best skills in employing their aircraft and delivering weapons in various situations.

In 2014, the best attack helicopter crew came from the 393rd Air Base of Army Aviation (AB AA), stationed at Korennovsk (also known as military unit 35666), flying the Ka-52, while second and third places were claimed by crews from the Torzhok-based Army Aviation Combat Training Centre (military unit 45095), which is subordinated to the Lipetsk-based 4th State Field Trials and Aviation Personnel Training Centre. It is noteworthy that the aircrew ranked in second place also flew the Ka-52.

In 2015, the Ka-52's dominance continued in both the national and international phases of Aviadarts. The first part of the competition tested air navigation and aircraft handling technique, combined with a visual search for camouflaged ground targets. The crews were then

The Ka-52 is a very stable platform for firing rockets and the gun thanks to the vibration-free environment and the precise targeting system. This had been proven once again at the Aviadarts-series in 2015. (Andrey Zinchuk)

required to perform their aircraft handling proficiency demonstration in the form of a simple aerobatics routine flown at low altitude in pair formation. Entry of the pairs into the operational area had to be at a set time after the en-route navigation and air reconnaissance phases of the sortie. The helicopters were required to fly their aerobatics routines at altitudes between 200–400m (656–1,312ft). The competition's second part evaluated the gunnery skills. Accuracy of arrival in the assigned time slot at the initial point over the gunnery range was also included in the evaluation criteria. Upon arrival at the range, each crew was assigned targets to be hit in a total of three passes, one of these with 80mm rockets, the second with cannon and the third used as a 'spare', should problems arise during the first or second pass.

Rockets were required to be fired from ranges of 2,500m (8,200ft) down to 1,500m (4,920ft), and cannon from ranges between 1,500–800m (4,920–2,624ft). The helicopters flew in pairs, employing manoeuvres to avoid anti-aircraft fire and evade enemy fighters as soon as they entered the gunnery range.

During the post-sortie judging of the helicopter rocket and gun work, 100 points were assigned in the case of one or more direct hits scored. Hits within the perimeter of an area marked around a target scored 10 points.

The competition's third stage assessed crew fitness through basketball, swimming and pull-up events.

The best attack helicopter crews in the Aviadarts-2015 national phase, held in June at the Pogonovo range near the city of Voronezh, came from the 575th Air Base, stationed at Chernigovka, flying the Ka-52, while second place went to aircrews from the 39th Helicopter

Regiment at Dzhankoi, also flying the Ka-52. Third place was shared between the crews from the Torzhok-based 344th TsBPiPLS of Army Aviation, flying the Ka-52, and the 393rd Air Base at Korennovsk, flying the Mi-35M.

The Aviadarts' international phase, held in August 2015 at the Dubrovichi range near the city of Ryazan, witnessed a total Ka-52 domination. The aircrew from the 39th Helicopter Regiment in Dzhankoi were ranked as the best attack helicopter crew, followed by the 575th Air Base in Chernigovka and the 344th TsBPiPLS of Army Aviation in Torzhok.

Taking so many prizes in several gunnery competitions in succession is hardly a random success, as the Ka-52 aviators train in all units shoulder-to-shoulder with their colleagues flying the Mi-24P, Mi-35M and Mi-28N, using the same syllabus and ranges. The demonstration of better overall results in these gunnery competitions could thus be easily attributed to the superior performance and better handling qualities inherent in the coaxial rotorcraft scheme.

A 'Gator gathering at Ryazan-Dyagilevo airfield during the international Aviadarts event in 2015, with as many as seven machines lined-up and ready to go. (Andrey Zinchuk)

The protocol on completion of the Ka-52's experimental operation was signed in April 2015. At the time, the total flight time amassed by the Alligator under this programme, launched in early 2011, had amounted for 11,172 hours. (Mikhail Lisov)

13

KA-52K FOR THE RUSSIAN NAVY

Early marinisation ideas

All earlier Ka-50 and Ka-52 developments had been related to improving the land-based versions. In fact, the original V-80 was never intended for shipborne operations by the Russian military, but the naval heritage of Kamov OKB had influenced its new attack helicopter design to some extent.

In the late 1980s, the technical projects department at Kamov outlined a design concept for a multi-role shipborne helicopter based on the Ka-50. This was a research project of the company, funded by the Soviet MoD, awarded in a bid to search for novel design solutions to satisfy naval warfare projected needs in the medium-to-long term.

The conceptual design, completed in 1991, represented a two-seat coaxial rotorcraft without armour protection, bearing little resemblance if any to the original Ka-50. The fuselage cross-section in the cockpit area was made much wider than that of the Ka-50, accommodating side-by-side seats for the pilot and navigator-operator, the latter situated to the right and slightly rearwards. The helicopter had a life support system for the crew exposure suits which would ensure survival in cold water, while the nose was shortened in an effort to improve the pilot's view downwards, an important consideration for ship deck landings. The Shkval-V TV/laser targeting system was replaced by a search radar working in the centimetric-length wavelength (X-band). The helicopter also lacked the gun turret and introduced a sealed weapons bay to accommodate an anti-submarine torpedo or depth charges. The empennage received two fins similar to those installed on the tried and tested Ka-27 *Helix*. The new naval helicopter also featured a rescue hoist installed to the port.

The design similarity of the proposed shipborne multi-role helicopter with the Ka-50 could only be found in the engine nacelles,

wings and undercarriage. The project, however, appeared at the wrong time, coinciding with the Soviet Union's break-up, and thus remained on paper only.

The next occasion when the Kamov OKB was asked if it could be able to offer a naval version of its attack model happened in December 2004. A company team, led by chief designer Alexander Vagin, was on a visit to the Marinha do Brasil (MB, Brazilian Navy). The main purpose of this visit was to promote the Ka-32A11BC model for firefighting and the Ka-31 for airborne early warning and control; at the time, the latter had already been inducted in service with the Indian Navy. At the meeting with the MB Commandant, Fleet Admiral Roberto de Guimares Carvalho, Vagin was asked whether the Ka-52 could land on a ship's deck and be armed with lightweight anti-ship missiles. It was a difficult question, but the Kamov OKB team had eventually confirmed that the two-seat Alligator could do the job. The huge expertise and experience in designing and operating shipborne helicopters encouraged the Vagin-led team that a navalised Ka-52 would be possible without any major and potentially costly redesign. Moreover, during the initial design of the single-seat Ka-50, its undercarriage and the stub-wings were made suitable for shipborne operations.

Upon returning home, Vagin reported to Mikheev about the interest expressed by the MB Commandant for a future shipborne version of the Ka-52. Then, based on the Brazilian interest, Mikheev ordered the Ka-52's design team to perform an in-depth analysis of the suitability of the helicopter for operations from rolling and pitching ship desks, where the undercarriage strength would be the limiting factor. The answer was, as expected, positive, because the designers who were responsible for the Ka-50's undercarriage in the past had considered

The first prototype of the Ka-52 during ship suitability trials onboard the large anti-submarine warfare ship *Vice-Admiral Kulakov* sailing in the Barents Sea in 2011. As Mikheev commented, the results from this testing campaign confirmed the expectations, with the 'Gator faring pretty well, even in rough seas. (Vitaly Lebedev archive)

The first Ka-52 prototype landing on French Navy ship *Mistral*. (Sergey Mikheev)

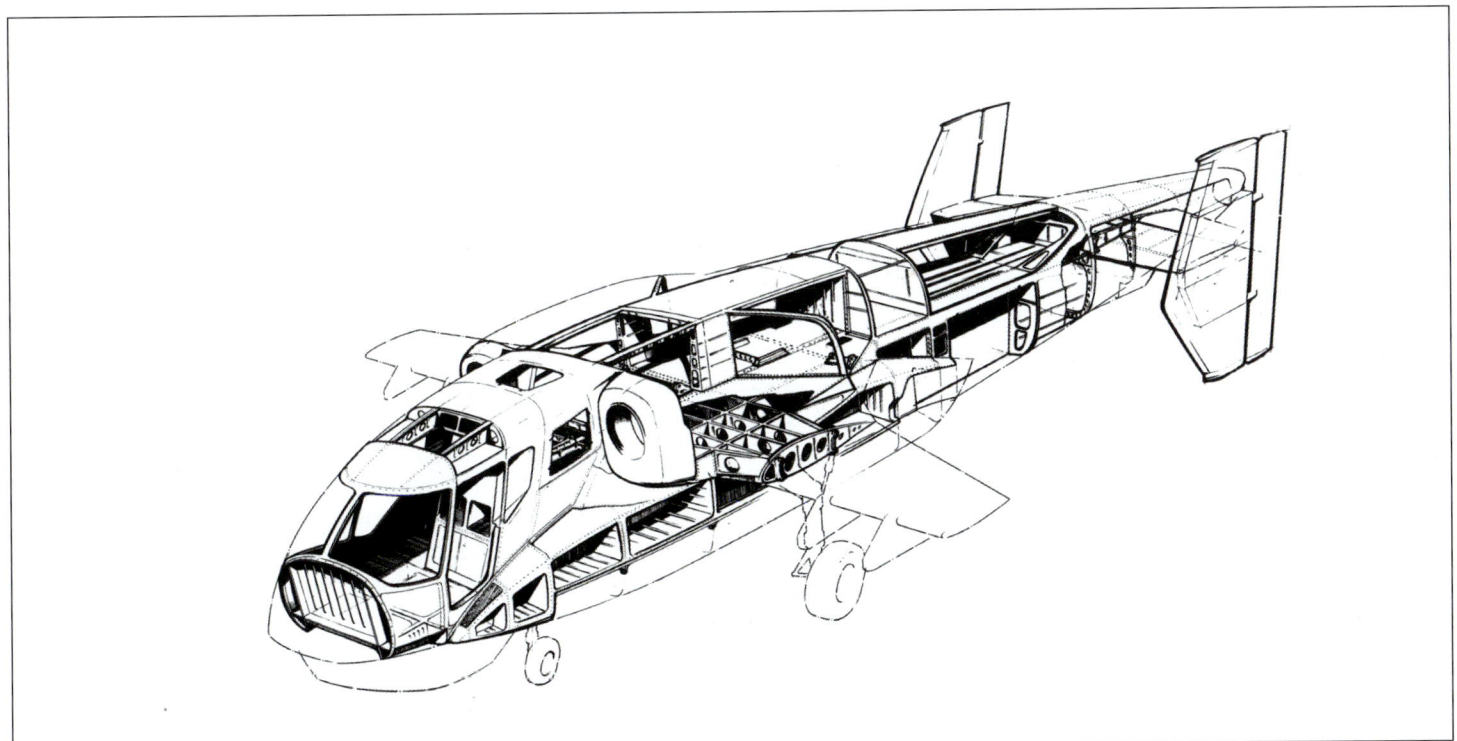

A concept design of the two-seat naval helicopter offered on the Ka-50's base, with an all-new fuselage, optimised for shipborne operations. (Kamov OKB)

Kamov's chief-designer, Alexander Vagin, presents the Ka-52 to Brazilian Navy Commandant, Fleet Admiral Roberto de Guimares Carvalho. (Mikhail Lisov)

such extreme loads. There were no issues at all with the anti-ship missiles, as the Kh-35 had already been tested from the Ka-27; its integration onboard the Ka-52 was deemed to be a straightforward undertaking, provided that funding was made available.

The interest in a shipborne Alligator derivative reappeared four years later when the Russian MoD decided to buy four amphibious assault, command and power projection ships. The aviation group of each ship was to include up to 16 helicopters — a mixture of attack Ka-52Ks, assault transport Ka-29s and transport/SAR Ka-27PSs; the ratio between the three types would depend on the specific mission requirements.

In fact, as Sergey Mikheev recalls, the requirement for a dedicated landing deck-capable derivative of the Alligator in the late 2000s was an unexpected but otherwise welcome turn for the Ka-52 programme, that happened only thanks to the Russian Navy's interest in procuring the *Mistral*-class ship. He also asserted that during the design phase of the Ka-50 in the early 1980s, the Kamov OKB built in a set of solutions that would make it suitable for shipborne operations.

Mistral deck trials

The first Ka-52 prototype carried out the evaluation of the deck suitability and undercarriage design, operating off the flight deck of French Navy amphibious assault ship *Mistral* during her visit to St Petersburg in November/December 2008. It was the pinnacle of the large-scale promotional campaign sponsored by the French government. This was, in fact, a personal undertaking by French President Nicolas Sarkozy, who had energetically promoted the *Mistral* sale to Russia. His Russian counterpart, Vladimir Putin, had

eventually agreed to purchase the ships – this act was portrayed as an appreciation of the much-needed French political support that Russia received soon after the war with Georgia over the territory of South Ossetia in August 2008.

The ship sale was also a significant support that the French government was keen to provide to national shipbuilder DCNS, which had been struggling with an unimpressive order book. All previous attempts by France to find new export customers for the rather expensive *Mistral*-class ships had proved fruitless in the face of fierce competition from other European manufacturers.

In order to meet the Russian legislation governing public procurement contracts, the Russian MoD had to organise a formal tender, where the other bidders were Spanish and South Korean shipbuilding companies. In the event, their offers were rejected as non-compliant and the French proposal was deemed the only one fully meeting Russian Navy requirements.

In November 2009, even before the completion of the tender that had to select the preferred contractor to build the Russian Navy's new power projection ships, the French government had sponsored a visit of *Mistral* to St Petersburg, with the chief intent to show that the ship could meet the helicopter suitability and other requirements raised by the potential customer. The Kamov OKB was also invited to visit the ship and bring its helicopters onboard *Mistral* for conducting limited compatibility tests.

The Kamov OKB team, led by designer-general Sergey Mikheev, embarked onboard the *Mistral* on 24 November to perform a survey of the flight deck, hangars and electronic systems. In addition, three helicopter types were slated to be tested – one Ka-52 owned by

French Navy ship *Mistral* during her visit to St Petersburg in November 2008. (Sergey Mikheev)

the Kamov OKB plus a Ka-27PL and Ka-29, both belonging to the Russian Naval Aviation Service (AVMF), operated by the Northern Fleet's 380th Independent Helicopter Regiment at Severomorsk-1 airfield near Murmansk.

The Ka-52 prototype departed the company flight test centre at Zhulebino, and during its ferry flight to Levashovo near St Petersburg was crewed by company test pilot Alexander Smirnov and a military test pilot, as this mission had been integral to the type's intense flight testing programme. The ferry flight, however, proved to be very difficult and tense due to the bad weather. The first refuelling stop was made at Torzhok, where the helicopter landed with a navigation system failure in very low visibility conditions. Nevertheless, the landing approach was performed in a safe manner thanks to the flying skills of Smirnov, who had to use back-up instruments. The helicopter was promptly repaired by a RPKB team dispatched personally by the company designer-general, Givi Djandzhava, to fix the helicopter, enabling it to arrive in St Petersburg just on time for the deck trials.

Early the next day, the Ka-52 continued its flight to Levashovo airfield near St Petersburg, but arrived late. The Ka-27PS and Ka-29 had already departed for their *Mistral* trials. The Ka-52 crew had to compensate for the delay and were notified that they would be restricted to only using the ship's rearmost landing spot. The reason for this was related to the concern of jettisoning the rotor blades in the event of crew ejection due to a bad landing approach. In addition, the Ka-52 was required to be without weapons on its external pylons. There was no time to remove the mock-up weapons, so it was decided the helicopter be despatched as it was because *Mistral* was about to leave the Gulf of Finland, having no time to wait for the Ka-52's arrival.

In the event, the Ka-52 crew managed to take off from Levashovo and find *Mistral* at sea, literally at the last possible moment, while

its avionics, which had been creating serious troubles during the ferry flight, worked flawlessly. After establishing visual contact with the ship, Smirnov made a low pass over the deck and entered into a left-hand turn, aiming to land on the rearmost spot. Mikheev, who monitored the landing, later commented that the helicopter had arrived and touched down on the deck 'just like it was at home'. The *Mistral* deck servicing crew promptly approached the Ka-52 with a fuel hose, demonstrating the ability to perform 'hot' refuelling with rotors turning. After filling the tanks with gas, the helicopter lifted off to applause from the guests and hosts from the *Mistral's* crew. The landing and refuelling cycle was repeated three times, and the helicopter departed for Levashovo after performing a low-level/high-speed pass over the deck. All the senior officers of the ship cheered the Alligator and greeted Mikheev and the Russian Navy CinC, Admiral Nikolay Kuklev.

The ship survey had revealed that the height of the hangars and aircraft elevator size was sufficient to house both the Ka-52 and Ka-27/29 families, but next to the elevators the height was lower than the minimum required, rendering it impossible to move the Ka-27 and Ka-29 from the elevator into the hangar and back. This, together with a good many other elements of the ship structure, had to be redesigned; the list of improvements added to the *Mistral's* Russian derivative had also included strengthening the hull for operation in extreme Northern conditions with ice on the sea surface, providing a heating system for the flight deck (needed for operating in extreme cold weather conditions, avoiding ice accretion) and arming the ship with SAMs for self-defence as well as installing Russian-made navigation and communications equipment.

The Ka-52's return flight home also proved an adventure as the navigation system failed once again when the helicopter approached

Ka-52 '061' ready for lift-off on *Mistral's* deck, with two members of the deck-servicing crew rushing to remove the chocks. (Sergey Mikheev)

While the Ka-52 is being secured on the flight deck, a group of *Mistral* deck-service crewmen line-up for a photo in front of it. (Sergey Mikheev)

Ka-52 '061' streaking over the *Mistral's* deck in a high-speed pass. (Sergey Mikheev)

Moscow. The helicopter then hit bad weather, with torrential rain and almost zero-visibility en-route, but skilled pilot Smirnov once again managed to cope with the difficult situation. He first got to the Moscow ring road, and then, flying above this distinctive landmark, managed to reach Zhulebino, landing there at dusk in the worst possible visibility conditions.

The contract between the Russian MoD and a consortium made up of France's DCNS and Russia's United Shipbuilding Corp. for purchasing the ships was eventually agreed in June 2011. It covered the purchase of two modified *Mistral*-class ships, to be built at the STX shipyard in St Nazaire, France, with an option for two more to be built in Russia at a later stage using all the technical documentation developed for the first pair.

The first of the two France-built ships ordered for the Russian Navy, named *Vladivostok,* was slated to be ready for hand-over in November 2014, earmarked to be operated by Russia's Pacific Fleet. The second ship, named *Sevastopol*, was slated to follow soon afterwards, again to be delivered to the Pacific Fleet.

Naval-specific design features

The supplement to the Ka-52's technical and tactical assignment (specification) issued by the VVS and AVMF called for the development of a dedicated shipborne version designated Ka-52K (internal Kamov OKB designation *Item 820*). It was required to have a newly designed rotor column with manually folded rotors, new radar, all-new aircrew life-support system, new air conditioning unit, newly added emergency flotation gear and new navigation aids for deck landings. The airframe also had to feature enhanced corrosion resistance, while the stub wings were required to fold, together with the rotor, in order to reduce the footprint when stored inside a ship's hangar or on crammed flight decks.

The shipborne Ka-52K, christened by Mikhev 'Katran' (Spiny Dogfish), retained unchanged both the targeting suite and weapons mix of the baseline model, as well as the powerplant and transmission.

The most complex task at the Kamov OKB was to design the folding rotors, as the design solution used in the 1970s on the Ka-27 could not be implemented as it was on the Ka-52K. The reason for that was the novel design of the Ka-52's rotor blades that feature semi-rigid suspension and torsion bearings in the form of steel plates. The design solution was a non-standard one and offered manually folding rotor blades, with a folding and unfolding time of around one minute; the blades have no additional operating limitations imposed compared to those of the land-based variant.

As Mikheev explained, the Ka-52K's wings were initially planned to fold upwards, and a scale model with this folding scheme had even been demonstrated at several defence shows. However, it turned out that such a wing-folding scheme would be incompatible with the engine cowlings when opened to enable the ground personnel to perform routine engine inspections or maintenance. As a result, a new folding scheme was offered, with the shortened movable sections of the wings stowed aft, rotating around a hinge on the trailing edge, next to the weapons pylon. This new wing-folding scheme had no adverse effect on the flight performance and combat load, but due to the shorter-span wings (compared to the wings of the land-based variant), the shipborne Ka-52K was provided with only four weapons pylons compared to six on its land-based forebear, while retaining the same load-carrying ability.

Moreover, as Mikheev noted, the inner wing pylons had been strengthened in a bid for each to be able to carry up to 1,000kg (2,200lb) of weapons. This, in turn, would enable the Ka-52K to take onboard two Kh-35 anti-ship missiles. This new ordinance load, however, would require integrating an all-new radar for long-range target detection and missile designation. The current Ka-band FH-01 Arbalet-52, inherited from the ground-based Alligator, is optimised for overland use and would be ill-suited for anti-ship missions due to its insufficient range, extending to no more than 20km (11nm). That is why the Ka-52K is planned to be equipped in the future with an X-band radar boasting a meaningful range against sea surface targets, exceeding 150km (81nm) when employed to detect and track large ships.

For the Ka-52's shipborne derivative, Phazotron-NIIR had proposed a new dual-band radar, based on the FH-01 Arbalet design and featuring an additional centimetric-wavelength channel (working in the X-band, emitting at 3cm wavelength). It would be optimised for detection of sea surface targets, capable of detecting large ships at a distance of between 150–180km (81–97nm).

Phazotron-NIIR's designer-general, Yuriy Guskov, maintained in 2012 that, in principle, the dual-wavelength capability could be provided by both the original mechanical-scan parabolic antenna of the FH-01 Arbalet-52 (by utilising two separate emitters for the millimetric and centimetric wavelenths) or by introducing a purpose-designed electronic scan active phased array. The former option, however, is considered far more affordable and may be implemented in the late 2010s.

The Russian MoD had not yet made a firm decision on the radar type to be used on the follow-on Ka-52Ks, as the four pre-production examples built at the AAC Progress plant in 2015 and 2016 retain the Ka-52's original millimetric-wavelength set.

The huge Kh-35 anti-ship missile had already been test-fitted onto the inner wing pylon of the second Ka-52 prototype, serialled '062', which was also used as a test-bed to evaluate in flight the rearward-folding wing design and rearwards-folding rotors.

More sea trials

In August 2011, the Ka-52's first prototype underwent extensive ship suitability trials, operating off the small deck of the Russian Northern Fleet's large anti-submarine ship (Project 1155) *Vice-Admiral Kulakov*, sailing in Kola Bay in the Barents Sea. The choice of this ship was a compromise solution since the landing deck of *Vice-Admiral Kulakov* was judged to be too small, able to accommodate only two Ka-27 helicopters. However, there was no better alternative to be used for sea trails at the time, since the lone Russian aircraft carrier, *Admiral Kuznetsov*, was in prolonged repairs. The only real choices included Project 1155 ships (such as *Vice-Admiral Kulakov*) and the Project 956 destroyers, but the latter offered an even smaller helicopter deck.

The helicopter was flown by Vitaly Lebedev, a Kamov test pilot with great naval flight operations expertise and experience under his belt. It was accumulated on the Ka-25 and Ka-27 helicopters, flown predominantly from small-size ships. The second crew member was test navigator Evgeniy Savin.

Ka-52 '061' deployed to Severomorsk-1 airfield near Murmansk and commenced the deck suitability flight testing campaign on 31 August. In two weeks it accumulated 35 sorties, with numerous landings on the deck of *Vice-Admiral Kulakov* when moored and on the move in Kola Bay, exploring in full the capabilities of the Ka-52 to land and take-off from rolling and pitching decks. The maximum deck pitch during these operations reached 5° and the wind speed was 20m/s (3,936f/m). The ship's stern displacement experienced at maximum pitch was around 0.5m (1.6ft) in sea surface state one (with wave height of just 00.1 metres/00.33ft), making landings on the small deck much more difficult than those on the much more stable large amphibious assault ships.

Lebedev flew the shipborne trials with landings performed in all possible methods, including in parallel closure with subsequent lateral movement to hover over the deck centre. The programme

A Ka-52 '061' during testing on the landing deck of the large ASW ship *Vice-Admiral Kulakov* near Murmansk, September 2011. (Vitaly Lebedev archive)

Sergey Mikheev with test pilot Vitaly Lebedev (on the left) and test navigator Vladimir Yurtaev. (Vitaly Lebedev archive)

also included exploring the go-around capabilities of the helicopter in various emergency situations; the crew members noted that the Ka-52 could perform a safe go-around at any point of the glideslope and also during a rough landing. The list of shortcomings revealed during this testing campaign included the poor visibility over the nose when closing to the deck, which size was limited by the hangar wall. Mikheev, however, commented that the Ka-52K was intended for operations from the decks of larger ships so this problem was not so acute and would not necessitate any radical redesign. At the same time, Lebedev noted that the Ka-52 was even better suited for shipborne operations compared to the Ka-27 family, thanks to its lower maximum height (by 410mm) and corresponding lower centre of gravity position, in combination with the longer undercarriage base (the distance between the front and main undercarriage units). As a result, these features rendered the Ka-52 much more stable when on the moving ship deck. In addition, the design of the main undercarriage unit shock absorbers enabled a shorter lift-off time.

In development and production

The Ka-52K development contract between Kamov and the Russian MoD was eventually signed in 2012. It called for full-scale development works and construction of four pre-production aircraft at the AAC Progress plant. The contract price amounted to 3,396 billion roubles (equating to about US$110 million at the time). A contract between Kamov and AAC Progress for the production of four prototypes was then signed on 16 September 2013, with all the helicopters originally slated to be handed over by October 2014. Following this, a batch of 32 production-standard Ka-52Ks were to be delivered to the Russian Navy's aviation service from 2015 onwards, under a separate contract

signed between AAC Progress and the Russian MoD.

The original development programme schedule called for the first experimental Ka-52K to be handed over to the Kamov OKB for full-scale testing and evaluation in 2013, while all four examples ordered had to be delivered by October 2014. The programme, however, suffered from a serious delay due to the need to solve numerous technical issues, with all the new technical solutions initially tested on the Kamov-owned Ka-52 prototypes and pre-series machines. The main reason for this slippage had been attributed to the constantly changing requirements of the customer, the Russian Naval Aviation, leading to a good many design alterations that required time and effort to be tested and then implemented on the production line.

The first pre-production Ka-52K shipborne helicopter (c/n 01-01) made its maiden flight on 7 March 2015 at manufacturer AAC Progress' airfield in Arsenyev, Russia, flown by the Kamov OKB test pilot Nail Azin and test navigator Alexander Shveikin. Four months later, this machine was displayed in public for the first time at the Naval Salon in St Petersburg held in July 2015; next to it, the Kh-35U and Kh-38E missiles proposed for integration were shown. The Ka-52K was then displayed at the MAKS-2015 air show, held at Zhukovsky airfield near Moscow in August.

The eagerly anticipated contract covering the delivery of 32 production-standard Ka-52Ks was signed on 8 April 2014 by the Russian MoD and AAC Progress. The first 12 of these Katrans were to be ready for delivery during 2015, but the handover date later slipped to 2016 and then 2017. Also in 2014, Russian simulation technology specialist TsNTU Dinamika was awarded a contract for the delivery of two simulator training complexes for the Ka-52K, with delivery deadline set at 25 November 2014. The first of these was required

Ka-52 '061' hovers next to the prow of *Vice-Admiral Kulakov*. (Vitaly Lebedev archive)

to be set up at the Russian Naval Aviation training centre at Yeisk, while the second was earmarked for installation at the naval airbase in Nikolayevka, north of Vladivostok.

Mistral deal cancelled

The Ka-52Ks was originally intended to be operated from the two *Mistral*-class amphibious assault ships, with each of these able to take on board up to eight Ka-52Ks, in addition to eight more Ka-27/29s.

After the French government's eventual refusal to hand over the ships in 2014 due to newly raised tensions surrounding Russia's involvement in the crisis in Ukraine, and the subsequent termination of the contract by mutual convenience in August 2015, the first batch of eight to 10 production-standard Ka-52Ks, originally slated to be handed over to the AVMF in 2015, was most likely to be delivered in 2016–2017 at the earliest and fielded with a newly formed shore-based attack helicopter squadron. It was expected to be established within the structure of the service's 7062nd Air Base at Nikolayevka, assigned to the Pacific Fleet, situated not far from Vladivostok.

The *Mistral* contract termination by mutual agreement was followed by the prompt return of the payment for the ships to Russia, to the amount of nearly 1 billion euros. At the same time, as Mikheev claimed in August 2015, nobody in Russia had been rushing to cancel the Ka-52K's production order.

The Russian Navy currently has only two ship classes that would be suitable, at least in theory, to carry the Ka-52 Project 1174 *Ivan Rogov* can accommodate up to four helicopters (but none of the three ships of the class is currently in operational use), while the newly built

Project 11711 *Ivan Gren'* and *Pyotr Morgunov* can take up to two. In addition, Russia's United Shipbuilding Corp claimed in 2015 that it could propose larger assault landing ships, capable of accommodating up to 16 helicopters, but the first of these would not be ready before 2022 at the earliest. There is not yet an order placed by the Russian MoD for such a class of ships, so it could be expected to materialise no earlier than 2018.

According to Mikheev, the Kamov OKB is well suited to develop follow-on Ka-50 and Ka-52 derivatives for naval use. One of his novel proposals calls for an airborne early warning (AEW) version, utilising an array of conformal radar antenna panels for 360° coverage and electronic boxes housed in external pods. Mikheev claimed that such a design would be better than the current Ka-31 designed in the late 1980s that features a large rotating antenna under the fuselage that creates huge stability and control problems and requires the use of a sophisticated automatic flight control system. The resultant AEW helicopter based on the Ka-50 or Ka-52 will be more compact and boast a considerably higher performance than the Ka-31.

In regard to the naval-specific features of the Ka-52, Mikheev is sure that some of these could also be used with success on the land-based version. This is especially true of the folding rotors, which are a useful feature for helicopters operating in desert or extreme cold conditions. The land-based Ka-52 with folding rotors and wings has a much smaller footprint, and can therefore be accommodated in smaller hangars for ease of its servicing in a hot climate. The same is true for helicopters operating in Arctic conditions, where small heated hangars can be used for helicopter maintenance and storage.

Ka-52 '062' was used as the test bed for the design novelties implemented on the Ka-52K such as the shortened, folding wings and the folding rotor blades. (Kamov OKB)

Ka-52 '062' on the ground, just before lifting off for a demo ride with the Russian Vice-Prime Minister, Dmitry Rogozin, in the right-hand seat. The helicopter is equipped with the new OPS-52 targeting payload. (Alexey Mikheev)

Ka-52's second prototype, '062', armed with a Kh-35U anti-ship missile on the reinforced inner starboard stub-wing pylon. (Kamov OKB)

The first pre-production Ka-52K, equipped with the new OPS-52 payload, with rotors and wings folded at the MAKS-2015 air show. (Author)

The first Ka-52K seen in flight during initial testing in Arsenyev, carrying a pair of 500kg (1,100lb) iron bombs under the inner pylons, used as ballast. (AAC Progress)

A close-up view of the Ka-52K's rotor column with blades folded. (Author)

The first pre-production Ka-52K, armed with Vikhr-1 ATGMs and rocket packs, and equipped with the GOES-451 payload, with the wings and rotors unfolded. (Andrey Zinchuk)

A close-up of the port wing in folded (stowed) position, carrying an APU-M six-round launcher unit for the 9M120-1 Ataka-1 ATGM. The left-hand wing with the outer weapons pylon is shown in the stowed position. (Author)

14

KA-52 FOR EXPORT

First export steps

At the MAKS-2013 airshow, Kamov and SAGEM of France signed a letter of intent for exploring the option of integrating the modern Strix optronic payload onto the Ka-52. First trials of the new system onboard the Alligator were tentatively slated for 2014, but this was eventually cancelled. The next step in the 'Westernisation' of the Ka-52, in order to be made more attractive for export, called for the integration of weapons upon customer request. European weaponry manufacturer MBDA was touted as the most likely supplier, but this never happened, so the export version of the Alligator offered in 2015 and 2016 retained an all-Russian armament and mission avionics.

Commissioning with the RuAF in the early 2010s had vastly improved the export chances of the Ka-52, and the most likely future customers are expected to come from the likes of traditional buyers of modern Russian weapons such as Algeria, as well as some ex-Soviet republics from Central Asia.

Alexander Mikheev, formerly deputy director general of Rosoboronexport, Russia's arms sales monopolist and now director general of Russian Helicopters Holding, claimed in public in June 2013 that the first export contract for the Ka-52 was set to be inked by the year-end, but he had refused to name the customer due to confidentiality considerations. Mikheev added that there were several Ka-52 versions on offer for export, each being tailored for performing a specific mission (i.e. equipped with a specific targeting suite and armed with the corresponding guided and unguided arsenal) such as attack, armed reconnaissance and counter-terrorism. In the event, no export contract was signed for the Ka-52 in 2013.

However, two years later, in August 2015, it was surprisingly revealed that a large-scale deal covering as many as 46 Kamov Ka-52 attack helicopters had already been agreed between Russia and Egypt. The news was confirmed for the first time in public during the detailed examination of the Ka-52K at the static display by a group of high-ranking Egyptian officers. This happened on the first day of the MAKS-2015 air show, held in Zhukovsky near Moscow, on 25 August 2015. According to eyewitnesses of the event (among whom was the author of this book), the Egyptian generals and officers already looked like the helicopter was theirs – in the way as buyers tend to review an elite stallion's teeth just after the purchase.

The first news of the Ka-52 contract for Egypt, which had become the launch export customer for the type, had actually surfaced just before MAKS-2015. It was a news release by the SPP NPK company, which developed a new observation and targeting day/night payload for the Ka-52 dubbed OPS-52. The company hinted that it had received an order for "about 50" OPS-52 systems intended to equip Ka-52s slated for delivery to Egypt between 2016 and 2019.

Egypt's strong interest in the Ka-52 had originated from its need to suppress the two-year insurgency raging across the Suez Canal in the Sinai Peninsula and the worsening internal security situation in neighbouring Libya, which threatened to evolve into a cross-border conflict in the foreseeable future.

Deal disclosed

Finally, on 29 December 2015, Russian Helicopters director-general Alexander Mikheev acknowledged the existence of a contract for 46 Ka-52 coaxial rotor attack helicopters for Egypt. It was placed through Rosobornexport, Russia's monopolist arms export agent, and the first deliveries were slated for early 2017. The production contract for the Ka-52 for Egypt was signed between Rosobornexport and AAC Progress in October 2015.

The export-standard Ka-52s to be built for the Egyptian military are set to be equipped with the new OES-52 targeting system installed under the nose. Developed by the Moscow-based SPP NPK company, it replaces the much bulkier and heavier UOMZ GOES-451 optronic payload which equips the RuASF Ka-52 and the AVMF Ka-52Ks.

At the same time, the export-standard Ka-52 is set to retain both the Ataka-1 and Vikhr-1 anti-tank laser beam-riding guided missiles (guided by sensors built in the OES-52 system), as well as the Igla-V air-to-air missiles.

The annual production output at the AAC Progress plant is set to increase threefold in 2017–2018, which means that the number of Ka-52 helicopters to be rolled out will rise to 25–30. This quantity would be enough to meet the annual delivery requirements of the VVS, AVMF and a couple of export customers.

In the event, the two long-suffering *Mistral* class amphibious assault ships were sold to Egypt and it is now expected the country will place an order for the Ka-52K shipborne attack helicopters. On 23 September 2015, Egypt and France finally agreed on the principle and terms of the acquisition of the ships originally built for Russia, rendered surplus after the termination of the purchase agreement. French President Francois Hollande's office confirmed this news after he spoke with his Egyptian counterpart, Abdel Fattah Al-Sisi, to agree the deal. The contract was eventually inked in October 2015, while paid about US$1 billion for the two ships, with a significant amount of the financing coming from Saudi Arabia.

In December 2015, a Russian government official confirmed that there were initial talks held between Russia and Egypt on the possible Ka-52K sale. He also claimed that in case of signing a Ka-52K export contract with Egypt in early 2016, the first deliveries could be possible in 2017. In late March 2016, Rossoboronexport officials confirmed that talks on the Ka-52K sales had been held with Egyptian military representatives.

In the meantime, sources from Moscow close to Rossoboronexport tended to hint that a production-standard Ka-52 was sent for a live demonstration in an unnamed country (believed to be Algeria), with a brief testing campaign conducted there in the second half of September 2015. The list of the demonstrations in that country had also included firing of five Ataka-1 missiles. One of these was launched tail-on at a very small, high-speed air target, simulated by a 9K11 Malutka subsonic ATGM, scoring a successful direct hit.

15
BUT WHAT ABOUT THE BLACK SHARK AND KAMOV?

Watching the Ka-52s participating in the Victory Day flypast over Red Square in Moscow on 9 May 2015, many Kamov OKB employees had sadly remembered the single-seat Black Shark. "Anyway, the Ka-50 looked like a real predator," they tended to say; this slogan was not new, as it had been repeated tens or hundreds of times during the testing effort of the two-seat version and during its air displays. The look of the Ka-52 is much more different when seen from the front and side-on, as the two-seater features a notably enlarged and somewhat fatter nose section that spoils the original sleek predatory appearance of its single-seat predecessor.

There had been many disputes on the subject of the single-seat Ka-50: including whether it was a conceptual mistake or not? Mikheev himself is more than confident that the single-seat configuration had been the right design solution at the time, and therefore it cannot in any way be called a mistake or compromise. The high level of automation of the flight control functions, including those in low altitude flight, in addition to the target search and missile guidance functions, are seen as being a worldwide trend now. But the Kamov OKB team had simply been ahead of its time, anticipating the game-changing technology and tactics developments in the late 1970s and early 1980s.

In the last decades of the existence of the Soviet Union, the trend to respond to the technical solutions pioneered by the everlasting opponent (i.e. USA) became omnipresent. So it had been expected that the Soviet response to the Hughes (now Boeing) AH-64 Apache would sport a good many similarities with it, including the same design layout and technologies. But this had not been the case with the Ka-50, as the head of the Kamov OKB decided to follow his own way. In the event, the Mikheev-led design house had proved able to design, test and launch into production a single-seat coaxial attack helicopter, seen as a completely different and capable beast.

Mikheev, however, would agree with the argument that a two-seat Ka-50 derivative had to be developed sooner or later for conversion training of pilots destined to fly the single-seat Ka-50. He still believes that there will be demand for a single-seat attack rotorcraft, which could also be offered in the form of an optionally piloted vehicle. The far simpler to fly coaxial helicopter is also much easier for automation of flight control functions than its conventional counterpart when converted to optionally piloted rotorcraft.

Kamov's team led by Mikheev had eventually succeeded in designing, developing and testing the Ka-50 and Ka-52, going through hard times, including the Soviet Union's break-up and the market economy establishment. Many of the team members, who had a sizeable contribution to the design, development, testing, production and introduction into service of the Black Shark and Alligator, had passed away, including designers Sergey Fomin and Genady Yakemenko, as well as pilots Evgeny Laryushin and Boris Vorobyov. The fathers of the Ka-50/52's long-range sting, the Vikhr ATGM, and its main bite, the 30mm 2A42 cannon, Arkady Gryazev and Vladimir Shipunov, had also died. In the summer of 2015, the company paid tribute to Leonid Ginsburg, a real commissar of the Kamov OKB, a long-time head of the Communist organisation and later on one of the closest associates of Mikheev.

Today, the Kamov OKB is a very different company than it used to be in the early 1990s as it has lost a lot of its capabilities. In the late 2000s, the company even lost its independence and now exists as a

The latest developments around the Ka-52K programme included a shipborne testing in the summer of 2016, and then a long cruise onboard the aircraft carrier *Admiral Kuznetsov* followed between October 2016 and February 2017, where the Ka-52K amassed both test and operations sorties in the Atlantic and the Mediterranean. (Alexey Mikheev)

fully owned business unit of Russian Helicopters, the state-controlled umbrella holding company that acts as the managing body of Russia's entire rotorcraft industry. The Kamov OKB, however, is not among the favoured companies within the holding, as it is in essence a non-profit organisation – the company has too many designers, its activity associated with too much design and development risk, too many new ideas and costs incurred during research and development activities. The historic company flight test station in Zhulebino, Moscow, where all its new rotorcraft types had made their maiden flights, including the Black Shark and Alligator, is also near the end of its existence. Russian Helicopters' top management has moved Kamov OKB personnel to the newly-built research and development centre in Panki and plans to sell the company's main building complex situated at 8 March Str in the Moscow suburb of Lyubertsi. This is a place with a historical significance for the Soviet/Russian rotorcraft industry, where the first Soviet-designed helicopter, the KASKR, made its maiden flight.

But this is not the end of the story for the famous Russian rotorcraft design bureau. The coaxial rotor specialist is still alive and actively working, with the Ka-226T, Ka-32A11BC, Ka-31 and Ka-52 running into production, while the new Ka-62 made its maiden flight in 2016, and there are a lot of new projects in the pipeline. The Kamov OKB also expects to regain its flight-test branch situated in Feodosya, Crimea, which had struggled for more than 20 years under

Mikheev meets Russian President Vladimir Putin at the company static display line during the MAKS-2005 air show. (Sergey Mikheev archive)

The Ka-50 single-seater sports much more predatory looks than its two-seat successor Ka-52, but the programme is now practically dead, with little chance of resurrection in the foreseeable future. (Dmitry Pichugin)

The Ka-50 open-air storage at Torzhok airfield in early 2015, with three Black Sharks sitting idle and awaiting their eventual fate. (Mikhail Lisov)

The assembly line at the AAC Progress plant had worked at full swing since 2010. (Author)

The two-seat 'Gator will eventually see service-wide operation within the RAA, becoming its principal new-generation attack type, with existing orders sufficient to equip no fewer than nine attack squadrons. (Mikhail Lisov)

Ukrainian jurisdiction. Furthermore, the Alligator is now routinely flying in Crimean skies, something that until recently was possible only in computer games. Finally, three Ka-52s were also deployed in March 2016 to Latakya/Hmeimim Air Base in Syria to take part in the Russian campaign against the full spectrum of radical Islamists and other anti-Assad militant groups. Life goes on, and the Ka-50/52 story also goes on, developing in a certain positive direction.

APPENDIX I

KA-52 TECHNICAL DESCRIPTION

Two-seat cockpit layout

The Ka-52 was originally designed in the late 1990s as a reconnaissance/attack helicopter for the twenty-first century, boasting a fully digital targeting suite for all-weather day/night operations and the capability to integrate into the command-and-control (C2) system deployed by Russian military forces onto the future battlefield. Its two-member crew was provided with sophisticated sensors and datalinks, allowing them to be all-seeing and all-knowing, while the Vikhr-1 and Ataka-1 ATGMs and the highly accurate 2A42 cannon made them all-powerful for knocking-out small hardened ground and sea targets.

Sergey Mikheev explained:

Our original design goal was to achieve as much commonality with the single-seat Ka-50 and that is why we introduced a new two-seat nose module only, while the rest of [the] fuselage [remained] untouched. This smart design solution greatly eased the launch of the series production effort and the AAC Progress aviation plant

in Arsenyev commenced manufacturing the machines of the first series batch by utilising a great proportion of existing Ka-50 components. Design commonality between the Ka-50 and Ka-52 is no less than 85 percent.

The unorthodox side-by-side accommodation of the Ka-52 crew, seen by many in Russia and abroad as a drastic departure from the traditional use of tandem, stepped cockpits, as featured on all such attack rotorcraft types since the Bell AH-1 Cobra, was actually a requirement supported by experienced combat pilots from the Torzhok-based combat training centre with a lot of combat experience under their belts. "When crewmen sit side-by-side, they enjoy much easier and faster communication between them [compared to the tandem cockpit configuration]. In most cases they can understand each other without talking at all, using body language only," says Colonel (Retired) Alexander Papay, the Kamov company's veteran chief test pilot and a former highly experienced military test pilot.

The absence of a tail rotor gives another notable advantage to the Ka-52, namely the ability to utilise all the effectiveness of the aircraft's directional control system to attain pretty high yaw rates. (Author)

The cockpit is equipped with dual controls and the left-seat pilot also has an ILS-31 head-up display for piloting and employing the forward-firing guided and unguided weapons. The pilot is responsible for handling, general system monitoring, firing cannon and rockets in addition to launching air-to-air missiles and ATGMs. The WSO is responsible for solving a multitude of tactical and navigation tasks, target search, detection, identification and acquisition, accuracy of fire assessment, self-defence, datalink operation and provision of external targeting to other platforms, in addition to assisting the pilot in handling the helicopter in high-workload situations.

Armour protection and aircrew rescue

The 40mm-thick flat armoured windshield can withstand hits of projectiles up to 12.7mm calibre, while an extra side-on protection for the pilots is provided by side armour and canopy scabbed-on armour screens. Further crew protection is provided as the pilots, wearing armour vests and sitting side-by-side, also screen each other with their bodies in case of projectiles and high-speed missile warhead fragments entering the cockpit.

The nose fuselage is also armour-protected side-on from projectiles up to 23mm calibre using dual-layer armour protection combining steel (outside) and aluminium plating (inside). According to Mikheev, the overall weight of the armour protection used in the Ka-52 proved less than that of an equally protected tandem-cockpit combat helicopter in the same weight class.

The Ka-52 retains the Ka-50's proven Zvezda K-37-800M ejection seats, ensuring simultaneous bailout of both crew members through the canopy after jettisoning the rotor blades. This is carried out by using explosive charges installed in the blade fastening, while the glazing of the two-part, sideways-opening canopy is jettisoned by explosive cord integrated in it. The crew members are then dragged

out by a rocket, with a subsequent immediate parachute deployment during the ejection sequence. The rocket is connected to a lanyard used to extract the aircrew, while the seat itself remains inside the helicopter. This fully integrated ejection system ensures aircrew safe bailout at speeds between 90–350km/h (49–189kt), and at altitudes from zero to 5,000m (16,400ft). The pilot and WSO are ejected at different trajectories in order to avoid midair collision between them. The system is cleared for ejection of aircrew wearing the ZSh-7VS (ZSh-7V) protective helmet with mounted NVG set. The crew members can wear MSK-5 immersion suits and NAZ-Ir emergency vests.

Each of the seats together with the rocket assembly housed in a large white cylinder on top weighs 57kg (126lb). Time from activation to crewmen landing during ground-level ejection is 46 seconds. Time from activation to escaping the rotor system is 0.71 seconds.

In case of emergency landing, survival of the crew is facilitated by the combination of a rugged and energy-absorbing landing gear and crashworthy 'stroking' K-37-800M seats.

Fuselage and rotor system design features

The aircraft-lookalike fuselage, with small cross-section, has mid-set stub-wings that lack high-lift devices, while the engines are installed in nacelles above the wing-roots. Each wing has a dual-spar structure and is provided with three armament pylons. The wingtip pods house self-protection equipment and have small vertical plates to the rear.

The all-moving small sweptback tailfin has a large trailing-edge tab and is used as a rudder for yaw control in high-speed flight. The high-set tailplane on the rear fuselage has endplate auxiliary fins. The tail is not a load-bearing structural element and the helicopter could continue flying in a safe manner after the tailboom had been torn off.

The skin panels are made from composite materials in the form of

The nose section has combined steel/aluminium armour protection to sustain hits of projectiles up to 23mm calibre. Extensive armouring is provided for the Ka-52's most vulnerable airframe areas, such as the cockpit sides, while the widely spaced engines are separated from rest of the fuselage by using firewalls. (Mikhail Lisov)

The two-seat Alligator was also set to retain the unique crew ejection capability, in which the rotor blades are first jettisoned. (Author)

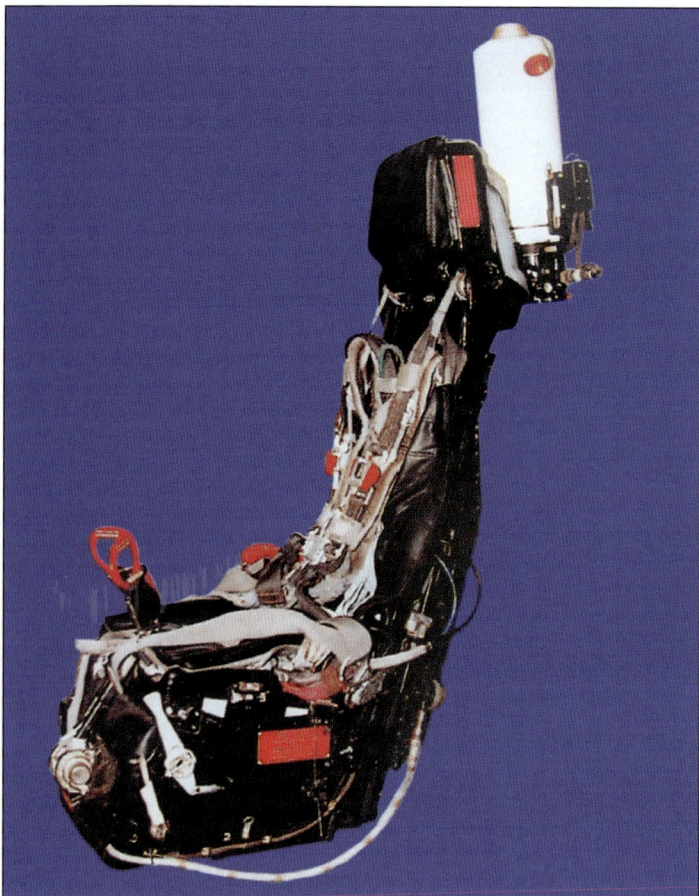

The Ka-37-800M ejection seat. (Zvezda)

A close-up view of the cockpit area from starboard
with the canopies opened. (Author)

three-layer panels and reinforced fibre-glass.

The coaxial rotor system features two contra-rotating rotors, widely separated and made from three blades each. The blades are the semi-rigid type, all-composite, with swept tips, attached to the hub by steel plates. Military requirements dating from the mid-1980s called for eliminating points in the helicopter design requiring lubrication at regular intervals; hence the Ka-52's rotor system has only three lubrication points. The upper rotor turns clockwise and lower one anti-clockwise.

Powering the Alligator

The first Ka-52 prototype was powered by a pair of Klimov TV3-117VMA turboshafts, each rated at 2,200shp take-off power, maintained up to 2,220m (7,280ft) and 30˚C ambient air temperature, equipped with IR emission suppressor devices installed on the exhaust ducts. The Ka-52 is also equipped with the AI-9V auxiliary power unit installed on top of the centre-fuselage, providing compressed air for engine start-up and for electrical power and hydraulic power supply needed for system checks on the ground.

The follow-on prototypes, pre-production and production-standard Alligators feature the more powerful and durable Klimov VK-2500-01 with take-off rating of 2,400shp and emergency rating in OEI conditions of 2,700shp that can be maintained at ambient temperatures of up to 45˚C for five minutes. It is rated at 2,400shp for take-off and in normal conditions (limited to 15 minutes), with a cruise rating between 1,500–1,750shp. The engine weighs 300kg (660lb).

Current service life figures cited by Klimov are 6,000 hours total life and a 2,000-hour TBO (4,500 and 1,500 hours respectively for the late production TV3-117VMA). These figures, however, are set at a later stage to be extended to 9,000 and 3,000 hours respectively.

The VK-2500-01 is fully interchangeable with the older TV3-117VMA version, and thanks to the increased OEI ratings it can provide a significant power margin during operations at high altitude and extreme heat. The increased power offered by the FADEC-controlled VK-2500-01 has resulted in a static-ceiling increase of some 1,000m (3,280ft), to a maximum dynamic ceiling of 7,000m (22,960ft), while the payload increase is between 1,000–2,000kg (2,200–4,400lb), depending on specific helicopter type. The performance-boosting features implemented in the VK-2500-01 design are said to centre on an all-new turbine section and a BARK-78 full-authority digital engine control and monitoring unit.

In 2012, the design team at the Kamov OKB hoped that further performance gains in terms of cruise speed, climb rate, IGE/OGE hover ceilings and payload capability could be achieved by using the even more powerful TV3-117VMA-SB1V, offered by Ukraine's Motor Sich company. It is fully interchangeable with the VK-2500 and was set to be approved by the Russian MoD, first for installation on the Mi-8MTV-5; its integration onto the Ka-52 and its 'navalised' derivative Ka-52K was touted as being possible at a later stage in the near-to-medium future.

The TV3-117VMA-SB1V is capable of maintaining its emergency power rating of up to 2,800shp for no less than 60 minutes at ambient air temperatures up to +52˚C; take-off power rating is up to 2,500shp, while cruise power rating is between 1,500–1,750shp. However, the integration of the new engine on the Ka-52 failed to happen due to the seriously deteriorating political relations between Russia and Ukraine after the annexation of Crimea peninsula by Russia and the following war in Eastern Ukraine in March/April 2014.

The VK-2500M is a new derivative of the TV3-117/VK-2500 family currently being developed by Klimov of St Petersburg, which would be used to power the Ka-52 follow-on derivatives, notably improving their flight performance in hot-and-high conditions and their safety characteristics. It features a big package of new technologies, such as a compressor, combustion chamber, free turbine and digital controls in a bid to increase power, cut fuel burn by 5 percent and reduce weight by 25 percent, as well as increasing the TBO. The VK-2500M will be OEI-rated at 3,000shp, with 2,800shp available for take-off, while its maximum continuous power rating will be set at 2,200shp. Its integration on the Ka-52 would be possible after 2020.

The helicopter has two primary fuel tanks, filled with reticulated foam, housed inside the fuselage box beam. Total internal capacity is

The Klimov VK-2500-01 turboshaft engine is a follow-on development of the TV3-117VMA, with a higher power rating and longer TBO and overall service life. (Author)

about 1,800 litres. Each tank feeds its own engine and has protection from layers of natural rubber for sealing the punctures caused by shells and high-speed fragments. Up to four external tanks, each with 500 litres, can be carried on the innermost and middle pylons.

General aircraft systems

The helicopter has dual hydraulically powered flight control systems without manual reversion and with spring stick trim. Yaw control in hover and low-speed flight is provided by differential collective pitch applied through rudder pedals, while at high speed, control is provided though the rudder only.

The landing gear is the hydraulically retractable tricycle type. All units retract rearward and are equipped with low-pressure tyres which are semi-exposed when retracted. The nose unit is steerable, with two wheels (400x150mm), while the main braking units are single-wheel, with KTA-23A wheels (700x250mm). At low altitude, the helicopter can fly with landing gear units locked in down position, without any speed restrictions, in order to be better-suited for emergency landing whenever needed.

The engine air intakes, rotors, AoA (Angle of Attack) and yaw sensors are provided with an electrical anti-icing system, while the windscreen and the canopy de-icing is provided by liquid spray.

The Ka-52 is considerably easier to produce and support than its predecessor Mi-24. Feedback on the maintainability, supportability and reliability of the Alligator provided so far from VVS units has been very positive. Yuriy Denisenko, managing director of AAC Progress, who amassed much expertise and experience of dealing with the Mi-24's and Ka-50/52's avionics suites back in the years he worked as an engineer at the plant, claimed:

No surprise for us, since the Ka-52 features a pretty advanced all-digital avionics suite that is much easier to maintain and fix in field conditions compared to the Mi-24's fully analogue avionics systems. The Ka-52 is also provided with lots of built-in test equipment for fault isolation and has very easy access to all systems and avionics bays; all these features contribute to the fast pre- and post-flight checks, prompt and easy fault rectification in field conditions.

All systems are configured for field maintenance on deployments away from the base for up to 12 days without the need of ground servicing equipment. Refuelling, avionics checks and weapons servicing can be performed from ground level.

According to maintenance data released by the Kamov OKB, pre-flight checks of the Ka-52 require only 2.15 man-hours vs 18.7 for the Mi-24, while checks between flights take 2.45 man-hours vs 13.25 and post-flight checks (including ammunition loading) take 3.2 man-hours vs 12.5.

Avionics outfit

The production-standard Alligator delivered to the RAA branch features the Argument-52 (also known as BREO-52 or K-806) digital integrated avionics suite of open architecture with a future growth capability. In its production form it is based on dual Baget-53-17 high-speed processors and a GOST R 52070-2004 digital data bus, equivalent to Mil-Std 1553B. Avionics integrator is the Ramenskoye-based RPKB company, now incorporated within the KRET defence avionics holding.

The Argument-52 incorporates multi-functional cockpit displays, inertial and satellite navigation systems, helicopter automatic flight control system, day/night targeting optronic payload, multifunctional radar and self-protection aids suite. The avionics suite also includes the PNK-37DM flight/navigation system and the BKS-50 communications system. Controls of the systems included in the suite are designed in accordance with the HOCAS concept.

The Ka-52 also comes equipped with the Briz two-way wideband datalink, allowing real-time datalinking of video footage. The helicopter can thus share video images in real time with ground C2 posts and other Briz-equipped helicopters. The main source of downlinked video image is the GOES-451 optronic payload; in addition, the Ka-52 can share radar and motion pictures derived from other on-board systems such as the HUD camera and flight/nav data, and can also provide the status of the engines and helicopter systems (as this information is displayed on the two centrally mounted cockpit displays).

The right seat is occupied by a WSO, known within the RAA as navigator-operator. He works with the sensors and is responsible for the launch of the ATGMs, but is also able to fly the helicopter if required. All the engine and systems information is displayed in the centre of the instrument panel, on two MFI-35 LCDs common for the pilot and WSO, while each of them uses two more MFI-35 displays for flight/navigation and targeting data one large and one small. The cockpit is equipped with dual controls, and the pilot in the left-hand seat also has an ILS-31 HUD with day and night modes. In addition, each crew member has one smaller display. There are also five back-up electro-mechanical instruments installed above the two centrally mounted LCD displays.

The Ka-52's sophisticated SAU-800 automatic flight control system provides control and stabilisation, enabling the pilot to fly the Ka-52 in manual and also in a plethora of automated modes to facilitate weapons employment or bad weather landing operations.

The Ka-52 has been commissioned in Russian military service without a helmet-mounted cueing and display system for steering the onboard sensors and gun turret, as well as displaying flight/navigation and targeting data. The reason for that is the lack of suitable Russian systems in operational readiness at the time of conducting the joint state flight testing effort in the late 2000s and early 2010s. Again, this capability is set to be added to the Alligator at a later stage, as the GRPZ and Elektroavtomatika are busy with developing new-generation systems.

Sophisticated targeting systems

"We are using an all-Russian-made optronic payload for targeting, weapons guidance and navigation, and therefore are no longer reliant on foreign suppliers," Mikheev noted. The Ka-52's SUO-806P weapons control system facilitates the use of the aircraft's guided and unguided ordinance, getting targeting information from the UOMZ GOES-451 payload; it also facilitates the use of forward-firing weapons by the pilot using the ILS-31 HUD for visual sighting.

The GOES-451 optronic payload, which is 640mm in diameter, is the core of the Alligator's sophisticated mission avionics suite, providing day/night target detection and designation for the employment of laser beam-riding missiles, guns and rockets.

The large and heavy turret assembly is installed under the nose and can be steered left and right at 230°, up to 30° and down to 80°. It houses the following devices: a gyro-stabilised platform with dual TV cameras (one with a narrow field of view, the other with a wide); thermal imager (FLIR sensor); laser rangefinder/designator; laser spot

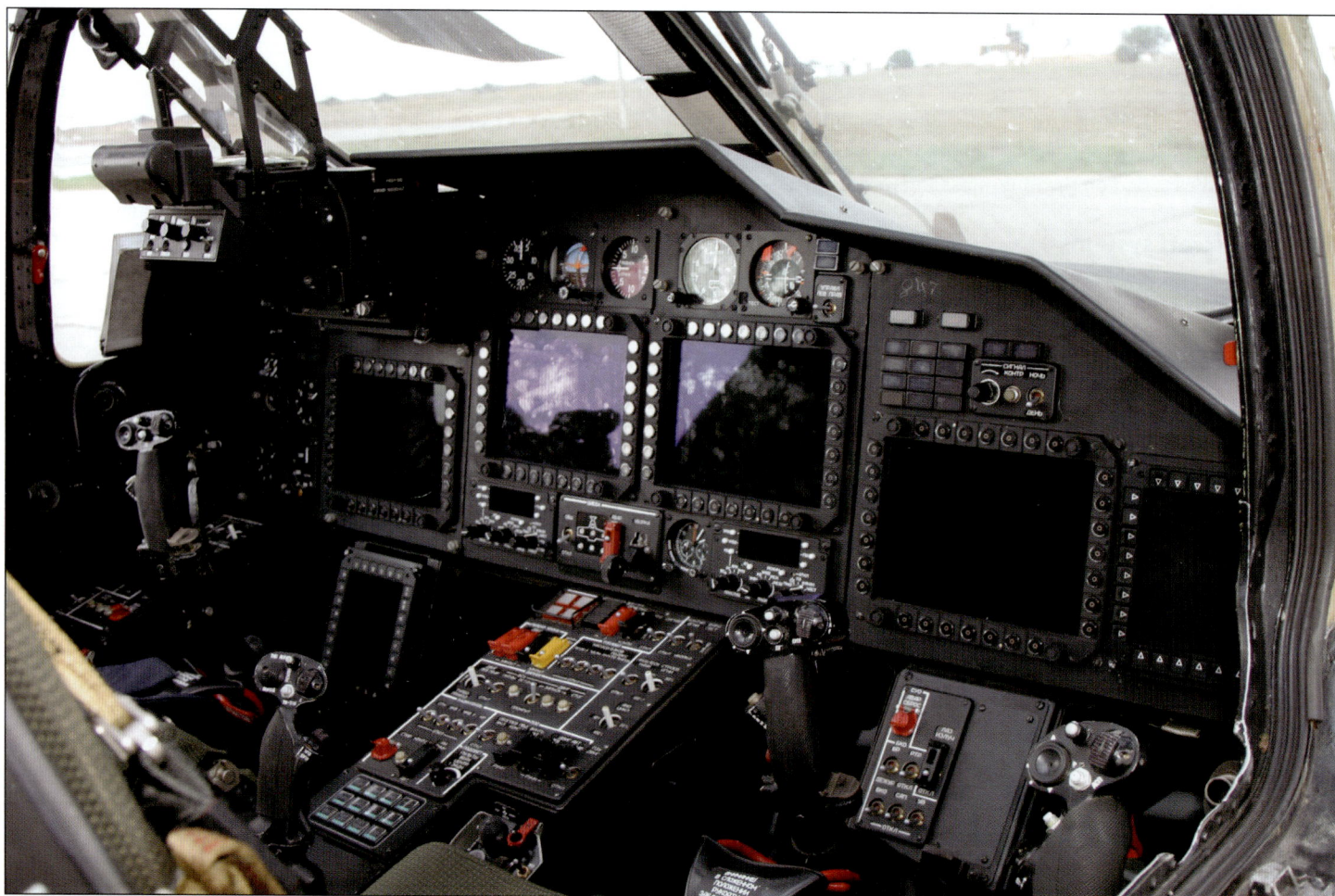

The cockpit of a production-standard Ka-52. (Andrey Zinchuk)

tracker; and ATGM laser beam-riding command guidance device.

The thermal imager uses a 320x240 element matrix. This is a relatively dated technology as Russia still has problems with launching into production new-generation thermal imaging technologies. The narrow FoV has a size of 3°x9° and it is claimed as able to facilitate detection of tank-sized targets at night within a 5–6km (2.6–3.2nm) range, and their identification at 3–4km (1.6–2.2nm).

During the day, the TV sensor package is used; it has two TV cameras with CCD sensors with x4 and x10 optical magnification (FoV of 0.6°x0.8°). The narrow FoV has useful detection ranges of up to 10km (5.4nm).

The laser rangefinder/designator has a range of up to 20km (11nm), with accuracy within 5m (16ft).

The GOES-451 is also integrated with the SOVI image enhancement system, which improves the quality of imagery supplied by both the IR sensor and the TV camera, aiding target classification and identification capabilities. The system, developed by the GRPZ and initially known as the Okhotnik, deals with the enhancement of the image (video footage) derived from the thermal imager and TV camera; it is advertised as capable of providing a good enough image in twilight and also in rainy and snowy conditions. The SOVI also enables the GOES-451 to perform automated target tracking, even in times of temporary excursion of the target outside the system's field of view for up to five seconds. Use of the SOVI system made possible the detection and tracking range to be extended 1.51.7 times.

The latest production derivative of the GOES-451 also supports low-level navigation at night by introducing an additional sensor package with a TV camera (with 30°x40° FoV) and an uncooled thermal imager, used to improve the aircrew's situational awareness. It can provide detection range of large terrain features at night at 1–1.5km (0.54–0.8nm), with large powerline poles at up to 600m (1,968ft).

The cockpit lighting is NVG-friendly and the Ka-52 pilots use the Geophizika-NV GEO-ONV1-01K NVGs. This version of a Gen 3 aviator NVG set was tailor-made for the Ka-52 and features a special pyrotechnic device for rapid decoupling of the power supply cable in case of crew ejection. The NVG set weighs 0.510kg (1.12lb) and is claimed to work sufficiently well at low-level, helping crew to detect electricity power poles, patches of woodland, individual trees or vehicles travelling through an open field out to a distance in excess of 1km (0.54nm) in average night lighting conditions. The GEO-ONV1-01K NVG set also enables the Ka-52 crewmen to perform take-off, hovering and level flight at altitudes between 50–200m (164–656ft) at night, maintaining constant visual contact with the terrain below and in front of the helicopter, as well as to fly approaches and landings onto unprepared and unlit landing zones.

Radar

The coaxial Kamov Ka-52 has a nose-mounted Phazotron-NIIR FH-01 Arbalet-52 (Crossbow) millimetric-wavelength radar using a large parabolic antenna installed in a deep radome in the nose. The first four radar-equipped production-standard Alligators were taken on strength by the VVS in December 2011.

The FH-01 Arbalet-52 radar was developed in the mid-1990s, initially conceived for export customers, and a version for the Ka-52 fleet was launched in 2002. An experimental radar set was installed onto the first prototype, and based on the initial test results obtained during a series of 17 sorties in 2004, Phazotron-NIIR's design team introduced a plethora of software changes to the system in order to increase range and improve the radar's sector search performance.

Mikheev explained:

A close-up view of the GOES-451 sensor turret in its latest version, featuring IR and TV additional sensors added to enable low-level navigation at night. (Author)

The Ka-52 has a nose-mounted Arbalet-52 radar and I could say that its integration effort proved to be [a] very smooth undertaking thanks to the significant radar experience and expertise of our company[,] accumulated during the development of the Ka-25 and Ka-27 families of naval helicopters, equipped with sophisticated radars at the time. In the event, we chose to walk away from the idea of installing the radar on the rotor mast because the nose location provides some weighty advantages. For instance, there are no constraints regarding the antenna size and the size/weight of the radar electronics black boxes; furthermore, the nose is also a vibration-free location, which is another radar-friendly feature.

As claimed by both Kamov and Phazotron-NIIR, the radar's principal advantage compared to the day/night optronic observation and targeting payloads is in its ability to provide reliable targeting information under various weather conditions because its performance is not degraded by rain, clouds or smoke on the battlefield and it also has a much faster scan cycle of the underlying terrain.

Thanks to the combination of these abilities, the radar can provide better situational awareness, target detection and safety of flight in adverse weather conditions, thus enhancing the Ka-52's overall battlefield effectiveness and survivability.

In its initial production version, the FH-01 Arbalet-52 lacks the non-cooperative identification capability of surface targets of the kind featured on the Lockheed Martin's AN/APR-78, which is installed on the Boeing AH-64D Apache Longbow. However, according to sources from Kamov, a series of enhancements is planned for introduction in the foreseeable future.

That is why in its current production configuration and state of integration, the FH-01 Arbalet-52 could not yet be considered to be a completely independent target acquisition, classification and identification sensor. The target engagement cycle, when using the radar, still requires visual detection and identification before engaging it with either guided or unguided weapons. This next step of the radar development i.e. to be able to be used as an independent targeting sensor, capable of target identification for subsequent engagement is set to take place in the near-to-mid future by progressively adding new software and hardware increments.

The FH-01 set was initially offered by the Phazotron-NIIR with an additional L-band decimetric-wavelength channel (known as Arbalet-L), with a single mast-mounted antenna or multiple

To the left of the GOES-451 on the development helicopters, another smaller turret is installed: the UOMZ TOES-520, housing a TV camera and thermal imager used for navigation purposes at night. This is the second prototype, '062', toting Ataka-1 ATGMs and 20-round packs for 80mm rockets (Author)

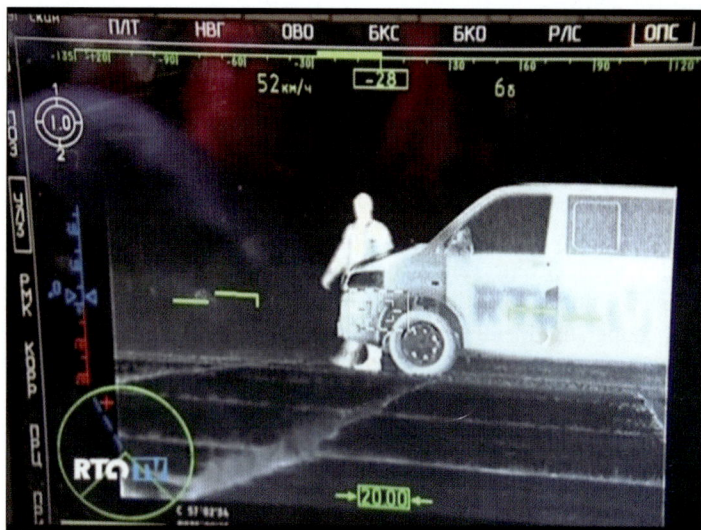

An IR image of a ground vehicle derived from the GOES-451's thermal imager. (via author)

conformal antennas providing a 360° scan capability using common processing hardware and software. This enhanced capability, however, was eventually rejected by the VVS for its production-standard Ka-52 in order to simplify the development and qualification effort and reduce the radar's development, testing and production costs.

As mentioned by Mikheev, the nose-mounted antenna works in a vibration-free environment with unobstructed field of view in the forward hemisphere, and the radar can be used at a minimum altitude of 10–50m (33–164ft). The radar weighs 140kg (309lb) and its large parabolic antenna scans a 120° sector in front of the helicopter – 60° left and right.

The millimetric-wavelength chosen for the radar of an attack helicopter, which typically conducts missions at low and ultra-low altitudes, is less sensitive to ground clutter and can provide high-resolution mapping of underlying terrain, detecting radar-reflecting stationary and moving objects.

It works in the Ka-band and is used for detecting ground, sea and air targets and supporting precision engagement by cueing the helicopter's GOES-451 optronic payload for visual identification and subsequent firing of both the 9M120-1 Ataka-V and 9A4172 Vikhr-1 laser beam-riding guided missiles or engaging the target with gun and rockets.

Arbalet's initial flight tests on the Ka-52 in 2004 confirmed the performance expectations of the design team with the helicopter flying at between 15–40m (50–130ft), the maximum detection range of a large railway bridge was 32km (17.3nm), while air targets were detected at 11–15km (6–8nm), MBTs at 12km (6.5nm) and power lines at 20km (11nm).

Range resolution is quoted as being under 20m (66ft), and angular resolution amounts to 20 angular minutes. There is also a weather mode that can detect dangerous meteorological occurrences and air turbulence zones, while another mode provides obstacle-avoidance data for ultra-low-level flight.

The moving target indication (MTI) mode, also tested for the first time in 2004, facilitates detection of a moving vehicle (travelling at speeds over 10km/h/5.4kt) at a maximum distance of 16km (8.5nm).

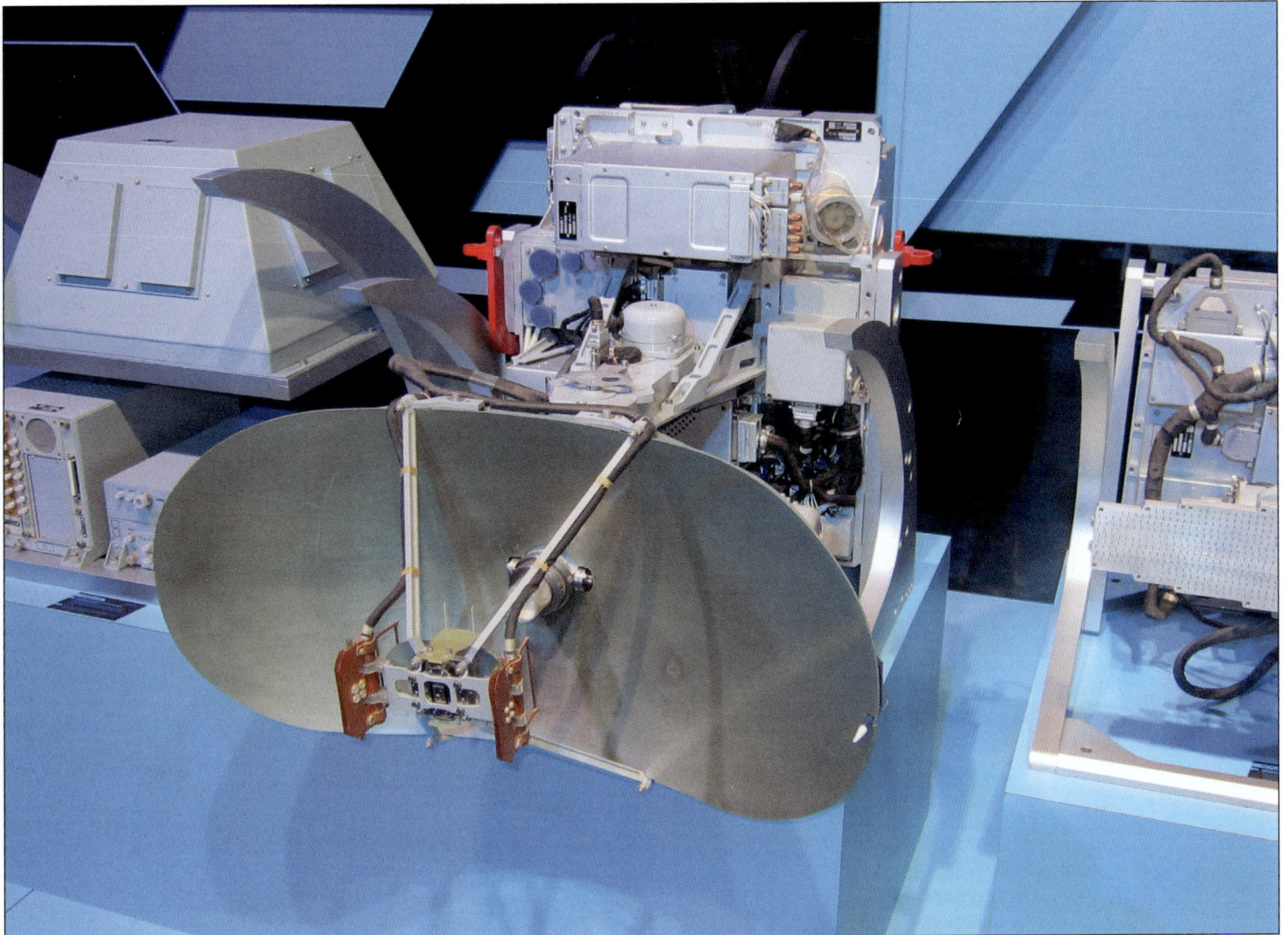

The Arbalet-52 millimetric-wavelength radar. (Author)

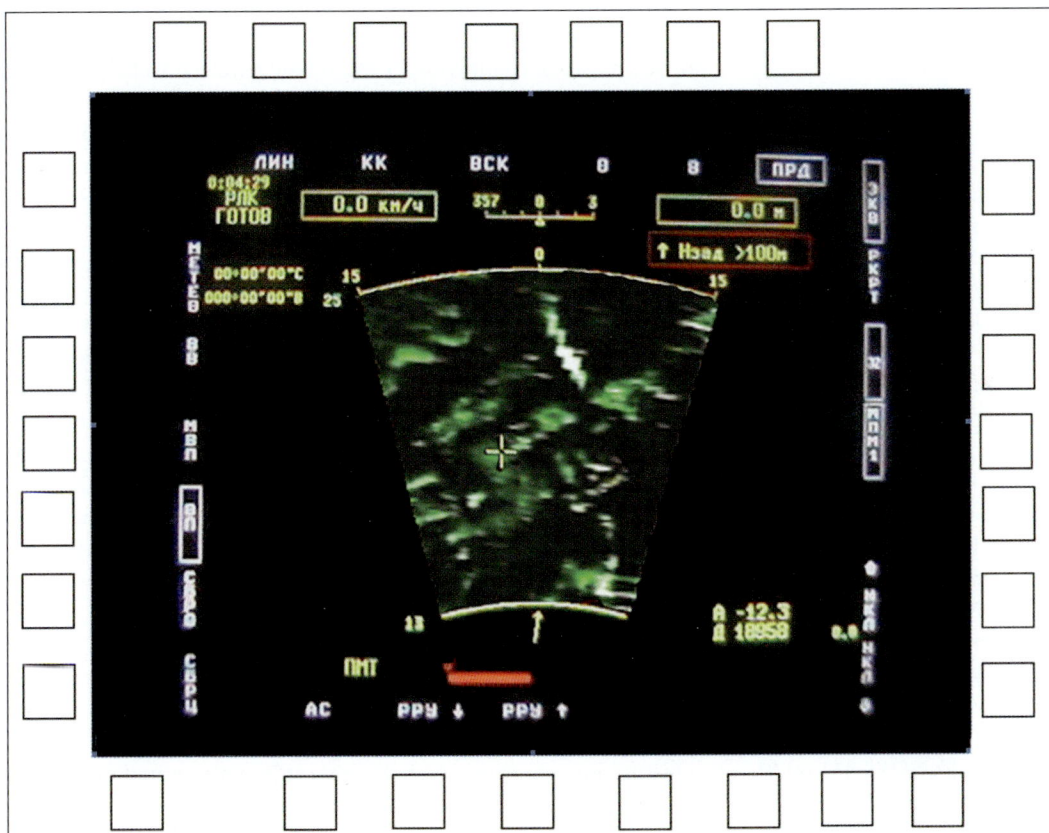

Radar picture of the underlying surface derived from the Arbalet-52 as shown on the MFI-35 colour display. (via author)

A close-up view of an APU-M six-round launcher for the Ataka-1 ATGM in the foreground, with a Vikhr-1 ATGM in the background, suspended on an Alligator, by using the APU-6 launcher. (Author)

The helicopter crew also commented that during the initial test campaign in 2004, the radar was able to precisely locate a motorway thanks to the detected flow of moving vehicles.

Guided missiles
Vikhr-1 ATGM

The Vikhr-M (NATO AT-16 *Scallion*) is the latest all-new ATGM system commissioned in service with the RAA. It was originally designed in the early 1980s by the Tula-based KBP, and its first derivative, the 9A4172 missile, entered service in 1985. The improved 9K121 Vikhr-M derivative with the 9A4172 Vikhr-1 missile followed suit in 1990 and was commissioned in Russian military service in 1995.

The Vikhr-1 is the principal anti-tank weapon for both the Kamov Ka-50 and Ka-52 attack helicopters. They carry up to 12 missiles on two six-round APU-6 launcher mounts.

When employed by the Ka-50, targeting is provided by the I-251V Shkval-V day-only TV/laser targeting search and acquisition system, with sufficient resolution to enable missile launches at armoured targets to a maximum distance of 10km (5.4nm) in clear weather.

The Ka-52 uses the much more modern UOMZ GOES-451 electro-optical payload, with a much wider steering envelope in azimuth and elevation than those of the Shkval-V. The system's FLIR targeting channel enables night ATGM launches at tactically useful engagement distances of up to 6km (3.23nm). The Vikhr-1's laser beam-riding ATGM guidance comes integrated with the Ka-52's GOES-451 multi-sensor payload, which features a built-in laser-beam guidance device for tracking the missile and generating steering commands.

Both the Ka-50's Shkval-V and the Ka-52's GOES-451 targeting systems feature laser generator units for laser-beam ATGM guidance, forming a special-pattern beam scanning the target in order to provide steering commands to the missile while travelling towards the designated target. This specific laser-beam command guidance method keeps the missile centred on the beam and is designed in such a way that it constrains the weapon's angular deviation in flight within an imaginary tube with a diameter of only 1m (3ft 3in) all the way to the target. Such small angular deviations, in turn, guarantee a pretty high probability of a hit when launched against small moving targets.

The 9A4172 Vikhr-1 missile is 130mm in diameter and 2,750mm long. Together with its storage/launch tube, it weighs some 59kg (130lb) and features a canard aerodynamic layout with a folding pair of rudders at the rear and folding canards (forward-mounted wings). The missile comes equipped with a tandem warhead, weighing 12kg (26.5lb), with some 6kg (13.25lb) explosive charge, said to be capable of penetrating 1,000mm of reactive armour dealing with dynamic protection at a 90° angle of arrival. It is fitted with both contact and proximity fuses, and the specific type of fuse can be selected by the pilot before launch, depending on the target type. The proximity fuse is activated at about 5m (16ft) from the target.

When the proximity fuse is selected, the Vikhr-1 can also be employed as an effective air-to-air weapon, as it is advertised as capable of hitting air targets flying at speeds of up to 800km/h (431kt).

The laser-beam providing steering commands to the missile is said to feature low-emitting power because it is not required to create a powerful laser spot and keep it on the target, as is the case with the semi-active laser guidance The emitted power is initially low and

The Igla-V air-to-air missile in launch tubes installed onto a twin-round Strelets launcher unit on the outermost wing pylon. (via author)

This Ka-52 from the Ostrov-based 15th Army Aviation Brigade sports a bizarre weapons load, suspended only for display purposes. Under the starboard wing it carries a B-8V20A rocket pack, UPK-23-250 gun pod and external tank, while under the port wing an external tank and another rocket pack are suspended. (Russian MoD)

The 2A42 30mm cannon was chosen by Mikheev ahead of purpose-designed aircraft guns for its reliability, particularly in the presence of dirt and sand, and ability to use standard land forces' ammunition. (Andrey Zinchuk)

30mm ammunition for the 2A42 prepared in a belt ready for loading into the ammunition box, with a mixture of fragmentation/high-explosive/incendiary and fragmentation/tracer rounds. (Mikhail Lisov)

increases as the missile closes to the target in order to grant reliable transmission of steering commands to the moving away missile. As a result, it would be difficult for it to be detected in time by laser warning systems equipping all modern MBTs and IFVs. The laser beam-riding guidance, combined with the missile's high, supersonic speed, could grant resistance to any known kind of optical jamming. Vikhr-1's 'brochure' probability of hit is claimed to be 0.80 when launched against moving targets.

The guidance system supports either a single missile or a two-round salvo against the same target. The missile, propelled by a two-stage rocket motor, has a maximum speed of 610m/s, and the flight time for a 4,000m (13,120ft) distance is nine seconds, while the maximum range of 10,000m (32,800ft) is travelled in 28 seconds. Minimum engagement range is 500m (1,600ft), and launch altitude is between 5–4,000m (16–13,120ft).

Ataka-1 ATGM

The 9M120-1 Ataka-1 version (NATO AT-6 *Spiral*) is the latest derivative of the weapon system designed for use by the Ka-52, featuring a laser beam-riding guidance mode in addition to the radio beam-riding one. This makes it possible to be guided using the Ka-52's GOES-451 optronic payload, which has a laser-beam ATGM guidance system originally designed for employing the Vikhr-1 ATGM.

The baseline 9M120 Ataka-V is still regarded as an affordable and reliable helicopter-launched weapon, offering a reasonable engagement envelope. Developed in the 1980s specifically for the Mil Mi-28 new-generation attack helicopter by the Kolomna Machine-Building Design Bureau (known in Russian as KBM), the Ataka-V is, in fact, an improved derivative of the proven 9M114 Shturm-V radio beam-riding missile used on the Mi-24V/P gunships.

The Ataka-1 has the same guidance and dimensions as its predecessor Shturm-V, but features an improved warhead, higher launch weight and extended maximum range increased from 4,000–6,000m (13,200–19,680ft). The minimum engagement range is 1,000m (3,280ft) and its launch altitude can stretch up to 3,050m (9,300ft). In addition to stationary and moving ground targets, it can also be used against low-flying air targets, travelling at a speed of up to 400km/h (216kt).

The two-stage missile is housed with its wings and control surfaces folded in a fibreglass transport/launch tube weighing 49.5kg (109lb), while the missile itself weighs 42.5kg (94lb). The Ataka-1 has a high top speed, up to 530m/s (1,738f/s), and its average velocity is 400m/s (1,312f/s). The anti-armour version comes equipped with a 7.4kg (16.3lb) tandem warhead of telescopic design, capable of perforating

850mm of rolled homogeneous armour after piercing reactive armour.

The flight time when engaging a target at a range of 5,800m (19,024ft) is only 14.5 seconds, and when travelling 4,000m (13,120ft), the missile has a flight time of less than 11 seconds.

The Ataka-1 is advertised as well suited to hitting small windows and other hardened targets with square shapes sized at 1x1m (3ft 3inx3ft 3in). The probability of hit when fired against MBTs at 4,000m (13,120ft) is quoted as being between 0.65 and 0.90.

There are two additional versions of this missile system currently in production, outfitted with high-explosive/thermobaric and blast/fragmentation warheads respectively, using proximity fuses for improved lethality. The latter, known as the 9M120-1F-1, is also promoted as a highly effective weapon against air targets, while the former, known as the 9M120-1F, is intended for use against personnel in the open or hiding in buildings, bunkers and caves. A load of up to 12 Ataka-1 missiles can be carried on two six-round launchers.

Hermes-A ATGM

The Hermes-A is the latest development on offer from the Tula-based KBP missile design house. The long-range missile with a powerful warhead is promoted as a universal solution for a wide variety of tactical situations, including the 'fire-and-forget' option at extended ranges. The missile's basic design concept dates back to 1999, when KBP had commenced the development of a new family of long-range missiles to be launched from air, sea and land platforms. All of the variants are based on KBP's proven 57E6 missile design, originally used in the 96K6 Pantsir-S1 (SA-22 *Greyhound*) self-propelled, low-to-medium-altitude SAM system. The eventual aim of the design team was to create an advanced anti-armour missile system capable of being fired from well outside the extended reach of lethal modern air defences. It is a heavy, long-range, two-stage missile; the first stage calibre is 130mm, while the booster is of 170mm. The transport/launch tube is 3.5m (10ft 9in) long, and the whole package weighs around 107kg (48.5lb), while the high-explosive warhead weighs 13kg (28.6lb) (in TNT equivalent).

The Hermes-A ATGM was test-fired by the Kamov Ka-52 in 2003; the maximum and minimum ranges reported during these firings were 18 and 0.8km respectively (9.7 and 0.43nm). The missile demonstrated a maximum speed of 1,044m/s (3,424f/s), while the average speed at a 15km (8nm) range was 524m/s (1,719f/s).

The missile employs inertial guidance in the initial and mid-course phases of flight (with optional radio correction), while in the terminal phase, a semi-active laser seeker is used, and the control system allows for a top-attack profile, to hit armoured targets in their most vulnerable place with less protection. This way, the system is provided with both 'fire, observe and correct' (with man-in-the-loop guidance in the midcourse phase of flight) and 'fire-and-forget' capabilities.

In 2013, KBM claimed that it was set to continue the development of its long-range ATGM family line for both export and domestic use, expecting it to be able to complete the Hermes-A testing and evaluation effort by 2018.

Igla air-to-air missile

The VVS requirements also called for the integration of the KBM 9M39 Igla-V heat-seeking air-to-air missile with a maximum launch range of 5.8km (3.1nm). The Ka-52 can carry up to four of these suspended on two 9S846 Strelets twin-round launcher units on the outer wing pylons.

The missile is 82mm in diameter and 1,639mm long, weighs 10.8kg (23.8lb) and its speed is 570–600m/s (1,870–1,968f/s), while the operating altitude is between 10–3,500m (33–11,480ft). It can be fired at targets flying at a speed of up to 1,400m/s (4,592f/s). The warhead is of high-explosive/fragmentation type, weighing 2.15kg (4.74lb), and the contact fuse provides delayed detonation in order for the missile to initially penetrate inside the target and then detonate the remaining rocket propellant.

The missile has a dual-spectral seeker working in the IR wavelength and has flare rejection capability; it is also immune to modulated IR jamming.

Each missile, housed in the Strelets twin-round launcher unit, is provided with two thermal batteries good for up to one minute of operation during the engagement cycle, including visual aiming, acquiring the target, lock-on and launch. Aiming of the missile on the target until getting a lock-on solution is performed visually by the pilot, who has to turn the helicopter in the horizontal and vertical plane as the missile's heat-seeking guidance system is fixed in boresight position, looking forward, and cannot be cued off-boresight by the radar, EO/IR payload or manually by using a joystick.

Unguided ordinance

The Ka-52's arsenal includes up to four 250kg (551lb) and 500kg (1,102lb) free-fall bombs, napalm tanks, KMGU-2 bomblet/mine dispensers and 80mm (3in) S-8 and 122mm (4.8in) S-13 rockets launched from 20-round B-8V20A and five-round B-13L pods respectively.

Kamov OKB test pilot Alexander Papay boasted:

The S-8 80mm rocket in particular proved a very precise weapon when fired from the Ka-50 and Ka-52 thanks [to] the combination of a stable helicopter flight (due to the coaxial rotor system with low levels of vibration) and the highly-precise targeting system. That is why the S-8, when launched by the Ka-50 and Ka-52, can be no longer considered as an area saturation weapon; instead it is now known as an effective point-killer.

The S-8 family of folding-fin rockets, launched from B-8V20-A packs, are usually fired from a maximum distance of 1,500m (4,920ft) in shallow dive or level flight, while their maximum range can reach 6,800m (22,300ft) when launched in pitch-up firing attitude that allows the rockets to follow a ballistic trajectory – this specific delivery profile is useful for area suppression purposes.

The basic S-8 rocket has a shaped-charge/fragmentation warhead while the improved S-8M and S-8KOM derivatives feature warheads with enhanced fragmentation effects. The latter also has much better armour penetration capability at ranges of up to 400m (1,310ft), while its fragments remain lethal within a radius of 12m (39ft). The missile

has a circular error probability of around 3m (10ft) when launched at a distance of 2,500m (8,200ft).

Guns

2A42

The Shipunov 2A42 is a 30mm gun with dual feed and 460 rounds. It has an adjustable rate of fire and was originally 'borrowed' from the BMP-2 infantry fighting vehicle. Widely regarded as a feather in the Ka-52's cap, it is touted as being among the most powerful if not the most powerful guns installed in a helicopter. It is also remarkably resilient to jamming and heavy dust contamination, and is cleared for operations in a temperature range from -50 to +50˚C, including in rainy, snowy and icy conditions.

The 2A42 weighs some 115kg (254lb), while the barrel itself weighs 40kg (88lb), and the overall length is 3,027mm. Barrel life is 4,000 shots. The NPPU-80 mount, together with the cannon, weighs 280kg (617lb).

The Ka-50 and Ka-52 have the 2A42 cannon installed in a NPPU-80 hydraulically-driven limited-movement turret installed on the starboard side of the fuselage near the centre of gravity in an effort to alleviate the effect of the powerful recoil. The complex NPPU-80 mount assembly has a hydraulic control system that rotates the gun 3.5˚ up (elevation) and 37˚ down (depression), as well as up to 9˚ to the right and 2˚ to the left.

Some Western analysts have questioned the wisdom of having such limited movement in the cannon. In fact, its rapid aiming in the horizontal plane is achieved by yawing the whole helicopter, while the limited turret rotation in the horizontal plane is used for fine aiming, applying corrections as calculated by the weapons control computer. It is noteworthy that the Ka-50/52's amazingly high yaw rate in a pedal turn is said to be comparable to the speed of rotation of the Mi-28N's bulky undernose turret containing the same type of cannon together with the ammunition load.

The 2A42 is provided with a two-sided ammunition feed system (also known as dual-feed) that allows for feeding armour- piercing/tracer rounds from one box as well as fragmentation/high-explosive/incendiary (OFZ) and fragmentation/tracer (OT) rounds from the other. The ammunition boxes are installed in the fuselage with short feeds to the breech.

The gun uses three types of shells OFZ, OT and armour-piercing/tracer (BT). The ammunition is housed in two boxes with different sizes. The first one is loaded with 230 OFZ and OT rounds, in a four-to-one ratio. The second one contains 240 BT rounds.

The OFZ and BT shells are used against manpower, soft-skinned ground and air vehicles. Each OFZ shell weighs 390g and is filled with up to 40g of explosive charge and has an impact fuse, while the self-destruction mechanism is activated at the 14th second of flying, allowing it to travel 3,900–5,300m (12,792–17,384ft). The OT round weighs 385g, has a smaller explosive charge and is fitted with a tracer enabling visual monitoring of its trajectory. The tracer is operable for 10 seconds, corresponding to a range of 4,300m (14,104ft)

The BT armour-piercing shell weighs 396g, has no explosive and is intended for destruction of armoured vehicles and other types of hardened targets. Its tracer burns for only 3.5 seconds, which corresponds to a range of 2,300m (7,544ft), while the effective range of the BT shell is 2,000m (6,560ft). It can penetrate 15mm of steel plate from a range of 1,500m (4,920ft).

The 2A42 has a maximum effective aiming range of 4,000m (13,120ft). It can fire in rapid rate at 900rpm and slow rate of 200–300rpm, and can also unleash single shots. Muzzle velocity is some 980m/s (3,214f/s). The strengthened muzzle is able to expend its

Ka-52 'Yellow 96' (c/n 05-01), produced in 2011, sports the definitive production-standard configuration with the Vitebsk-52 self-protection suite and Arbalet-52 radar. It was delivered to the RAA training centre at Torzhok in January 2012. (Author)

UV-26M chaff/flare dispensers are housed in the wingtips to counter heat-seeking missile threats. The four units have a total capacity of 128 PPI-26 heat-emitting flares that can burn for five to eight seconds after ejection. (Author)

entire ammunition load without needing to make intermediate cooling stops. The one-second salvo weight when using the high rate of fire amounts to 5.33kg (11.7lb), while at the slow rate it is reduced to 2kg (4.4lb).

The 2A42 is also promoted as a very precise weapon in both the trainable and fixed forward-firing modes of the NPPU-80 for destroying hardened point targets.

"We routinely achieve firing preciseness in the region of 1.2–1.4 mils, which means that from a firing distance of 1,000m (3,280ft) at least half of the unleashed projectiles would hit a target measuring 1.5mx1.5m," noted test pilot Alexander Papay, who had amassed hundreds of sorties with gun firings.

GSh-23L

The Ka-52 can also use two UPK-23-250 gun pods with 250 rounds each. It is a highly lethal and accurate gun system using one GSh-23L 23mm twin-barrel cannon. It is a rapid-fire lightweight and compact cannon, developed in the early 1960s, capable of unleashing 174–196gram rounds at a muzzle velocity of 680–730m/s and at a rate of fire of 3,200rpm. Its effective range is up to 1,800m (5,900ft) and the fragmentation/high explosive shells, which each weigh 174g, have a muzzle velocity of 715m/s (2,345f/s), advertised as effective against soft and light armour-protected targets. The one-second salvo weight amounts to 9.33kg (20.6lb)

Self-protection suite

The Ka-52's fully integrated L370V52 Vitebsk-52 self-protection suite was commissioned in November 2011, together with the Arbalet-52 radar. This integrated self-protection suite is advertised as the first sophisticated and effective suite ever employed on a Russian helicopter type.

It integrates four L370-2-01 UV missile approach warning sensors, four L140 Otklik laser warning sensors for a 360° coverage and four UV-26M chaff/flare dispensers (with a total of 128 rounds). The system also incorporates a new-generation IR jammer system with two L370-5 downwards-pointing jammer heads of lamp type located side by side beneath the fuselage to cover a sector of 360° in azimuth and 90° in elevation (i.e. fully covering the lower hemisphere). The Ka-52 also has provision for the installation of the L150 Pastel radar warning and homing receiver system.

The L370-5 IR direction jammer uses a sapphire lamp, mated to an optical system for firing a narrow beam of IR energy at incoming heat-seeking shoulder-launched SAMs and their air-launched derivatives.

The beam is modulated, using a pattern of smart algorithms, in order to affect the missile's guidance system and cause a miss at a safe distance, beyond the range of its proximity fuse.

The IR directional jammers work in close cooperation with the UV missile warning sensors on the nose and tail used to detect the missile launch and its direction of arrival by tracking the movement of its plume. The jamming effect is also enhanced by using the PPI-26 series of 26mm IR flares, pumped from the wingtip-mounted UV-26M dispensers units. Each wingtip houses two dispensers, each loaded with 32 rounds. To enhance the jamming effect of the integrated self-protection suite, the Ka-52 also has IR emission suppressor devices installed on the exhaust ducts of the VK-2500-01 turboshaft engines. These are used to reduce the temperature of the exhaust gases, which range from 400–600°C on non-protected ducts to around 300°C when IR suppressors are used.

Table 1
Alligator's survivability features

• Cockpit side armouring of double-layer spaced design with steel plating making the outer layer, while the inner layer is made of aluminium alloy plating, said to be capable of withstanding hits by rounds of up to 23mm calibre. The 40mm-thick flat windshield can withstand hits of armour-piercing rounds up to 12.7mm calibre, as well as high-speed missile warhead fragments. Scabbed-on steel screens are installed on the side canopies.

• Strengthened rotor mast and protected swashplate, able to retain operability when damaged by direct hits of artillery rounds of up to 23mm calibre.

• Twin-spar composite rotor blades capable of retaining operability in case of damage to one of the spars.

• Main gearbox shielded from direct hits by artillery rounds and high-speed missile fragments by other less-important pieces of equipment and fuselage structural elements. The gearbox has a 30-minute run-dry capability. The shafts, connecting the main and intermediary gearboxes (used to transfer torque from the engine output shafts to the main gearbox), feature increased diameter for extra strength.

• Engines separated from rest of the fuselage by using firewalls and engine bays equipped with effective extinguishers. Automatic fire-extinguishing system.

• Strengthened and dual-redundant extended control runs, dual-

Both Ka-52 crew members are provided with full sets of flight controls, but the one seated in the left-hand seat is the pilot while the other in the right-hand seat acts as WSO. (Andrey Zinchuk)

redundant power supply, distribution of the systems in many different locations inside the fuselage to prevent damage of two or more important systems by a single hit.

• Capability to land with heavily damaged or even missing vertical and horizontal tail surfaces.

• Undercarriage and fuselage designed to offer maximum energy absorption during forced landing.

• Fuel tanks filled with reticulated polyurethane foam for explosive wave and fire suppression and lined with twin-layer thick porous resin protectors for protection against the explosion of kerosene vapours and to prevent large leaks when punctured by projectiles or high-speed fragments. Fuel tanks are also made crash-resistant, retaining their integrity in case of crash landing to avoid fuel leakages.

• Repairability of combat damages in field conditions.

Table 2
Ka-52 specifications
Dimensions
Fuselage length, 13.53m
Length with rotors turning, 16.00m
Wing span, 7.30m
Height, 4.95m
Main rotor diameter, 14.50m
Weights
Empty weight, 7,800kg
Maximum take-off weight, 10,800kg
Maximum take-off weight with external tanks, 12,200kg
Max combat payload, 2,500kg
Internal fuel, 1,487kg

External fuel*, 17,320kg
Performance
Max speed, 300km/h
Max cruising speed, 260km/h
Max rate of climb at sea level, 12m/s
Max rate of climb at 2,500m, 9m/s
G-limits, +3.5/-1.3
Service ceiling, 5,500m
OGE hover ceiling in ISA (International Standard Atmosphere) conditions, 3,900m
IGE (In Ground Effect) hover ceiling in ISA conditions, 4,350m
Combat radius, 200–220km**
Range on internal fuel, 460km
Ferry range, 1,110km

* in four underwing tanks

** on internal fuel and a 5% reserve

V-80-1 prototype (c/n 800-01), serialled '010', wore a white 'smart' paint scheme with a black flash, in which it made its maiden flight on 17 June 1982 in the skilled hands of Kamov OKB test pilot Nikolay Bezdetnov. The first prototype lacked weapons and sighting system and was intended for flight performance assessment and testing the operability of various onboard systems. V-80-1 was also tested with various types of empennage and in its initial configuration had its stub-wings installed with anhedral of 120 deg, later reduced to 6 deg.

V-80-1 prototype (c/n 800-01), serialled '010', seen here wearing an overall black scheme. It was applied shortly after the start of the flight testing and also featured a false second cockpit and a door in the rear fuselage outlined in yellow on the fuselage sides. The first prototype of the Ka-50 was lost in a fatal crash on 3 April 1985 in Lyubertsi, killing Kamov OKB test pilot Evgeny Laryushin.

V-80-2 prototype (c/n 800-02), serialled '011', was the second prototype, seen here in its initial overall black paint scheme, lacking the cannon mount and the sensor nose. Later on it received the NPPU-80 mount with a 2A42 30mm cannon and the Shkval-V TV/laser targeting system and saw an intense participation in the flight test effort, including the testing and evaluation of the Vikhr ATGM system. V-80-2 took to the air for the first time on 16 August 1983 and after retirement in the early 2000s it has been put in storage at Kamov's flight test station at Zhulebino.

Peter Penev

V-80-2 prototype (c/n 800-2), serailled '011', seen here in a silver paint scheme with turquoise underside, which was applied in the second half of the 1980s. At the time it also got a sensor nose, in addition to a 30mm cannon mount and stub-wings with pylons for carriage of ATGMs and unguided ordinance. The new sensor nose housed the Shkval-V TV/laser targeting system and a mock-up of the Merkuriy night-vision system on the top. The hard-working V-80-2 played a significant role in the early flight testing. It amassed a total of 620 flight hours, spending some 9,400 30mm rounds and launching 100 Vikhr ATGMs during its highly-productive career as noted on the nose.

Ka-50 '25' (c/n 800-05) was the last aircraft built at the OKB Kamov's experimental plant in Lyubertsi near Moscow. It enjoyed a very productive test and evaluation career spanning over 19 years. Flown for the first time in April 1990, 800-05 initially wore the serial '015' and was used as the pattern aircraft for series production. It was also the first Ka-50 to be equipped with the Zvezda K-37-800 rocket-based ejection seat. A veteran from the Chechen war and Rubezh-2004 exercise in Kirgizstan, it saw use in numerous test and evaluation programmes, and was upgraded in 2003 with the Vitebsk-50 integrated self-protection suite which completed its flight-test effort in 2009.

Ka-50 '018' (c/n 00-01), known also as the V-80Sh-1, was the first Black Shark to be produced at the AAC Progress plant in Arsenyev. It took to the air for the first time on 22 May 1991 while in February 1992, it was handed over to the Russian Air Force's flight-test centre for the participation in the second stage of the Ka-50's comprehensive flight test and evaluation effort. In 1997, 00-01 was upgraded with the Samshit-50 optronic payload and flew for the first time in its new guise on 4 March that year under the new designation Ka-50Sh. In 2007, 00-01 was displayed at the MAKS-2007 airshow in a new night-capable configuration, shown here, which featured two electro-optic payloads in the nose – the GOES-330 on the bottom and the TOES-520 installed on the top.

Ka-50 'H318' (c/n 01-01) was the second production-standard machine built at the AAC Progress plant, receiving the serial '020'. In September 1992, it was displayed at the Farnborough SBAC airshow in the UK wearing a new overall mat black colour paint scheme. Its fin sported a striking logo representing a lone wolf head and the name 'Werewolf'. Later on, this machine was used for various test works at the Kamov OKB and made its last flight on 13 December 2005.

Ka-50 'H347' (c/n 01-02) was the third Black Shark rolled out at the AAC Progress plant at Arsenyev, originally wearing the serial '021'. It was displayed, together with '020', at the Paris Air Show in June 1993, wearing an overall mat black colour scheme with a striking Black Shark logo on the fin. In 1996, this machine was converted as the first prototype of the Ka-52 Alligator two-seater, receiving an all-new two-seat nose section while the remainder of the airframe and the general systems was unchanged.

Peter Penev

Ka-50 '22' (c/n 01-03) was the fourth Ka-50 built at the AAC Progress plant. Here it is shown in a striking 'Black Shark' paint scheme, including a sharp tailfin shape and a large shark mouth. 01-03 was handed over to the Russian Army Aviation service on 13 December 1993 but proved to be a short lived as it was lost in a fatal accident on 17 June 1998 during an aerobatic display practice sortie over Torzhok airfield, killing the pilot, Maj Gen Boris Vorobyov.

Ka-50 '27' (c/n 03-04) was among the last three Black Sharks produced at the AAC Progress plant. It was formally delivered to the Russian Army Aviation Service on 24 November 2009 but saw a brief service. Operated by the the Torzhok-based combat training and aircrews conversion centre, 03-04 made its last flight on 29 October 2012 and currently the machine is held in a long-term storage at Torzhok airfield awaiting its eventual fate.

Peter Penev

Ka-52 '061' (c/n 00-01) was the first two-seat prototype converted from production-standard single-seater, c/n 01-02, with conversion works performed at the Kamov OKB's experimental plant in Lyubertsi in the first half of 1996. It took to the air in its maiden flight in hover on 25 July 1997 and then the first Alligator prototype was used in the factory test effort and the first phase of the flight-test effort, powered by the new and more powerful VK-2500 engines. It also saw a lot of use in several international customer demonstration flight programmes. Here 00-01 is shown in a configuration dated from the early 2000s, featuring an UOMZ Samshit-B-1 mufti-sensor payload behind the cockpit in addition to a smaller TOES-520 turret installed under the nose. The helicopter wears the original black colour scheme combined with an orange-painted deep nose radome housing the Arbalet-52 airborne radar, working in the Ka-band and looking in the forward hemisphere. It also sports a mock-up of the Arbalet-L L-band radar mounted on the top of the rotor mast.

Ka-52 '062' (c/n 00-02) was the second Alligator prototype and the first one to be produced at the AAC Progress plant in Arsenyev. It was built using the fuselage of incomplete Ka-50, c/n 03-01, which received a new nose section. 00-02 took to the air for the first time on 27 June 2008 and after completing the brief factory flight test programme was handed over to the Kamov OKB for participation in the Ka-52's joint state testing and evaluation effort. The helicopter was used, and is still in use, by the design bureau for various test works. Here it is shown in its latest configuration, revealed in 2015 and used to test various new design features planned to be implemented in the Ka-52K shipborne version, including the shortened, backwards-folding wings and the folding rotor blades. The helicopter is armed with a Kh-35U anti-ship missile to show its expanded list of roles when operated from ships.

Peter Penev

Ka-52 '063' (c/n 00-03) is the third Alligator built, also converted from an incomplete Ka-50 fuselage. Flown for the first time on 28 October 2008, it was used as the first pre-production Ka-52. The helicopter was displayed at the 2011 Paris airshow wearing a newly-applied camouflage resembling the colour pattern of an alligator's skin. It is shown armed with the Vikhr-1 ATGMs.

Ka-52 '52' (c/n 01-02) was the second pre-series Alligator built at the AAC Progress plant in 2009 to be used in the concluding part of the second stage of the comprehensive state testing and evaluation effort. It was lost in a non-fatal crash landing on 29 October 2013 at Zhulebino in Moscow due to a rotor system mechanical problem, upon completion of a sortie aimed at testing onboard equipment intended for use on the Ka-52K shipborne version.

Ka-52 '92' (c/n 03-02) was among the initial-production Ka-52s built at the AAC Progress in 2010 and delivered to the 344th Combat Training and Aircrew Conversion Centre at Torzhok north of Moscow in December that year. It is in the initial production configuration for the Russian Army Aviation, lacking nose-mounted Arbalet-52 radar and the Vitebsk-52 integrated self-protection suite, but featuring provisions for their retrofit at a later stage.

Ka-52 '96' (c/n 05-01) is an Alligator built in late 2011 at the AAC Progress, which features the full production configuration, including the Arbalet-52 nose-mounted radar and the Vitebsk-52 integrated self-protection suite consisting of missile warners, laser warners and directional infrared jammers. It was delivered to the 344th Combat Training and Aircrew Conversion Centre at Torzhok in January 2012 for use in the research and conversion training roles.

Peter Penev

Ka-52 '061' (c/n 00-01), wearing a two-tone grey camouflage, was used in this new configuration which lacked a nose-mounted radar and featured only the GOES-451 payload. In this configuration the first Alligator prototype was involved in ship compatibility trials. The initial phase of these trials was flown off the desk French Navy amphibious assault ship *Mistral* in December 2008. In August 2011, more trials were amassed using the landing desk of the Russian Navy large anti-submarine ship *Vice-Admiral Kulakov*.

Ka-52K (c/n 01-01) is the first of the four pre-series shipborne helicopters built at the AAC Progress plant in 2015, with its maiden flight reported on 7 Match that year. This machine features the new OPS-52 payload (intended to equip the Ka-52s ordered by Egypt) shown for the first time installed at the MAKS-2015 airshow in August 2015, just for demonstration purpose. During the flight testing performed by the Kamov OKB, 01-01 flew equipped with the UOMZ GOES-451 payload, the same as that installed on the land-based version built for the Russian Army Aviation service.

APPENDIX II
AAC PROGRESS PLANT

The Arsenyev Aviation Company Progress (abbreviated as AAC Progress) is among the five big rotorcraft production facilities in Russia. It is regarded as benefiting from the most modern manufacturing technologies available to produce the most sophisticated and advanced Russian military rotorcraft. The plant works hard to gradually increase productivity and output in a bid to meet the sharp upswing in orders for the Kamov Ka-52 received from the Russian MoD, and after 2016 for foreign customers the first of them Egypt with first deliveries scheduled for early 2017, while Algeria is also expected to follow suit in the foreseeable future.

The plant is also ready to launch one new rotorcraft production line in the near future: the Kamov Ka-62 medium twin-engine helicopter, promoted as suitable for both commercial and government/military operations. The current favourable business situation at the company follows some 15 years of struggling for survival in the harsh post-Soviet economic environment, with very few orders.

Growing business

Since 2009, the company's business has been growing at a fairly rapid rate. Sales in that year amounted to US$110 million, then in 2010 and 2011 a sharp increase in output was reported thanks to the upswing of Ka-52 deliveries to the Russian MoD; 2010 revenues totalled 7,889 billion roubles (equating to about US$260 million), while those in 2011 reached 10.3 billion roubles (US$340 million). In 2012, the figure was 22.5 billion roubles (US$681 million), but in 2013 it dropped to 15.19 billion roubles (US $460 million) before growing once again in 2014 to 18.391 billion roubles US$279 million.

This huge manufacturing complex employs about 6,000 people in

The second Ka-52 prototype '062' seen in flight head-on, carrying external tanks, test instrumentation pods and equipped with ribbed engine exhaust suppressors. Assembled using the airframe of the Ka-50 with a new nose section, it took to the air for the first time in Arsenyev on 27 June 2008. (AAC Progress)

Arsenyev, a relatively small city of some 59,000 inhabitants situated in Russia's remote Far East, about 200km (110nm) from Vladivostok, an important Pacific port and economic centre, also known as the capital of the Primoriye region, no fewer than seven time zones east of Moscow.

The AAC Progress administrative building and main gate. (AAC Progress)

The Ka-52 fuselage is built around a high tensile strength steel torsion box beam, measuring 1m (3ft 3in) in width and height, with the gearbox installed above and engines to the sides. It also provides attachment to the equipment bays covered by external panels from composite materials forming the external outline of the rear airframe. (Author)

A Soviet-legacy production mega-facility dealing with helicopters and missiles, AAC Progress is the biggest employer in Arsenyev – indeed the small city had been developed between the 1940s and 1960s for the sole purpose of supporting aerospace production at the giant plant.

Back in Soviet times, there were around 15,000 employees. In the mid-to-late 1980s, the plant rolled out no less than 150 Mi-24 *Hind* attack helicopters a year. This remarkable output coincided with the Soviet Union's war in Afghanistan and the rapid expansion of the Soviet Army Aviation branch. Between 1970 and 1990, as many as 2,443 Mi-24s rolled off the line. This figure includes 10 Mi-24s, 240 Mi-24As, around 240 Mi-24D/DUs, 160 Mi-24Rs, 170 Mi-24Ks, 1,000 Mi-24Vs and no fewer than 600 Mi-24Ps.

In addition to the omnipresent *Hind*, the plant specialised in producing the 3M80 Moskit (SS-N-22 'Sunburn') ship-launched supersonic anti-ship missile. This huge and deadly Mach 2.5 ramjet-powered missile has a warhead weighing 320kg (705lb) and boasts a maximum range of up to 120km (65nm).

Next, the company switched to the Kamov Ka-50 Black Shark, which was originally earmarked as the Mi-24's successor in RAA service. The first Black Shark took to the air in May 1991. However, this rather unorthodox coaxial single-seat attack helicopter appeared at just the wrong time, during the dissolution of the Soviet Union and the start of abrupt cuts to Russia's defence budget.

As a result, orders disappeared almost overnight, leaving a number of incomplete Ka-50 airframes at the factory. In the event, only 13 production-standard examples were manufactured and delivered to the Russian MoD between 1991 and 2009, including three airframes completed as late as 2008–2009.

In the event, in the turbulent 1990s and early 2000s, AAC Progress managed to stay afloat thanks to the production of the Moskit anti-ship

The forward section, still lacking armour for side-on protection of the air crew. (Author)

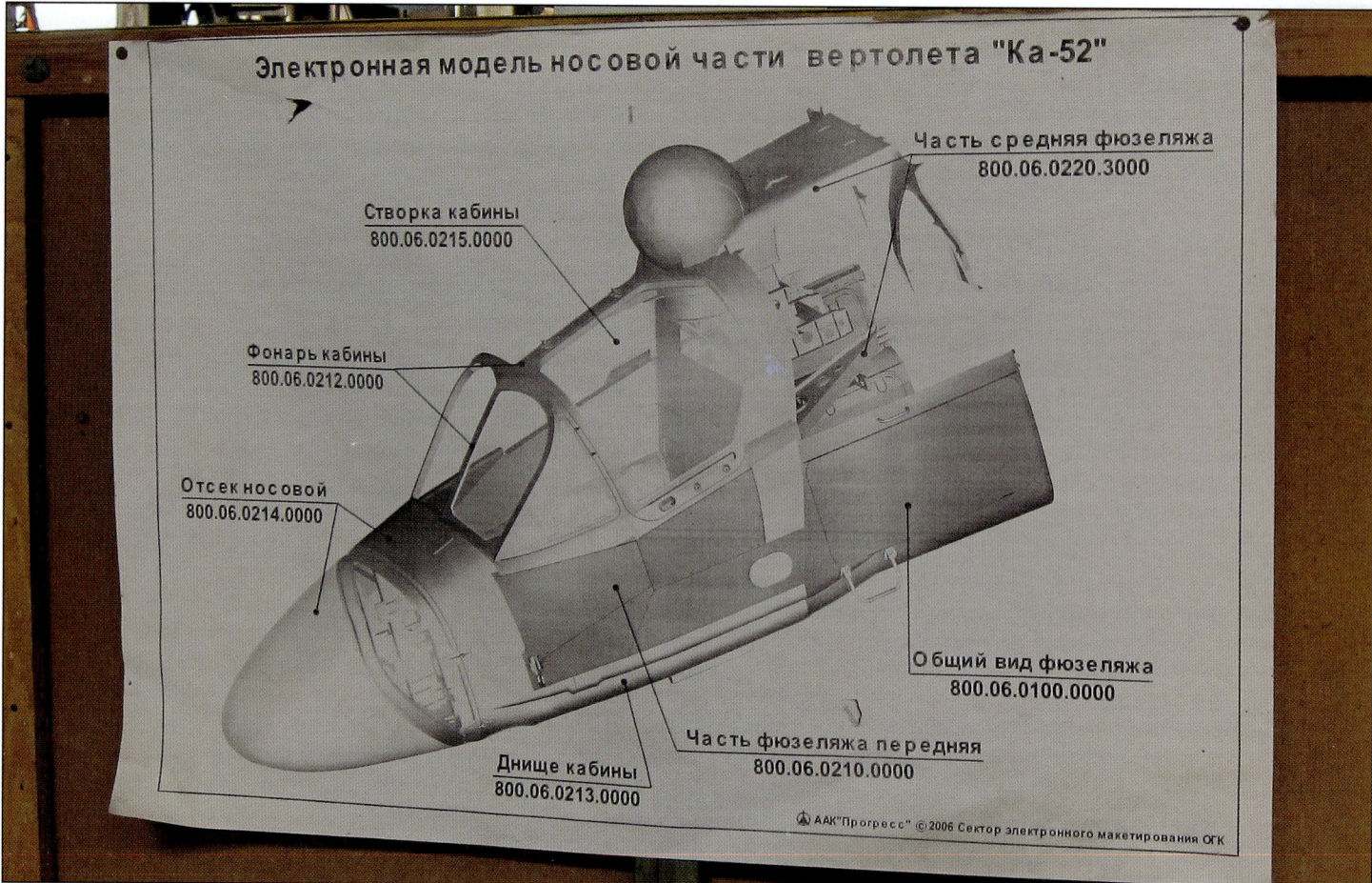

An electronic model of the Ka-52's front fuselage section this is an old configuration, with a roof-mounted optronic payload, used for general familiarisation purposes with its components. (Author)

missiles ordered in large quantities by the Chinese and Vietnamese naval arms.

Attempts to launch civilian aircraft production in the early 1990s proved unsuccessful, as only 13 Mil Mi-34 *Hermit* light single-engine helicopters rolled off the line between 1993 and 2002. In addition, the company has since produced 110 Yakovlev Yak-55 and five Yak-54 piston-engine high-performance aerobatics aircraft.

Currently, only military aircraft are produced at the AAC Progress, plant, although this is expected to change in the foreseeable future when the Ka-62 6.5-tonne civil helicopter goes into serial production.

'Gator production process

Despite the expected traditional repressive secrecy that has been characteristic of the Russian aerospace industry, often compared to spy mania particularly in regard to its defence products during his March 2012 visit, the author was granted access to all shop areas of the plant and there were very few photography restrictions, applicable only to the 'Gators in the final assembly hangar and those undergoing ground and flight tests.

"The Ka-52 is the principal product manufactured by the AAC Progress," the company's managing director, Yury Denisenko, told the author. "We have enough space within the production facilities to accommodate a second set of jigs in an effort to establish a second fuselage assembly line and thus increase the production rate, provided that we receive significant export orders."

The traditional Soviet-era aerospace industry approach of separating design and mass production activities is still in force within the contemporary Russian rotorcraft industry. As a result, the Arsenyev-based company is engaged in serial production of

The fuselage assembly shop. (Author)

the Ka-52, while all the major development and design works are still the responsibility of the Moscow-based Kamov OKB. The latter maintains its own office at the AAC Progress plant in order to exercise quality control over the manufacturing process and oversee the implementation of engineering changes on aircraft on the production line.

Cooperation between AAC Progress and Kamov OKB is now formally conducted within the framework of the Russian Helicopters holding company, which acts as the managing and coordinating body for the entire Russian rotorcraft industry. Since the late 2000s, the newly established holding company has consolidated many major production facilities and design houses and now also deals with the coordination of the marketing, R&D and after-sales activities within the sector.

Mechanics installing control runs in the cockpit. (Author)

Final assembly works on a Ka-52 fuselage before towing it to the final assembly shop. (Author)

The tail and rear fuselage sections have entirely composite non-load-bearing skins with large removable panels for easy servicing. (Author)

The export of helicopters to military customers is only handled through Rosoboronexport, the sole agent for almost all Russian defence exports. Government sales to the Russian MoD, the so-called 'state defence orders', are handled by AAC Progress itself.

About 25 percent of the current workforce is made up of people with higher engineering education, and there have been lots of young specialists hired over the last five years, bringing the average age of personnel down from 49 in 2008 to 42 in 2012 and about 40 in 2015. The average salary for qualified production line personnel in 2012 was around US$1,000 a month. It is noteworthy that the current labour component within the cost structure of helicopters produced at Russian plants is only 10 percent, while Western helicopter manufacturers calculate labour costs between 30–40 percent of their eventual production cost.

Production cycle

AAC Progress deals with the complete production cycle of the fuselage, rotor blades and other systems, as well as final assembly, system integration, ground/flight testing, delivery, after-sales service and through-life support activities. Virtually no outsourcing is used in the Ka-52 fuselage production process, and almost all components are consequently produced in-house.

It takes about 9–12 months to build a helicopter at the tempo sustained in 2012 and maintained until 2016; as Denisenko noted, there is a lot of effort currently being made to double the output.

The production process starts with raw materials, blanks and preparations coming in, together with crates containing all the necessary vendor-supplied items, such as accessories, avionics boxes, engines, rotor columns and transmission components, while output is in the form of ready-for-delivery helicopters.

Component manufacture is handled by several large workshops outfitted for mechanical processing and forming of metallic components, as well as a dedicated shop for producing carbon-based composite parts, including large panels and assemblies for the fuselage, and a large composite rotor-blade shop. There are about 2,500 people employed in the production unit.

The company has invested a lot of funds in purchasing Japanese-made digitally controlled multi-axis milling machines and machining centres that reduce labour by a factor of 10 and provide a much more precise output. There is also a very modern Italian-made moulding line for iron, aluminium alloy and magnesium alloy castings of complex shapes, which had turned the AAC Progress plant into a 'centre of excellence' for the casting work of complex parts within

Russian Helicopters Holding. Funded by the Russian government, investment in the factory began in 2008 and was completed by 2015. By 2012, investment amounted to some 7 billion roubles (equating to around US$233 million).

The composite blade shop, integrated into the main factory, produces blades for both the Ka-52 families and the Ka-62. The blades are produced by laying up a number of composite sheets on a profile pattern and then baking the resultant blade in an autoclave. A set of additional processes is applied after baking, including installation of a titanium grip for connection to the rotor mast.

Structurally, the streamlined, fixed-wing aircraft-like fuselage is built around a steel torsion box beam, which acts as the main load-bearing component of the fuselage, onto which the gearbox, cockpit section, tail section, engines, main landing gear legs and cannon mount are attached, while the wing centre section passes though the box.

The large tailboom provides plenty of room for installation of equipment boxes, placed behind easy-access panels, allowing simultaneous access for checks and maintenance by several technicians. The empennage has a fixed tailplane with endplate fins and a central tailfin with trailing edge rudders with a yaw damper.

The built-in test equipment and easy-access arrangements minimise the need of dedicated ground servicing equipment, an important consideration for autonomous operations outside the base for prolonged periods, up to two weeks.

Final assembly and testing

All parts and assemblies are in turn moved to the fuselage assembly line, where helicopter bodies take shape first assembled by moving step-by-step onto the jigs, and then completed in a special area before

Ka-52 component manufacture and assembly work is handled by as many as 16 shops at the AAC Progress plant, most of which deal with metallic parts and assemblies. All parts and assemblies are finally moved to the 'Gator's fuselage assembly shop, where helicopter bodies take shape. This Ka-52, c/n 08-01, was delivered to the Korennovsk-based 393rd AB in 2013 and then transferred in late 2014 to the 39th VAP at Dzhankoi. (Author)

The final assembly of this Ka-52 is almost done and very soon it will be handed over for electrical system checks. (AAC Progress)

It takes about nine months to build a helicopter at the tempo of 12–20 helicopters a year sustained from 2011 to 2015, but it was set to be accelerated in 2016 in order to double the output thanks to the presence of an export order for Egypt and an order from the Russian naval air arm. (Author)

being handed over to the final assembly line, the so-called Workshop No. 26. After camouflage paint has been applied, fuselages are handed over to the final helicopter assembly line, situated in a spacious heated hangar. Here, positioned on a single station, they receive powerplants, systems and mission equipment.

Between late 2011 and early 2014, all Ka-52s coming off the production line were painted in the new RuAF standard single-tone dark grey, which has replaced the two-tone green camouflage. From early 2014, however, the old-style two-tone green paintwork with light blue underside was adopted once again, while the Ka-52K shipborne derivative retained the dark grey camouflage.

Final assembly at Workshop No. 26 takes about four weeks, so long as the supply chain for important vendor-supplied equipment works in a smooth manner. After the completion of the series of detailed electrical system checks, the freshly-assembled 'Gators are transferred to the Flight Test Station (FTS), which occupies a remote hangar at the plant's own airfield. It has a 1,100m (3,630ft) grass runway and several concrete pads connected by a small taxiway. This last link of the factory's production chain is responsible for the ground/flight testing and flight safety, as well as customer delivery activities and furnishing assistance to the customers during the ferry fights.

Four weeks are dedicated to all the necessary ground and flight checks and pre-delivery activities. A minimum of six functional check flights are required for each newly assembled helicopter. In 2012, the FTS had only two qualified production test pilots, Vladimir Utva and Alexander Kukla, who are rated on the Ka-52 and Mi-8T (replaced in 2015 by a Mi-171). Both of them have a civil aviation background, flying the Mi-8T, and were then qualified as production test pilots on the Black Shark/Alligator in 1997 and 2010 respectively.

The FTS personnel commence work on each freshly assembled machine with the weight and centre of gravity (CoG) check to see whether there are any deviations in the CoG position. Completion of the so-called technical passport (including all the necessary preparations for the flight testing) follows; this activity covers adjustments of various systems, flushing the fuel tanks, filling with fuel and lubricants, installing rotor blades, etc.

Phase two of flight test preparation includes setting up the Ka-52's VK-2500-01 engines in working conditions. Their synchronization takes around 15 start-ups, running in modes from idle to auto, and runs at maximum and emergency power settings then follow.

Flight tests begin following completion of engine and rotor system functional checks and adjustments. The first sortie is in hover only and includes a dynamic balancing of the rotors, first at an altitude of 10ft (3m), then 16ft (5m) and finally at 50ft (15m). Vibration levels are measured and, if necessary, the blades receive additional balance weights until the vibration problem has been solved.

The second sortie, up to one hour long, is dedicated to control and stability evaluation in forward flight. The third sortie explores the Ka-52's performance limits within approximately one hour and is dedicated to checking performance, including maximum level speed at 3,000m (9,900ft), maximum rate of climb, performing manoeuvres with the maximum allowable pitch and bank angles as well as autorotation, commencing from 1,500m (4,950ft) at minimum engine-power settings.

The last three sorties deal with checking the in-flight functionality of the flight, navigation and communication systems, as well as of selected parts of the helicopter's mission suite.

In addition to the testing and checking performed by the FTS, flight checking and certification of newly produced helicopters also requires a separate, independent inspection programme undertaken by the flight crews of the Military Acceptance Service. This is an all-encompassing quality assurance organisation subordinated to the Russian MoD, dealing with overall supervision of the quality of the manufacturing process and end product, for both domestic and export military and civil customers of all Russian aviation and defence industry plants.

After successful completion of this stage of testing and certification, all documentation generated during the ground and flight checks is collected in a file that is preserved by AAC Progress during the entire life-cycle of the newly manufactured helicopter. The average time needed for setting and adjusting the systems, checking the functionality of the helicopter on the ground and in the air, and certifying it as ready for customer delivery is between two weeks and one month, provided that no major technical issues surface during the process.

The first series-production machines were rolled out in the second half of 2010, with their delivery reported in December 2010, while the first front-line attack squadron assigned to the 575th AB took on strength its first 'Gators in May 2011. (AAC Progress)

A close-up view of the Ka-52's scabbed-on armour plating on the fuselage and canopy, used to protect crew members, their ejection seats, the cockpit avionics and control system. (via author)

A gunship grey-painted Ka-52 in March 2013 in the final assembly shop. (AAC Progress via Alexander Mladenov)

Company production test pilots Vladimir Utva (right) and Alexander Kukla. (via author)

Ka-52 c/n 05-05, later delivered to the 393rd AB at Korennovsk and wearing serial 'Red 42', undergoes rotor cone adjustments at the Flight Test Station in March 2012, with only its lower rotor blades installed. (via author)

An early-production Ka-52, still unpainted, in a functional check flight. From time to time, Ka-52s are handed over to the factory FTS before getting their camouflage paintwork, which is then applied only after completion of the flight check programme. (AAC Progress)

The flight test station team at the AAC Progress plant at Arsenyev captured by the camera posing together with Kamov OKB test pilot Nail Azin and test navigator Alexander Shveikin (in the centre) just after the Ka-52K's maiden flight on 7 March 2015. (AAC Progress)

The Ka-52K underwent its extensive sea trails at Severomorsk and Murmansk areas, with operations off the desk of Russian navy aircraft carrier *Admiral Kuznetsov* and even took part in a real-world night search and rescue operation to assist fishermen in distress. (Alexey Mikheev)

The Ka-52 attack helicopters were spotted in Syria for the first time on 15 March 2016 in still partially disassembled state – this tends to indicate that the helicopter had just been offloaded from an An-124 Russian transport aircraft. The baptism in fire for the Hokum took place during the battle for Al-Qaryatayn, an important town near Palmyra that was recaptured by the Syrian government forces from Daesh on 3 April. The Ka-52s were seen on video footage in shallow dive attacks firing 80mm rockets from B-8M20-A packs. In addition, during the battle of Al-Qaryatayn these were also reported to have fired some 9M120-1 Ataka-1 ATGMs as well. (via Author)

Ka-52 'White 51', c/n 10-05, was produced by the AAC Progress plant in 2013 and delivered to the 15th AAB at Ostrov in early 2014. (Andrey Zinchuk)

This Ka-52, wearing the blue-colour serial '11', serves with the 39th VAP at Dzhankoi in Crimea. The regiment was newly-established in December 2014 and in 2015 it took on strength a dozen of Ka-52s, that were originally delivered in 2013 to the 393rd Air Base (Army Aviation) at Korennovsk. (via author)

The first 12 Ka-52s for the Russian Army Aviation were ordered in 2008 and their delivery was made in late 2010 and early/mid-2011. This machine is from the first batch, operated by the Torzhok combat training centre for experimental operation. Here it is seen during Esen-2011 exercise at Privolzhsky airfield in southern Russia, where it was used in the close air support role firing 80mm rockets. (Andrey Zinchuk)

The Ka-52 is considerably easier to produce and support than its predecessor with the RAA, the Mi-24, thanks to its high automation and lots of built-in test equipment. Pre-flight checks of the Ka-52 require only 2.15 man-hours vs 18.7 for the Mi-24, while checks between the flights typically take 2.45 man-hours vs 13.25 and post-flight checks take 3.2 man-hours vs 12.5. (Andrey Zinchuk)

The Alligator will be eventually used for equipping no less than 12 Russian Army Aviation front-line squadrons. By early 2017 the type was inducted in the inventory of no fewer than five squadrons and the feedback from the aviators and technicians has been positive. The Ka-52 saw its baptism of fire in April 2016 in Syria where three examples have been deployed for combat operations. (Author)

This machine, wearing the red-colour serial '46' (c/n 06-05) was among the batch of 16 Ka-52 originally delivered in early 2013 to the 393rd Air Base (Army Aviation) at Korennovsk, and in 2015 it was transferred to the Alligator-equipped squadron of the 39th VAP in Crimea. (Andrey Zinchuk)

The Ka-52's experimental operation with the Russian Army Aviation took place between September 2011 and April 2015, which saw the type amassing 11,172 hours. The general conclusion was that the Ka-52's overall performance meets the Russian military requirement and the type can be operated within the scope of the intended combat tasks. This Alligator, Red 73, is among the four machines from the 13th and 14th production series handed over to the 55th OVP in Korennovsk in the Southern Military District in December 2016. (Mikhail Lisov)

Kamov OKB's test crew – navigator Vladimir Yurtaev (to the left) and pilot Alexander Tcherednichenko seen at aircraft carrier *Admiral Kuznetsov* in front of a pre-series Ka-52K undergoing sea trails in September 2016 in the Kola Bay off Murmansk. Both of them wear orange MSK exposure suits used for flights over cold water areas. While engaged with test sorties in Murmansk area, the Ka-52K crew was also scrambled to perform a real-world search operation and it found a group of fisherman who had an incident at sea but managed to survive on a remote coastal shelter. The Ka-52K used its infrared camera of the GOES-451 sensor payload to find the survivors and then directed rescue boats to provide first aid. (Alexey Mikheev)

Commissioning with the RuAF has vastly improved the Ka-52's export chances. The most likely future customers were expected to pop out from the league of the traditional buyers of modern Russian weapons such as Algeria as well as some ex-Soviet republics from Central Asia. In the event, Egypt proved to be the first export customer, with an order for 46, the first of which are set for delivery in the first half of 2017. In addition, Egypt is being regarded as a firm customer for the shipborne Ka-52K for operations off the desk of its two Mistral-class amphibious assault ships purchased in 2016 from France. (Mikhail Lisov)